CHANGING CHILDHOODS

local and global

CHILDHOOD: THE SERIES

This book is the fourth of four which have been prepared as the core teaching texts for the Open University course U212 *Childhood*. The growing field of childhood and youth studies provides an integrative framework for interdisciplinary research and teaching, as well as analysis of contemporary policy and practice in, for instance, education, health and social work. Childhood is now a global issue, forcing a reconsideration of conventional approaches to study. Childhood is also a very personal issue for each and every one of us – scholars, policy-makers, parents and children. The books therefore include children's and parents' voices as well as academic discussion of childhood in diverse societies and points in history. The recognition of childhood and youth as a focus of study, debate and personal reflection provides the starting point for this introductory series.

Book 1 *Understanding Childhood: an interdisciplinary approach* asks 'What is a child?' and introduces a range of perspectives within childhood and youth studies. Topics in this book include the history of beliefs about childhood, the growth of scientific approaches to studying children, the significance of gender, debates around children's rights and how far children are seen as innocent or knowing.

Book 2 *Childhoods in Context* examines the interplay between family, work, schooling and other influences in the daily lives of children and young people. Topics include changing family patterns, debates about school versus work, and current concerns about child labour. Issues in early childhood are also discussed, as well as the transition from child to adult.

Book 3 *Children's Cultural Worlds* looks at the distinctiveness of children's cultural worlds by exploring the everyday activities of young children through to teenagers. Topics include friendships and the significance of play, how children use language to construct relationships and identities, the role of print literature, other media and information technology in children's lives, and their growing power as consumers.

Book 4 *Changing Childhoods: local and global* considers the status of children in society, and the significance of children's rights, recognizing that childhood is both a local experience and a global concern. Topics include the effects of poverty and other adversities, including violence, on children's health and well-being. Finally, the book illustrates the ways in which children and young people become engaged with social issues, including issues surrounding their status as children.

Further details on The Open University course U212 *Childhood* and other courses in the BA Hons *Childhood and Youth Studies* degree can be obtained from the Course Information and Advice Centre, PO Box 625, The Open University, Walton Hall, Milton Keynes, MK7 6YG, United Kingdom. Telephone +44 (0)1908 653231, e-mail general-enquiries@open.ac.uk, web site http://www.open.ac.uk/courses.

WILEY

The Open University

CHANGING
CHILDHOODS

local and global

edited by
Heather Montgomery, Rachel Burr
and Martin Woodhead

First published 2003 by John Wiley & Sons Ltd in association with The Open University

The Open University
Walton Hall
Milton Keynes
MK7 6AA
United Kingdom
www.open.ac.uk

John Wiley & Sons Ltd
The Atrium
Southern Gate
Chichester
PO19 8SQ
www.wileyeurope.com or www.wiley.com

Other Wiley editorial offices: John Wiley & Sons Inc., 605 Third Avenue, New York, NY 10158–0012, USA; Jossey-Bass, 989 Market Street, San Francisco, CA 94103–1741, USA; Wiley-VCH Verlag GmbH, Pappelallee 3, D-69469 Weinheim, Germany; John Wiley & Sons Australia Ltd, 33 Park Road, Milton, Queensland 4064, Australia; John Wiley & Sons (Asia) Pte Ltd, 2 Clementi Loop #02–01, Jin Xing Distripark, Singapore 129809; John Wiley & Sons Canada Ltd, 22 Worcester Road, Etobicoke, Ontario, Canada M9W 1L1.

Library of Congress Cataloging-in-Publication Data

A catalog record for this book is available from the Library of Congress.

British Library Cataloguing in Publication Data

A catalogue record for this book is available from the British Library.

ISBN 0 470 84695 X

Edited, designed and typeset by The Open University.

Printed in the United Kingdom by Scotprint, Haddington.

Contents

Contributors

Rachel Burr is a lecturer in Childhood Studies at The Open University. She has worked as a social worker and trainer in England, Ireland and Vietnam. Between 1996 and 1998 she lived in Vietnam where she did child-focused research for a doctorate in anthropology. Her research interests are in child-focused human rights, the role of child-focused international aid agencies, and children of the streets and orphanages in Vietnam (she is currently investigating the effects of HIV/AIDS on the lives of those children). She has taught anthropology in the US. Her recent publications include 'Global and local approaches to children's rights in Vietnam', *Childhood*, **9**(1), and 'Ethics of doing anthropological fieldwork', *Anthropology Matters*, **3**. She is currently working on a book on children and their rights in Vietnam, to be published by Rutgers University Press in 2004.

Perpetua Kirby is an independent research consultant and a visiting research fellow at South Bank University. She researches and evaluates children and young people's projects within the UK, and has a special interest in projects that promote children's participation in decision-making. Her publications include *Involving Young Researchers: how to enable young people to design and conduct research* (Joseph Rowntree Foundation, 1999) and 'Involving young people in research' in *The New Handbook of Children's Rights* (edited by Franklin, Routledge, 2002). She is currently working on a national study of good practice on involving children and young people in decision making (with the National Children's Bureau).

Heather Montgomery is a lecturer in Childhood Studies at The Open University. She is an anthropologist who has conducted fieldwork in Thailand among young prostitutes and is the author of *Modern Babylon? prostituting children in Thailand* (Berghahn, 2001). She has held post-doctoral positions in the USA, Norway and Oxford and is the author of several articles on children's rights, child abuse and the anthropology of childhood. Other publications include 'Imposing rights? A case study of child prostitution in Thailand' in *Culture and Rights* (edited by Cowan, Dembour and Wilson, Cambridge University Press, 2001) and 'Abandonment and child prostitution in a Thai slum community' in *Abandoned Children* (edited by Panter-Brick and Smith, Cambridge University Press, 2000).

Catherine Panter-Brick is a reader in anthropology at the University of Durham where she teaches medical anthropology. Her research interests focus on health, human reproduction and nutrition, street children, risk, poverty and adversity. She has published widely on aspects of children's health, including a review article on street children, human rights and public health in *Annual Review of Anthropology* (vol. 31, 2002). She has edited the volume *Biosocial Perspectives on Children* (Cambridge University Press, 1998) and, with Malcolm Smith, *Abandoned Children* (Cambridge University Press, 2000).

Martin Woodhead is a senior lecturer in the Centre for Childhood, Development and Learning at The Open University. He has contributed to courses in child development and education, and has carried out research in child development, early education, sociology of childhood, child labour and children's rights. He has been a Fulbright scholar in the USA and a consultant to international organizations including the Council of Europe, Save the Children and OECD. He is a co-editor of the journal *Children & Society*. His publications include *In Search of the Rainbow: pathways to quality in large-scale programmes for young disadvantaged children* (Bernard van Leer Foundation, 1996), and the three-volume series *Child Development in Families, Schools and Society* (Routledge in association with The Open University, 1998, edited with Faulkner and Littleton). Martin chaired the course team for the Open University course U212 *Childhood*, for which this book is a core text.

Introduction

In 1909, the Swedish reformer Ellen Key claimed that the twentieth century would be the 'century of the child' (Key, 1909). She envisaged a world where children would take their rightful place alongside adults as full and equal participants in society. From our vantage point at the beginning of the twenty-first century, how does her prediction look? How has the status of children changed over the past hundred years?

On the one hand, children are a source of concern as never before. From the wealthiest children of North America, Europe and Japan to the poorest children in the countries of sub-Saharan Africa and Asia, children's lives are of critical interest to the media, to governments and to international agencies. Their development and well-being is researched, legislated for and debated at every level. Childhood is recognized as a global as well as a national and local concern. The 'century of the child' has seen the birth of international charities (such as Save the Children) and international organizations (such as the United Nations Children's Fund, UNICEF) dedicated to improving children's welfare throughout the world.

The twentieth century also saw the recognition of the idea that children have rights, which began with the Geneva Declaration of the Rights of the Child, 1924, and was continued in the United Nations Convention on the Rights of the Child, 1989 (UNCRC). By ratifying the Convention, governments have agreed to incorporate its provisions into their national laws and to place children's interests at the centre of policy-making, as the first call in the allocation of resources, not as an optional extra to be funded when resources are plentiful.

Yet despite the progress made during the 'century of the child', at the end of it more than 10 million children under the age of five still died every year, 150 million were malnourished, 600 million lived in poverty, and 100 million were without schooling (UNICEF, 2000). Adequate nutrition, water supplies, sanitation and basic medical care would prevent many of these deaths. At the beginning of the twenty-first century, new health challenges undermine children's well-being, notably the HIV/AIDS pandemic. Poverty, social upheaval and violence continue to threaten children's security, with millions of children forced out of their homes and communities, living as refugees, on the streets or in shanties. And the challenges for childhood are not just in the poorer countries of the world. Significant numbers of children live in poverty or suffer from abuse, exploitation, discrimination and racism, even in the wealthiest countries.

So, childhood issues have become more visible, at global as well as at local levels, and there has been progress in tackling some, but by no means all of the adversities threatening children's well-being. But there is another story to be told, which is about our vision of the future of childhood in a globalized world. To talk about 'the child' seems to ignore the significance of the plurality of children's experiences, in all their diversity, related to age, gender, ethnicity, geography, cultural, economic and political circumstances. Towards the end of the century, critical voices asked about the appropriateness of applying universal standards for children's well-being, notably the UNCRC, to the specific circumstances of children's lives in local contexts. Questions were raised about how far children's health and well-being are, in part at least, cultural constructs. For example, the social anthropologist Jo Boyden drew attention to the risks when cultural images of particular kinds of childhood masquerade as universal truths about children's nature and needs:

> As the twentieth century has progressed, ... highly selective, stereotyped perceptions of childhood – of the innocent child victim on the one hand and the young deviant on the other – have been exported from the industrial world to the South.... It has been the explicit goal of children's rights specialists to crystallize in international law a universal system of rights for the child based on these norms of childhood.

(Boyden, 1990, p. 191)

Changing Childhoods examines why the status and well-being of children has become such a central issue and reviews some major areas of concern, notably in relation to poverty, ill-health and violence. This book (like its companion volumes) starts from an appreciation of the diversity of childhoods within contemporary societies. These diversities can be studied at a local (or micro) level, e.g. in terms of gender or ethnic differences within communities. They can also be studied at a global (or macro) level, e.g. in terms of distribution of resources, health and education services, as well as children's prospects for survival, health and growth. What makes this fourth book in the series distinctive is the perspective we take on these issues. When 'diversities' are examined under the lens of children's rights they frequently look more like 'adversities', 'deprivations', 'inequalities' and examples of 'social exclusion'.

The opening chapter begins by discussing some major adversities, and the ways young people can be physically and/or psychologically vulnerable, but also sometimes resilient. Specific adversities – poverty, ill health and violence – are the subject of the next three chapters. The local/global theme runs through each of these chapters. An individual child's experiences of malnutrition or violence may be caused by local hardships, disasters, or conflicts; but they may also be linked to global environmental issues, economics and politics.

Inequalities at international, national and familial level feature strongly in these chapters, which acknowledge the very different ways inequalities are expressed in different social and cultural contexts. A child's gender, their age, ethnicity, religion, or whether or not they are the first or last born, may have very different implications for the ways they are treated; awareness of factors such as these should prevent over-generalization about what counts as adversity.

What becomes apparent when reading through these chapters is how interconnected the problems are that children face. Poverty and ill-health, for example, compound and reinforce each other. A child is much more likely to become ill if she or he lives in a poor family and this illness may well make the family's poverty worse if they take time off work to care for the child or struggle to pay medical bills. Economic hardship can strain family relationships and place children at risk of ill-treatment or violence. Of course, children may experience violence in a variety of contexts: at home, at school, on the streets, as well as in civil conflicts or major wars. And wars don't just make children into victims of violence. Children may also perpetrate violence; in 2003 there are an estimated 300,000 child soldiers in the world. It is salutary to note that when this book was being written, the wars that affected children – both as casualties and combatants – were based in some of the poorest countries in the world. Sub-Saharan Africa, for example, was beset by problems of war, civil unrest, poverty and AIDS. In contrast to the rest of the world, rates of infant mortality were actually rising in these countries. In some ways, it is artificial to divide adversities into discrete categories. The interconnections between poverty, ill health or violence are all-important, especially from children's points of view.

This interconnectness encourages a holistic approach to children's well-being. Well-being is not only about children's physical health but also their emotional and psychological health. It encompasses children's ability to make friends, to participate fully in the social life of their community, to fulfil their potential and abilities, to have access to services and to realize the possibility of changing their own lives. This definition of 'well-being' helps guard against over-reliance on the narrow range of indicators that are often used in statistical reviews of the state of the world's children. Infant mortality rates, poverty rates and levels of school enrolment have been very important measures of progress towards achieving children's rights, but they need to be seen as part of a bigger picture. The broad definition of 'well-being' also allows authors of these chapters to look at the difficulties that children face even when they are relatively wealthy, healthy and living in stable societies. Affluence can cause its own pressures, perhaps less tangible and life-threatening than hunger or ill health, but just as significant for the children concerned.

A final theme of the book is about changing responses to childhood adversities, and about the role of children in contributing to change. At the beginning of the book, we acknowledge that children are especially vulnerable, but we also review evidence of children's capacities for resilience in coping with – and even surmounting – the effects of poverty, ill-health or violence. This theme surfaces again in later chapters, as part of a review of major approaches to intervening in children's lives. A rights-based approach is one of the most important legacies of the 'century of the child'. It recognizes that children have a right to be protected, but also that they are entitled to participate in society and to have their voices heard on the issues that most affect them. In other words, children have a role to play in 'changing childhoods', in so far as they are able to shape their own personal futures as well as the institutions within their society, their families, schools and community. This is not just about adults granting children rights. It is about children's own assertion of their rights. Here we encounter one of the inevitable imbalances in the study of the child. It is a story written almost entirely by adults, and this book is no exception. The risk is that the potential and actual role of young people is diminished, even though they have a rich history of social and political activity, from the twelve year olds who led the Children's Crusades in 1212 to the children who were at the forefront of the fight against apartheid in South Africa during the 1970s. As Judith Ennew put it, 'Children may be permitted to make history, but they are excluded from making policy' (Ennew, 2000, p. 46). It is only during the latter years of the twentieth century (and even more so during the first few years of the new century) that children's status as citizens has begun to be more fully embraced, for example through child consultations, schools councils, youth forums and children's parliaments. We have tried to represent children's perspectives in this book. All the authors have extensive experience of conducting first-hand research with children, interviewing them about their lives and listening to them tell their stories. Children's voices feature prominently in many of the chapters.

Chapter 1 'Adversities and resilience' asks how adversity is defined, by whom, and how children live and cope with it. It looks at various dimensions of adversity and the impact of these on children's physical, emotional, social and political well being. This chapter emphasizes that children's experiences of adversity are diverse and that they respond actively, and sometimes even positively, to adversity. The second half of the chapter examines children's resilience when faced with adversity, looking at why, given the risks that children face, certain children fare much better than others. It looks at the protective factors, both at an individual and at a social and cultural level, which have been identified as bolstering children's resilience.

Chapter 2 'Children, poverty and social inequality' focuses on the material aspects of adversity. The chapter's authors discuss the different effects of poverty on children in a wide variety of contexts, and emphasize that living in poverty has psychological as well as material effects on children. It also examines the links between poverty and other forms of adversity, notably ill health. The chapter starts by looking at the often contested definitions of poverty, especially at the distinction between absolute and relative poverty. Poverty is not just about lack of material possessions. It is also about stigma, inequality and the social exclusion of certain groups of children. The chapter explores inequalities at global and local levels, looking at how macro-economic policies affect children's lived experiences within communities and families. It focuses particularly on the unintended effects that the structural adjustment programmes imposed by the World Bank have on children in countries of the South.

Chapter 3 'Achieving health for children' argues that ill health can affect all children, wherever they live, and that affluence is not necessarily a guarantee of good health. While certain diseases and conditions such as dehydration, diarrhoea or measles are rarely fatal to children in the affluent North, in contrast to countries of the South, other diseases such as obesity, diabetes and asthma are disproportionately found in the North. The chapter asks why so many of the world's children continue to die, especially children under five, despite targets and promises being made to improve children's health at an international level. As in the previous chapter, the authors draw attention to inequalities in health at local as well as at a global level, including a discussion of gender differences. These issues are set in the context of debates about definitions of child health, including broad definitions of emotional health and well-being. By contrasting Western bio-medical approaches with other societies' beliefs about child health, it is possible to argue for a wider and more holistic understanding of children's health issues.

Chapter 4 'Children and violence' starts by noting the ambivalent relationship between children and violence in Western thought, examining contradictory constructions of childhood as inherently innocent and also as inherently cruel and violent. This chapter explores children's various roles as perpetrators, witnesses and victims of violence. It focuses on three of the main sites where violence takes place against children and where they commit violence: at home, amongst their peers and in armed conflict. Within each of these three sites, the chapter examines the relationship between children as victims of violence and as perpetrators of it. Taking in a broad geographical sweep, this chapter looks at children and violence in a variety of circumstances, from seventeen-year-old soldiers in the UK to victims of genocide in Cambodia. It analyses violence in its widest possible terms to encompass not only physical pain and injury but also psychological violence and bullying.

Chapter 5 'Intervening in children's lives' looks at adults' attempts over many centuries to improve children's lives. It explores the reasons for adults' concern with children's well-being and focuses on three main explanations. The first is that children are victims, vulnerable through no fault of their own, and therefore special, innocent and apolitical. The second views childhood as a formative period and children as an investment. The third sees children as worthy of support and respect in their own terms, not because of their vulnerability or future potential. Each of these conceptualizations of children is linked to a different form of intervention; namely, rescuing children, fulfilling their potential and ensuring and implementing their rights. The chapter is illustrated through examples spanning three centuries, of Thomas Coram's Foundling Hospital, Head Start programmes in the USA and the work of Save the Children.

Chapter 6 'Children's participation in society' continues Chapter 5's discussion of participatory rights by looking at children as agents of change, highlighting the critical role that children play in contemporary societies, as well as the obstacles they face. The chapter begins with a discussion of the meaning of participation in the context of the UNCRC, including debates about children's competence to participate as well as adult responsibilities for guiding participation. There is a discussion of models and strategies of child participation, including the importance of listening effectively, with examples drawn from early childhood through to the teenage years. Child participation projects are reviewed, including child-to-child health projects as well as children's role in research. Finally, the chapter looks at children and young people's role in democratic processes, such as schools councils, youth forums and children's parliaments.

In preparing these chapters, we aimed to draw on examples from a wide range of geographical locations and periods in history. Making comparisons between childhoods according to economic context, cultural tradition or world location is fraught with difficulties. Numerous terms are in circulation, notably Third World, industrialized countries, developing countries, or most recently minority world and majority world. Generally, the authors use the labels 'North' to denote the richer, more industrialized countries, and 'South' to denote the poorer, less industrialized ones. Also, they use the label 'Western' to denote the cultural beliefs and practices associated with highly industrialized societies, which have their roots in the philosophy that developed in Europe and North America in and around the eighteenth century, during the historical period sometimes called 'The Age of Enlightenment'.

Preparation of this book (and the others in the series) has been linked to the production of audio-visual case studies of childhoods in three locations – Cape Town (South Africa), Chittagong (Bangladesh), and Oakland (California) (the books and audio-visual material together make up the Open University course U212 *Childhood*). Many of the themes of the book were explored with children, parents and communities in these three locations, and quotations are included in several of the chapters.

We would like to thank all those who contributed at each stage in the preparation of this book, especially Dr Jo Boyden (University of Oxford, Refugee Studies Centre), Dr Judith Ennew (University of Cambridge, Centre for Family Research) and Dr Allison James (University of Hull).

Heather Montgomery, Rachel Burr and Martin Woodhead
The Open University, 2003

References

BOYDEN, J. (1990) 'Childhood and the policy makers: a comparative perspective on the globalization of childhood' in James, A. and Prout, A. (eds) *Constructing and Reconstructing Childhood: contemporary issues in the sociology of childhood*, London, Falmer Press.

ENNEW, J. (2000) 'The history of children's rights: whose story?', *Cultural Survival Quarterly*, **24**(2), pp. 44–8.

KEY, E. (1909) *The Century of the Child*, New York and London, G. P. Putnam and Sons.

UNICEF (2000) *Poverty Reduction Begins with Children*, New York, UNICEF.

Chapter 1

Adversities and resilience

Martin Woodhead, Heather Montgomery and Rachel Burr

CONTENTS

I WELL-BEING AND ADVERSITIES

This book is about the challenges faced by children and young people in the world today, and about their role in the process of change. Chapters 2, 3 and 4 will examine three particular forms of adversity – poverty, ill health and violence. Chapters 5 and 6 will look at how adults attempt to alleviate the effects of adversity on children, and at children's contributions to changing the institutions that shape their lives. This chapter introduces these issues, looking at how adversity is defined and what research can tell us about the main risk factors, as well as considering the ways that children can show resilience in the face of threats to their well-being.

Promoting children's well-being is a central theme of this chapter (and book). Children's well-being is based on a holistic understanding of their needs, a recognition of the importance of both their physical needs (for food, sleep, shelter etc.) and their psychological/emotional needs (such as to feel loved and secure, to be given opportunities for play and learning). While a broad measure of agreement can be achieved about what constitutes children's needs and their well-being, any definition is necessarily rooted in both time and culture. Beliefs about childhood vary between different cultures, societies and times in history, particularly in terms of the kinds of care, play and learning that are considered good for children, as well as the goals of development, socialization and education (Woodhead, 1997).

This is one of the reasons children's rights have become so important. A rights framework can draw on international agreement among diverse societies about universal requirements for protecting children and promoting their well-being, as in the 1989 UN Convention on the Rights of the Child (UNCRC). An approach based on the UNCRC has other advantages: rights are constituted in international law, and not merely dependent on the benevolence of well-intentioned adults. Rights also emphasize children's own stake in the conditions that promote their well-being, and that they must be consulted about matters that affect them. Even so, a rights-based approach still leaves room for negotiation about what constitutes well-being, notably in the UNCRC's Article 3 which states that the 'best interests of the child shall be a primary consideration' (see Burr and Montgomery, 2003).

Put simply, adversity is about situations or events that fail to meet children's needs, violate their rights and threaten their well-being. Resilience is about the ways children react to adversity. As you will see, situations that might threaten one child's well-being may not pose the same risk to another child, and, in a different context, may be seen as posing no risk at all. Both the adversities that children face and their vulnerability or resilience in the face of those adversities must be understood by looking closely at the specific circumstances of individual children as well as at broader social and cultural factors.

SUMMARY OF SECTION 1

- 'Well-being' is a holistic concept which recognizes the importance of understanding and supporting children's physical and emotional needs and their rights.
- Adversity occurs in any situation which threatens children's well-being. Resilience is about the ways in which children react to adversities.

2 DIMENSIONS OF ADVERSITIES

Allow about 20 minutes

ACTIVITY 1   **What threatens children's well-being?**

Think about and make a list of some major things you think can be harmful to children's well-being. Then try to group them in terms of kinds of adversity.

You may find the illustrations on pages 4–5 helpful in thinking about this activity.

Children collecting insects to eat during a famine in Sudan.

Children playing on the walkway of a run-down public housing estate in the UK.

Young child playing in the streets of Bangladesh.

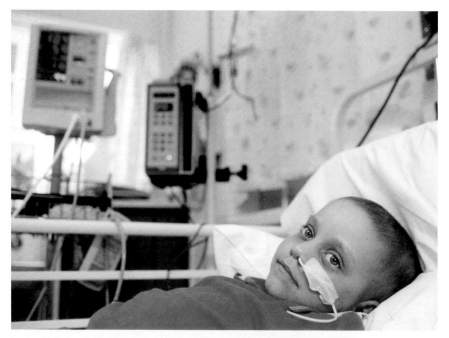

Child with leukaemia
being treated in
Exeter hospital, UK.

Parental argument
witnessed by a child.

COMMENT

This is how we grouped our list of adversities:

1   natural disasters (e.g. floods, earthquakes, droughts);

2   ill health (e.g. becoming seriously ill, having a road accident);

3   poverty (e.g. not having enough to eat, having to live in an overcrowded slum or shanty town);

4   family problems (e.g. death or divorce in the family, a parent becoming ill or alcoholic and unable to care for a child);

5   exploitation (e.g. having to work long hours in unsafe conditions);

6   abuse (e.g. physical, mental or sexual abuse);

7   discrimination (e.g. due to racial or religious prejudice);

8   violence (e.g. in the home or in the community, being bullied, war situations);

9   living in a dangerous environment (e.g. at risk from pollution or street crime).

You may have come up with other suggestions or you may disagree with some of the suggestions or groupings in the list above. For example, living in slums or shanty towns is associated with poverty, but some might feel living in a modern high-rise apartment block, socially isolated and without outside play space, is, in its own way, just as harmful to children's well-being. Also, while most would agree that emotional security is important for children's well-being, not all children experience the divorce of their parents as an adversity.

This activity illustrates the many different types of adversity that children experience as well as the difficulties in some cases of identifying them as necessarily harmful. So it is important to ask why these events are considered adverse for children. Some seem obvious: a flood or a famine affects children because it means they have nowhere to live or they cannot get access to food. Similarly, children living in poverty or in a war zone are at risk because their physical health, and even life, is threatened. In other instances, however, the threat to their well-being is primarily an emotional one; living in a family where a parent has died or is absent through divorce, or where parents continually shout at each other or the children, can cause serious emotional distress. Being racially abused or suffering discrimination can also be disturbing to children and, when coupled with racist violence, can clearly also have physical consequences.

It is also necessary to relate children's experiences of adversities to the political, social and economic circumstances in which they live. While some adversities, especially natural disasters, affect whole countries or regions, many others affect particular groups in a society, for example, those who are poorest, most vulnerable or most at risk from discrimination. Living in an affluent country or one less prone to natural disasters may protect many children from certain kinds of adversity, but it may expose them to others, for example risks from road traffic, urban pollution and street crime. Wealthy children may also experience ill health, physical, emotional or sexual abuse or an acrimonious parental divorce.

Finally, it is important to consider how adversities are felt by children themselves. Sometimes children can suffer the trauma of a specific event – an illness, accident or family crisis. In fact, some difficult moments are part of everyone's experience of childhood. The focus of this chapter will be on more enduring difficulties, which may include specific traumatic events, but where these are part of an underlying pattern of adversities. Bear in mind that classifying kinds of adversity as in Activity 1 is in some ways artificial. Children rarely experience the effects of the adversities in their lives in this way, any more than adults do. Childhood adversities are often about chains of difficult circumstances, hardships and trauma, undermining the economic, physical and psychological well-being of vulnerable children and families in ways that are multiple and cumulative, direct and indirect, and sometimes passed from generation to generation. Very often children will not be aware of why childhood is so difficult for them, or even recognize that it is difficult.

For example, think about what might happen to children faced with a serious adversity, such as a famine. Shortage of food will have an immediate impact on their health and well-being. The youngest children and those already weakened by illness or disability will be especially at risk. But there will be other, more indirect effects of food shortage, notably because parents and other family members on whom children depend are also weakened, physically and psychologically, and so are less able to provide adequate care or to work. Parents themselves may become sick and children may be orphaned. Certain ethnic groups may be discriminated against in the provision of food, shelter and health facilities. Sometimes, famine occurs not just through natural disaster but as a consequence of civil war, so vulnerable children may already have been traumatized by violence. Even where there is political stability, communities are very likely to have been disrupted. For example, schools may be closed and resources diverted to deal with the immediate crisis. If the famine is acute, families may be forced to leave their villages to migrate in search of food and work, perhaps ending up sleeping on pavements in an already overcrowded city. This in turn may expose children to a whole new set of risks, for example contaminated water supplies and inadequate sanitation. Resulting extreme poverty may mean children have to work to support their family, and they may be exploited or abused by an unscrupulous employer, or risk accidents or injury from working in a dangerous environment.

Thus, while the immediate impact of a famine situation may be relatively short term, it could trigger other kinds of adversities, with repercussions for children's long-term health, family stability and future prospects as they become adults. Adversities experienced during a person's childhood may in turn affect the well-being of their own offspring. The long-term and intergenerational effects of malnutrition in particular are discussed in more detail in Chapter 3.

We have deliberately used the term 'adversities' in the title of this chapter (and this section) to signal the multiple difficulties that millions of children face. Sometimes these difficulties overwhelm children: their health deteriorates, their learning is disrupted, they become disturbed, depressed or defiant and aggressive. But children are not always vulnerable victims of adversity. Sometimes they seem to thrive despite all the odds stacked against them. Some adversities may give children the impetus to overcome difficulties and even to achieve great things. The rest of this section will look at the effects adversities have on children, and the extent to which the social environment affects the scale of adversities. Section 3 then reviews research into children's vulnerability to adversity as well as the factors that can make them resilient. Finally, Section 4 refers to studies (notably by social anthropologists) which draw attention to the way adversities – and their effects on children – vary between contexts and cultures.

2.1 Studying the effects of adversities

Longitudinal research typically measures aspects of children's development at intervals throughout childhood. Information may also be collected about children's social background, home circumstances, school experiences etc.

This section briefly summarizes two major areas of research. The first is the impact of poverty – specifically the effects of a major economic crisis. The second is about difficult family relationships – the impact of parental conflict, separation and divorce on children's well-being. Many of the studies described in this chapter have been carried out by psychologists, using a longitudinal research design to find out about major influences on development and well-being.

Economic hardship and children's well-being

Around 1930, research teams in California began two of the very first major longitudinal studies. The Oakland Growth Study followed a sample of children born in 1920–1. Children in the Berkeley Guidance Study were around eight years younger, born in 1928–9. What neither research team could have known as they began their work was that the 1930s would turn out to be a time of acute economic hardship for many American families, with inevitable impacts on the children in both studies – their childhoods were dominated by the Great Depression. A decade later, the USA would become involved in the Second World War, creating new challenges and opportunities for the children in the studies, some of whom were by now young adults.

Migrant agricultural family in Nipomo, California, during the Great Depression (1929–34).

Many years later, Glen Elder and colleagues reviewed the impact of these events on the children in both studies, comparing children in families most badly hit by financial hardship (the 'deprived group') with children in families that had been less seriously affected. Children in the deprived group were adversely affected by the reduction in family income, as well as by the consequent shift in family roles and responsibilities, notably the greater reliance on mothers and older children to earn money to support the family. They experienced changes in their key relationships with their parents, with unemployed and frequently demoralized fathers tending to withdraw, while their wives took on greater power and emotional significance for the children. Frequently, the stress induced by economic hardship and role changes led to greater marital conflict, increased parental irritability and arbitrary and inconsistent discipline of the children, which was sometimes linked to their fathers' heavy drinking (Elder, 1974).

One especially significant feature of these studies is what they tell us about the way children were differently affected by economic hardship according to their age – the two cohorts were born eight years apart – as well as their gender. The 167 children in the Oakland Growth Study were already around ten years old at the onset of the Great Depression:

> Thus, they entered the Great Depression after a relatively secure phase of early development. Later, they avoided the scars of joblessness after high school by virtue of wartime mobilization. By contrast, the 214 members of the Berkeley cohort experienced the vulnerable years of early childhood during hard times and the pressures of adolescence during the unsettled though prosperous years of World War II.

> (Elder, Modell and Parke, 1993, p. 15)

In fact, the effects were even more subtle, especially in relation to gender. Many of the boys in the Oakland study looked for part-time work to supplement family income during their early teen years. They gained relative independence much earlier than would otherwise have been the case, spending more time away from home and with their peers. Girls in the Oakland study also took on more responsibilities, but their work tended to be within the home, especially where their mothers were the main breadwinners and younger siblings needed care. They did not earn money, so did not gain the independence enjoyed by their brothers or have as much opportunity to spend time with their peers.

Children's gender also shaped the impact of hardship for the younger children in the Berkeley study, but in this case it was the boys who appeared more vulnerable. They were more likely to develop behavioural problems, which in some cases lasted into adolescence, when their school achievement was frequently poorer than that of the girls, with lower self-confidence and poor motivation. The greater vulnerability of boys was very probably linked to their fathers' demoralization and irritability, unable to offer their sons a positive role model and tending to be more punitive in their use of discipline.

These studies of the children of the Great Depression demonstrate the effects of economic adversity in children's lives as well as the different patterns of effect according to children's age and gender. Another lesson from the studies is that many of the adverse effects on children are not direct consequences of economic hardship but stem from the social and emotional impact of hardship on parents. This in turn has serious repercussions for children's feelings of security, as well as for the quality of parent–child relationships. For the next example, we turn to studies more directly focused on the potential adverse consequences for children of marital disharmony, parental conflict and divorce.

Parental conflict and children's well-being

One of the comments made in Activity 1 was about how far should divorce be considered a source of adversity for children. This has been a major area for research in countries of the North (reviewed by Rodgers and Prior, 1998). Most studies confirm the distress caused to children, irrespective of age and gender, at least in the short term. But the evidence for long-term effects is much less clear. Most children appear to readjust, although they may of course still be affected by the experience. For a minority of children, however, parental separation and divorce is associated with long-term health and behavioural difficulties, poor school achievement and early drop-out. Drawing firm conclusions on what exactly causes these problems is made more difficult because parental separation and divorce can involve a range of potentially adverse experiences for children, very often spread over months or even years. Difficulties between parents may appear long before there is talk of separation. At worst, children may witness, or be drawn into, emotionally distressing scenes, which may be accompanied by actual violence between parents and towards the child. The process of separation may itself be drawn out and acrimonious, with children left confused and divided in their loyalties. The outcome may be a sharp reduction in living standards, and an isolated child living with a depressed parent. These are just some of the ways that some children's well-being may be put at risk. For other children, the experience may be quite different. Many parents are acutely sensitive to the adverse impact their difficulties can have on their children, and do everything they can to minimize this.

Witnessing parental conflict can be distressing and constitute a form of adversity for children.

Much less research has been done on how these issues affect children in the South. It would be extremely interesting to know how universal these findings are.

At this point, it is helpful to distinguish several different kinds of family adversity that can affect children's emotional and social adjustment (Rutter, 1981):

- privation – where children are denied affection, for example in a low quality orphanage;
- disruption – where bonds of affection are disrupted, for example when a parent dies or parents separate;
- distortion – where parents' relationship is antagonistic and family dynamics are disturbed.

A number of studies point to the third category, 'distortion', caused by antagonistic relationships before, during and after divorce, as a major contributor to long-term effects on children. A longitudinal study was carried out in New Zealand, based on a birth cohort of 1,265 children who at that time had been followed up at annual intervals to the age of thirteen (Fergusson, Horwood and Lynskey, 1992). It distinguished two broad patterns of family adversity, which closely match the second and third types identified above:

- family change (separations, reconciliations and other changes);
- parental discord (conflict, arguments and reports of assault).

The researchers then linked children's experiences of family change and parental discord to problem behaviour, based on records of offences committed by children between the ages of eleven and thirteen. Children who had experienced high levels of parental discord were at much greater risk of getting into trouble. Family changes did not in themselves appear to put children at risk, but they did amplify the adversity for children when they were combined with a high level of parental discord. The researchers also found that children who already had a history of behavioural difficulties before the onset of family problems were at greatest risk. Furthermore, boys who had experienced high levels of parental discord were more at risk of offending than girls (84 per cent versus 63 per cent). Of course, it is possible that girls were adversely affected in a different way from boys, which may not have been measured by the study.

One last point to note about researching the effects of adversities: even carefully controlled scientific studies do not allow for a final conclusion about the effects of family adversities on children's well-being, because the impact of those adversities may alter from one generation to the next, as circumstances change, and especially as attitudes and practices towards children facing adversities change. For example, Wadsworth (1986) reviewed the evidence about effects of separation and divorce from a British longitudinal study of children born in 1946. He notes there was a greater probability that children would show signs of psychological disturbance, such as bed-wetting, both at the time of the separation and on into their teenage years. They were also at greater risk of suffering from ulcers as young adults (if boys) and depression (if girls). The boys especially were more likely to become delinquent later on and commit violent or sexual crimes.

These results from a 1946 cohort appear to contradict more recent evidence that divorce is not in itself a major long-term risk factor. But, as Wadsworth pointed out, for children born in the 1940s, the experience of parents divorcing was significantly different from now. There was still a strong social stigma associated with divorce. Divorced mothers were often judged less favourably than married mothers by teachers, health visitors and social workers. Advice for professionals and parents tended to conclude that loss of a parent from the family home was likely to be 'utterly destructive to the moral fibre of the child who falls its victim' (quoted by Wadsworth, 1986, p. 124). Faced with this judgement, the burden of stress on parents and children was likely to be an added form of adversity. By the same token, the long-term impact of children's distress may be diminished in contexts where parental separation and divorce affect a large percentage of young people during their childhood, where they are not stigmatized and where support is available from other children or adults who have known the same experience, or have sympathetic understanding of it.

2.2 The social construction of childhood adversities

The research above demonstrates that risks to children's well-being do not inevitably follow from an impoverished environment or from disturbed family relationships. These risks frequently result from a complex combination of children's vulnerability, difficult circumstances and events in their lives. In some situations, the impact of adversity may also be amplified by social attitudes that stigmatize both the adversity and the children affected. In this sense, adversities can be socially constructed, as illustrated here in relation to disability, gender and race.

Adversity and disability

Allow about 20 minutes

A C T I V I T Y 2   **Saaid**

Read the short extract below about Saaid, a boy from Morocco. List the ways in which you think that his situation might be described as adverse. Then think about how far Saaid's disability is due to his muscular condition and how far it is to do with social attitudes.

> Saaid is ten years old and comes from a poor family in a suburb of Marrakech. He has a muscular condition which has left his arms and legs weak and limits his ability to move. Saaid would like nothing more than to participate in the games of other children in the neighbourhood and to help his family like his other brothers and sisters. 'I'd like to play football outside the house but the others don't let me play with them. They say I'll hurt myself and often my parents agree. I'm even prevented from doing ordinary activities within the house that I know I can do. Once at a party in our house I was sure that I could manage to serve the drinks for the guests. But my aunt's daughter prevented me. She told me that I was ill and that people like me couldn't do things like that.'
>
> (Save the Children, 2001, p. 31)

COMMENT

It is evident that Saaid does not see himself as a child with disabilities, rather as someone who is excluded from normal life with friends and family. Very probably, Saaid's confidence, self-esteem and skills are more undermined by feelings of rejection and social exclusion than by the muscular condition itself.

This example draws attention to the way social attitudes and practices can create childhood adversity. It can be argued that it is not that children are disabled and therefore suffering adversity but that society labels them as disabled and turns their disability into an adversity. If, for example, a child in a wheelchair cannot go to a mainstream school because there are not the facilities such as wheel ramps, lavatories and lifts, then it is not the child's disabilities which are causing adversity but the school's, and society's, attitudes and lack of provision (see also Stainton Rogers, 2003, p. 184).

Although many public buildings are accessible to children in wheelchairs, children are still sometimes disabled by lack of provision for their needs.

Adversity and gender

Another way in which societies can create adversity for children relates to gender. In certain parts of the world, it could be argued that being born (or indeed conceived) a girl is in itself a form of adversity, because of the lower chances compared to boys of reaching term, surviving infancy and achieving health and education. This is not due to an inherently greater vulnerability amongst female infants. On the contrary:

> Males are more vulnerable than females … more male fetuses are spontaneously aborted during pregnancy than females … they are more susceptible to prenatal and perinatal complications; more boys than girls die in infancy; and throughout life men remain more at risk for many diseases and accidents. Such differential vulnerability has its counterpart in psychological development: thus in determining what kinds of children are most susceptible to stress sex has quite consistently emerged as a predictor.

> (Schaffer, 1996, p. 93)

But in societies that place higher value on boy children, girls become vulnerable through the ways they are treated. In other words, it is not that being a girl as such is disadvantageous. It is people's reactions to, and expectations of, girls that turns being female into an adversity. One thirteen-year-old girl in Bangladesh expressed her feelings very clearly:

> Our society doesn't value girls and that's not right. They should value us. Girls are human, too.

> (The Open University, 2003)

Gender discrimination in terms of life chances and health opportunities is discussed in greater detail in Chapter 2, Section 3.3 and in Chapter 3, Section 3.4 (see also Stainton Rogers, 2003, Section 5).

Afghan refugees attending a UNESCO-sponsored school in Islamabad, Pakistan. Under the Taleban regime in Afghanistan, girls were not allowed to go to school and had few civil rights. For these girls, having been born female was a form of adversity.

Adversity and ethnicity

Racial prejudice offers another clear example of the social construction of childhood adversity. Being a member of an ethnic or religious minority is obviously not, in itself, an adversity. It is the social attitudes towards a minority group and its children that constitute the risk to their well-being (see, for example, Connolly, 1998). These processes can operate at an institutional and societal level, not just at an individual level.

For example, it is well known that children's health and well-being can be harmed by various forms of environmental pollution, such as from concentrated pesticide use, air pollution from industrial sites and high environmental concentrations of heavy metals, notably lead. As with material poverty and family discord, children are not equally at risk from these environmental hazards. For example, high levels of vulnerability are associated with urban poverty (such as poor housing and water supplies), specific geographical locations (such as industrial sites) or specific parental occupations (such as intensive agriculture). Via these factors, environmental risk is also linked to ethnicity. For example, Sharon Stephens draws on the concept of 'environmental racism' to account for the evidence in the USA that African-American children are reported to be two to three times more likely than white children to suffer from lead poisoning. 'This is largely because people of color do not have the same opportunities as whites to "vote with their feet" – to escape unhealthy physical environments by moving' (Stephens, 1998, p. 54). (See Chapter 3, Section 3.3 for further discussion.)

Saunders housing project and Marathon Oil Refinery, Texas City, USA. African-American and Hispanic children are two to three times more likely than white children to suffer the effects of lead poisoning and environmental pollution.

2.3 Adversity in children's best interests?

Poverty, family conflict, prejudice and discrimination are all widely recognized as having adverse effects on children's well-being – in terms of both their physical and psychological health. But there are other situations where the label 'adversity' does not immediately seem so appropriate. For

In both situations children do repetitive, boring tasks and, it can be argued, different forms of child labour.

A cram school in Japan.

A factory in Thailand using child labour.

example, take the situation of children in well-resourced classrooms in one of the world's most affluent countries – Japan. In the next reading, Norma Field makes the case for seeing some aspects of Japanese childhood as a form of adversity.

READING

Reading A discusses the schooling of relatively wealthy children from stable backgrounds. These children might be assumed to experience relatively little adversity in their lives, yet Field depicts these children as suffering. Under the heading 'Education as endless labor', she suggests that the situation of many Japanese children has much in common with that of children who are forced to work in hazardous and exploitative conditions in the poorest countries of the world. As you read this short article think about the following questions:

1   In what ways does the author think schooling is potentially harmful to Japanese children?

2   Why might parents choose this form of education as the best for their children?

3   Do you consider that the pressures of competitive schooling in rich societies are a threat to children's well-being?

COMMENT

Field describes the children in some Japanese schools as labourers because of the expectations placed upon them – the long hours of study, repetitive learning tasks, productivity in terms of exam results. Yet these children are not protected by any child labour laws.

According to her account, children can suffer both psychologically and physically. She draws an analogy with the pressures on sports and music prodigies – channelled into a narrow range of activities and stretched to reach higher and higher achievements, until they can no longer cope and become ill. Here adversity is about social pressure and expectation rather than poverty. Indeed, it could be argued that these children suffer *because* of their parents' affluence rather than despite it. Of course, one thing that makes these children's situation different from a child labourer in extreme poverty is that the parents are in a much stronger position to choose what is 'best' for their children. Many parents might claim that competitive schooling is desirable and believe it to be in their children's best interests. Far from exposing their children to harm, they are doing their very best to ensure their future prospects, preparing children for the demands of modern employment. They might also argue that short-term hardships during childhood are justified by long-term benefits to children and their families.

It is Field who labels this situation as damaging to children. She challenges arguments about choice, especially where children's choices are concerned, because of the medical evidence of adverse effects: '... the recent statistics are suggestive of how the bodies of children speak even when their tongues do not' (Reading A, p. 36). (See Maybin and Woodhead, 2003, for a more extended discussion about the impact of school and work in children's lives, in past as well as contemporary societies.)

The first lesson from this reading is that adversity is not just linked to material, economic and social deprivations. In extreme cases, children can be at risk within situations that are supposed to promote their best interests. Bear in mind that Article 28 of the UN Convention on the Rights of the Child does not just state that children have a right to education. It says that education should be compulsory – being required to attend school is seen as part of children's rights. Schools may be planned as benign environments for children but claims about high-pressure schools (as in Reading A), as well as evidence of bullying in schools (see Chapter 4, Section 3), are a reminder that children may experience these settings very differently. The same can be said about some aspects of health and social care provision, and about some juvenile justice systems. Cases of physical and sexual abuse of children in residential homes by those employed to care for them offer an especially stark reminder that vulnerable children can suffer adversity in the very settings designed to protect them (Green, 1999).

The second lesson from Reading A is about the controversies that surround what counts as adversity. The educational practices that Field views as harmful are also considered harmful by some parents and teachers in Japan itself, but certainly not by all. Many parents accept them as inevitable. In fact, some might argue that experiences of moderate adversity can actually be beneficial to children, by challenging their inner resources, helping them to cope with difficult situations and teaching them important life skills. The same might be said of those children in the Oakland Growth Study who adapted to the hardships of the Great Depression and found opportunities to become more independent and autonomous (see Section 2.1).

In short, there may be strong disagreements about what situations are adverse to children, and what constitutes damage to children's well-being in the long term. There is a difficult line to be drawn between acknowledging diversity in cultural beliefs and practices on the one hand and setting standards which identify certain beliefs and practices as harmful, or even abusive, especially since a stressful situation may be experienced as adversity by one child, but a challenge by another. Children's abilities to cope with adversities – their resilience as well as their vulnerability – are the subject of the next section.

SUMMARY OF SECTION 2

- Different kinds of adversity affect children in different ways. Adversity is often the result of multiple and cumulative events which threaten children's well-being.

- Longitudinal studies of children growing up in economic hardship illustrate how the same underlying set of circumstances can affect children differently according to their age and gender.

- Research into children whose parents experience marital difficulties, separation and divorce have identified parental discord and conflict as one of the major factors that put children at risk. In the past, some of the risk associated with divorce may have been due to social attitudes as well as the experience itself.

- Some adversities can be socially constructed, for example, where children are labelled, stigmatized or discriminated against because of their gender, race or disability.

- Children's well-being can be affected even within situations intended to promote their best interests, such as when they are under intense pressure to achieve in school.

3 VULNERABILITY AND RESILIENCE

Earlier sections of this chapter have concentrated on the adversities that young people may face throughout their childhood, examining how situations as diverse as poverty and environmental pollution, divorce and gender discrimination can adversely affect a child's well-being. Yet the examples we have looked at repeatedly draw attention to the limitations of many discussions of the effects of adversity, because of the marked differences in how children react, depending on context, age, gender and social attitudes.

Recognition of the marked differences in children's reactions to adversity has led to new ways of conceptualizing the topic. Researchers began to realize that most attention had understandably been on the ways adversities can harm children, but that this had led to the neglect of situations where children appear to thrive despite adversity. They began to ask 'What makes children resilient?' as well as 'What makes children vulnerable?' (e.g. Rutter, 1987; Masten, 1994). Having looked at how children respond to adversity, this section now looks in more detail at the specific risk and protective factors that exist in children's lives. It goes on to examine in detail a study that attempted to define such factors for a group of children growing up in Hawaii in the 1950s and 1960s. Finally, it considers children who develop resilience through caring for others.

3.1 Risk factors and protective factors

The concepts of vulnerability and resilience go hand in hand with two other important concepts – *risk factors* and *protective factors*:

> 'Risk' refers to variables that increase an individual's likelihood of psychopathology or their susceptibility to negative developmental outcomes. Some risks are found internally; they result from the unique combination of characteristics that make up an individual, such as temperament or neurological structure. Other risks are external; that is they result from environmental factors, such as poverty or war, which inhibit an individual's healthy development.
>
> (Boyden and Mann, 2000, p. 7)

According to this view, the greater the number of risks children face (internal and external), the greater will be their vulnerability to poorer health, developmental delay and psychological difficulties. Conversely, children's resilience will tend to be increased by the presence of protective factors. As with risk factors, protective factors can be internal or external – internal qualities, such as good health, emotional stability and adaptability; and external circumstances, such as adequate nutrition and emotionally supportive relationships – all of which combine to help an individual cope with misfortune.

Allow about 10 minutes

A C T I V I T Y 3   **An example of risk and protective factors**

As a simple illustration, think about the following (fictitious) example, involving two young children, Edward and David.

Edward has an affectionate and calm temperament. David is more irritable and restless. David's parents find their son hard to manage whereas Edward's parents find theirs easygoing. Just before they are due to start school, both boys experience the break-up of their parents' marriage. How do you think they might respond? How well do you think they will adjust to starting school?

Now consider the following. Both boys are very fond of their grandparents, who live in a nearby town, so they are used to seeing them once or twice a week. Unfortunately, three months after David starts school, his grandparents announce they have to move house to a town 100 miles away. At the same time, Edward's grandparents decide to live even nearer to their grandson, so that they can offer extra support. Again, think about how each child might be affected by this new change in his life.

Finally, how might the outcome be different if Edward's grandparents move away, and David's come to live nearby?

C O M M E N T

This example is designed to illustrate the way risk factors and protective factors combine to increase children's vulnerability or resilience in the face of adversity. The boys both experience their parents' separation – an external risk to their well-being. But this risk does not affect them in isolation. It interacts with other risk and protective factors. Put very simply, David's irritable temperament can be seen as an (internal) risk factor, making it more likely he would be seriously affected by his parents' separation, perhaps by becoming difficult or aggressive at school, or clinging to his mother or father and refusing to go at all. Edward's temperament can be seen as an (internal) protective factor, making it more likely he would cope with the adjustment to school.

If David's grandparents move further away, this would be an additional (external) risk factor threatening his well-being. He might experience this as another form of emotional rejection, very possibly adding to his vulnerability and his difficulties adjusting to school. By contrast, Edward's grandparents' decision to move closer would serve as another (external) protective factor for Edward, increasing his resilience. However, if the grandparents' planned moves were reversed, the boys' situations in terms of vulnerability–resilience would be more balanced. Edward's adjustment to school might be put at risk, while the increased support and attention from David's grandparents might help him come to terms with what had happened.

This example is not entirely hypothetical. The influence of children's temperament on their social adjustment is well established by research, as is the role of social support in protecting children from adversities (reviewed by Schaffer, 1996). Of course, in real situations of adversity, risk and protective factors influence children's vulnerability and resilience in much more complex ways. For example, Beardsall and Dunn (1992) studied pairs of siblings in the UK, where one sibling was six years old and the other older. They observed the impact of a traumatic event on each of the siblings, such as the death or illness of one family member, unemployment of the primary breadwinner, or parents' divorcing. They judged that the negative effect of these events on brothers and sisters was the same in only 31 per cent of cases.

> The following example illustrates the differing impact of 'shared' events on two siblings: in one family the father had to leave home for three months because of his job; this had far more impact on the first-born son than on his sister; the family was then involved in a car accident in which there was a fire, the father was injured and the driver of the other car killed. The first-born son was considerably disturbed by the events, his sister only temporarily upset. In another family, there was a rift between the parents and a close family friend – a supportive 'granny' figure, who then stopped visiting the family: this had a severe impact on one child, who had been especially close to the friend, and only a mild effect on the sibling.
>
> (Beardsall and Dunn, 1992, p. 353)

There are many reasons why these children might react differently to the same events. We could ask about their age, gender, birth order or their temperament and personality. We could ask about the intensity and quality of their relationships with other family members, the availability of emotional support from friends, teachers or others outside the family, and so on. By making a full assessment of both risk and protective factors, it becomes more possible to predict how well a child will cope with adversity – their vulnerability or resilience – as well as where intervention may be most needed and most effective.

3.2 A longitudinal study of vulnerability and resilience

One of the first major studies into children's resilience in the face of adversity was carried out on the Hawaiian island of Kauai by Emmy Werner and Ruth Smith. In a longitudinal study, Werner and Smith followed the progress of nearly 700 babies born in 1955, checking them at intervals throughout their childhood and on into adult life. This provided a rich resource of research data about the way adversities affected individual children, as well as the factors that helped many to cope. At the start of the study, the total population of Kauai was about 32,000, of mixed ethnic descent, living mainly in small towns scattered around the 30-mile-wide island. Initially the economy was based mainly on sugar and pineapples. However, it underwent significant change during the course of the study, notably through the growth of tourism as well as scientific and military installations, due to the strategic importance of Hawaii as a US state located in the Pacific Ocean (it achieved statehood in 1959). One of the remarkable features of this longitudinal study was its success in keeping track of children and families, with 88 per cent of the babies followed through to the age of eighteen.

Two Hawaiian girls in the 1960s.

About half the children were growing up in poverty, with many compounding risk factors such as perinatal complications, poor living conditions, family instability and low parental education. Not surprisingly, many of these high-risk children did indeed go on to suffer at school, get into trouble with the law or suffer from mental or physical health problems. However,

> … there were others, also *vulnerable*, exposed to poverty, perinatal stress and family instability, reared by parents with little education or serious mental health problems, who remained invincible [i.e. resilient], and developed into competent and autonomous young adults, who worked well, played well, loved well, and expected well.

> (Werner and Smith, 1982, p. xv)

Werner and Smith set out to investigate what factors protected some children from risk or, in their words, what made some vulnerable children invincible.

READING

Reading B is an extract taken from the concluding chapter of Werner and Smith's report in which they sum up the main findings of their study. They begin by setting out some brief details of the children's backgrounds and of the social changes during their childhood. They go on to explain the adversities facing these children which made them a high-risk group. As you read through the extract, make a list of the factors that distinguish 'resilient high-risk' children from 'vulnerable high-risk' children. For both groups, note internal qualities of the children (e.g. temperament, social responsiveness) and external qualities of their social environment (e.g. close, supportive relationships in family and community).

COMMENT

Out of a cohort group of 700, only 204 children 'developed serious behavior or learning problems at *some time* during the first two decades of their lives' (Werner and Smith, 1982, p. 2). As Werner and Smith explain, they became particularly interested in the children who developed into competent and autonomous individuals despite these high risks, whom they called the 'resilient high-risk' children.

Elsewhere in their report, Werner and Smith explain that the 'resilient high-risk' group included 42 girls and 30 boys, whereas the main comparison group of 'vulnerable high risk' children included 39 girls and 51 boys.

Werner and Smith offer some additional insights into the differential vulnerability of boys and girls, which shifted between childhood and adolescence. Note that Werner and Smith's evidence that girls show higher resilience than boys in the long term builds on the evidence of earlier sections in this chapter, and reinforces the point that gender becomes a form of adversity in societies that adopt discriminatory practices (see Section 2.2).

Werner and Smith's pioneering research into risk and protective factors associated with children's long-term vulnerability or resilience has been very influential on subsequent studies into the effects of childhood adversities. Of course, the identification of risk and protective factors raises new questions about precisely how these different factors combine in children's lives. Werner and Smith offer some suggestions:

> The physical robustness of the resilient children, their high activity level, and their social responsiveness were recognized by the caregivers and elicited a great deal of attention … The strong attachment that resulted appears to have been a secure base for the development of the advanced self-help skills and autonomy noted among these children in their second year of life.
>
> (Reading B, p. 39)

Note the emphasis given here to children's own roles in the processes that shape their resilience and vulnerability, as well as the ways in which characteristics of the child interact with the features of their caregivers. The image of children being presented through this research is not simply of passive victims of adversity. Of course, in one sense these children are victims, since they have no control over the quality of the environment into which they are born, especially the caregiving they receive during the earliest months and years. But children do play an active part in determining the outcomes of adversity in a more subtle sense, through the qualities they bring to each difficult situation they meet:

> Some children are better able to manage stress because of disposition or temperament. Thus, some of the protective factors such as resourcefulness, curiosity, a goal for which to live, and a need and ability to help others are largely matters of temperament and coping style. Generally, children who are able to remain hopeful about the future, are flexible and adaptable, possess problem-solving skills and actively try to assume control over their lives are likely to be less

vulnerable than those who passively accept their condition. Children who develop constructive coping techniques are normally better able to deal with their feelings and emotions than those who are less able to be hopeful and optimistic. Socially-competent children, capable of lateral thinking and problem solving, can enhance their coping by identifying alternative options to their current circumstances and devising creative solutions. The capacity to engage in critical thinking can also help to shield a child from simplistic interpretations of experience that are self-defeating and socially destructive in the long run. Personal history also has vital influence on coping. Children who have experienced approval, acceptance and opportunities for mastery are far more likely to be resilient than those who have been subjected to humiliation, rejection, or failure.

(Boyden and Mann, 2000, p. 8)

Separating these so-called internal qualities of the children from external protective factors is helpful but it does not tell the full story. As we discussed previously, they are often interdependent. For instance, one of the reasons children's temperament, level of activity and social responsiveness can be so influential on their resilience is because it affects the quality of their relationships, especially with those on whom they depend for survival, care and learning. Some children may be more effective than others in eliciting those very kinds of nurturance, emotional support and guidance which serve as protective factors.

Stories of children surviving situations of extreme adversity illustrate how children's own resourcefulness can enable them to form mutually beneficial relationships with adults. Apfel and Simon (1996) cite two cases: a twelve-year-old Cambodian girl in a refugee camp, whose acting talents attracted the attention of an American woman who subsequently adopted her; and Israeli writer Elie Wiesel, who as a thirteen-year-old boy in Auschwitz received an extra bowl of soup from other camp inmates in return for his stories about his home life before the war, and who survived. Of course, the converse is also sadly true, where children's chances of survival and healthy development have been reduced because they have been less successful in engaging positive adult attention, or have even provoked hostility.

Other children can also increase or undermine children's resilience. Peer relationships play a powerful role in children's social, emotional and cultural lives (see Kehily and Swann, 2003). Supportive friends can help buffer difficult experiences at home; rejection or bullying can do the opposite (see Chapter 4, Section 3). Box 1 gives an example of the importance of children's peers as a potential protective factor, even for very young children in situations of extreme adversity.

Box 1 Holocaust survivors

In October 1945, a group of six Jewish three-year-old orphans arrived at a country house in West Sussex, England. They were to be cared for by a small team of nurses, under the direction of Sophie and Gertrud Dann, who had worked with Anna Freud in setting up the wartime Hampstead nurseries in London. Later, Anna Freud and Sophie Dann wrote an account of their experiences with these children.

While the children's origins varied, all their parents had died in the Holocaust during the first year of their life. By the age of one, the babies were all together at the Theresienstadt concentration camp not far from Prague (now in the Czech Republic). They received basic care from other inmates, who were themselves undernourished, overworked and in constant threat of deportation to Auschwitz. The camp was liberated by the Russians in early 1945, and the children were taken to a holding centre for one month, before being flown to England in bombers. They went initially to a reception camp, in the Lake District, and then eventually travelled south to begin their new lives in West Sussex. At this point, they had experienced multiple deprivations and trauma, plus the disturbing effect of several complete changes of environment in a matter of months. One of the few constant features in these three-year-olds' recent lives was each other.

> During the first days after arrival they destroyed all the toys and damaged much of the furniture. Toward the staff they behaved either with cold indifference or with active hostility … They would turn to an adult when in some immediate need, but treat the same person as nonexistent once more when the need was fulfilled. In anger, they would hit the adults, bite or spit …

> The children's positive feelings were centered exclusively in their own group. It was evident that they cared greatly for each other and not at all for anybody or anything else. They had no other wish than to be together and became upset when they were separated from each other, even for short moments. No child would consent to remain upstairs while the others were downstairs, or vice versa, and no child would be taken for a walk or on an errand without the others. If anything of the kind happened, the single child would constantly ask for the other children while the group would fret for the missing child.

(Freud and Dann, 1951, pp. 130–1)

Refugee children, survivors from Theresienstadt concentration camp, Czechoslovakia, arriving in England on 14 August 1945 on the last flight of the airlift of twelve Lancaster bombers which carried the children from Prague.

3.3 Children who care

In some circumstances, protective factors are not just about children gaining support through relationships with adults or peers. They are about children finding resilience through taking responsibility for others. In the UK, it is estimated that more than 50,000 children take on significant day-to-day caring responsibilities for immediate relatives who are very often older than them – parents, grandparents, brothers or sisters who may be disabled, mentally or physically ill or in other respects dependent.

A young carer in the UK helps her mother.

Allow about 30 minutes

ACTIVITY 4 **Young carers**

Read through the description below of a sixteen-year-old carer called Julie. She lives in the UK and takes on substantial caring responsibilities for her brother. Some people might say that she is coping with a form of adversity, although it is obvious that she sees things differently. Based on what you have read earlier in this section, list all the risk factors Julie faces and then list the protective factors that boost her resilience. Overall, do you think that she is vulnerable or resilient?

> I don't think anyone would choose to be a 'carer' at any age, and while you are young it can be especially difficult. But I know that it is this that has made me who I am and has changed my life in many ways. All this despite the temporary difficulties. I like to see things in a positive

light and would like any young carers who may read this to think positively too.

At times being a carer is tiring and soul-destroying. I battle against an invisible disease in my brother that means his health deteriorates, but the signs are very visible and as a family we must deal with them. I am the only one who can give him emotional support when he is feeling down. Our parents drive him round the bend (surprise surprise!) and it's me who's left to make him smile when he's going through hard times. It's me who is there to make him laugh when there's absolutely nothing to laugh about. However much hard work it is to achieve this, it's always worthwhile for the smiles and look he gives me. However much I 'give' to him, the amount he 'gives' back in return far exceeds this.

The time I spend with my brother is based around making sure he has the time of his life now, because he may not later. I could live five times longer than him, so his quality of life is important to me. It's great when we go out somewhere excellent, or go on holiday, because he enjoys it even if it's not 'my idea of fun'.

Being a young carer teaches you so much, perhaps taking away childhood, but often giving you an awareness of life and how precious it is. Some would say I've had to grow up too fast, but I believe I've made more of my life because of it.

Sometimes I feel like I have to make up for what he can't do. I try to be two children in one. I did this in my GCSEs [public exams taken by many schoolchildren in the UK at the age of sixteen] and do it in my hobbies, in my social life too. But it all boils down to the fact that I don't want to waste any opportunity I have got because I've seen just what it's like to have none at all.

Some people do the things they want to because they choose to. Young carers don't always get the choice, but what we want is not sympathy and apologies for our supposed misfortune, but recognition and encouragement for what we do.

(Bibby and Becker, 2000, p. 69)

COMMENT

Julie is living in a household where her brother is seriously ill and she feels she is taking on most of the emotional support for him. She is making sacrifices in her personal life and in her education and is taking on a role that she did not choose. These might all be seen as risk factors. However, she also exhibits many of the personal qualities associated with resilience. She has a sense of humour, a clear moral framework and a sense of responsibility in terms of caring for others. She has constructive coping techniques and a long-term plan for her life. She also has family support and remains hopeful about the future. Julie's sense of responsibility and her mature reflections about her situation convey a very different image from that of the vulnerable child unable to cope with adversity.

| SUMMARY OF SECTION 3 |

- Evidence that children respond very differently to adversities led researchers to introduce new theoretical frameworks for studying the effects of risk and protective factors on children's vulnerability and resilience.

- Resilience can be defined as the ways in which children cope with, and even respond positively to, adversity. This may be due to a combination of positive personality traits as well as a supportive social environment.

- Werner and Smith carried out one of the first studies on children's resilience based on children born on the Hawaiian island of Kauai. Their study showed how children's temperaments interact with family and community factors to determine whether they are vulnerable or resilient.

- Internal protective factors, related to temperament, sense of humour, feelings of purpose, belief in a bright future and spirituality can protect children from some of the effects of adversity.

- External protective factors, such as an adult or peer who shows an interest in the child, may also promote a child's resilience.

- The case of young carers shows children who can become resilient through taking on responsibilities not normally expected at their age.

4 THE CULTURAL CONTEXT OF RESEARCH AND INTERVENTION

The theoretical framework set out in Section 3 was developed mainly from research in North American and European contexts. It has become increasingly influential in studies of the effects of adversity, especially amongst those working in developmental psychology and psychopathology (Masten, 2001). It has the advantage of encompassing both vulnerability and resilience, helping to account for individual differences, and suggesting where intervention is most appropriate. However, questions have been raised (especially by social anthropologists and cultural psychologists) about how far patterns of risk and protective factors apply to all societies and all children in all circumstances. There are two main issues:

- how far risk and protective factors need to be seen as context specific;
- whether too much attention is placed on the individual and not enough on community mechanisms for dealing with risk.

A refugee in Macedonia is comforted by her child.

Risk and protective factors in context

Specifying internal and external risk and protective factors must not overlook the extent to which expectations of children and of the ways they are treated are culturally defined. Arguably these cultural expectations will powerfully modify whether a particular type of personality or a particular set of experiences count as risk factors. (We have already touched on this issue in Sections 2.1 and 2.2 in relation to social attitudes, stigma and the social construction of childhood.)

For example, take the issue of how far children's age affects their vulnerability or resilience. Western research suggests as a general rule that younger children are more vulnerable than older children – although the sensitivity of the early years should not be exaggerated (Schaffer, 2000). But research carried out in Ethiopia has suggested that in some situations it is not chronological age itself that affects vulnerability/resilience so much as cultural expectations of the behaviour and activities at certain ages. In Ethiopia, many boys were conscripted into the army in the 1980s and 1990s to fight in the war with Eritrea. Some of these had gone through their initiation ceremony, which emphasized that they had made a transition to manhood and to full adult membership of their group. Warfare was sanctioned as a proper manly activity and these new initiates were encouraged to show their manliness by fighting. After the war, agencies involved in reintegrating boys back into their communities noticed a distinct difference in their ability to cope with civilian life and to come to terms with what they had done as combatants, depending on whether or not they had been initiated. Those younger boys who had not been initiated still viewed themselves as children, despite their experiences of war. They found it much harder to come to terms with what they had done and to reconcile the brutality they had experienced, and had inflicted, with their status as children (de Berry and Boyden, 2000). In this context, undergoing an initiation ritual was a key protective factor which improved these young men's resilience by sanctioning their experiences.

The idea that risk and protective factors are in part culturally defined connects with themes earlier in this chapter, particularly how Japanese children and parents view the pressures of competitive schooling. Another example of culturally defined risks and vulnerabilities relates to young people working. Until children are about sixteen years old, the main focus of concern within Western societies concentrates on potential adverse effects of work. But for young people a few years older, the concern reverses, and unemployment is seen as a greater risk to well-being. Arguably the difference in perceived risk has little to do with the age of children or the activities involved, and much more to do with cultural expectations about being a child versus a young adult (Woodhead, 1999). For an extended discussion of the significance of transitions between childhood and adulthood, see Morrow (2003).

Community response to risk

Risk and resiliency can be seen as cultural in an even more profound sense. The search for explanations for individual differences in responses to adversity in terms of a combination of internal and external factors is arguably an expression of Western ideas about the separate, individualized, developing child. Questions concerning the relevance of Western-inspired ideas about the relationship between the individual and the community become especially significant in relation to therapeutic interventions:

> In many … societies different conceptions of the self and its relationship to the social and the supernatural … mean that explorations of inner emotions and conflicts have less relevance than in the West. In short, helping to alleviate distress by the exploration of intrapsychic cognitions, emotions and conflicts is a form of healing somewhat peculiar to Western societies and of doubtful relevance to societies holding different core assumptions about the nature of the self and illness.
>
> (Bracken, Giller and Summerfield, 1995, p. 1075)

This point will be taken up again in Chapter 3, which challenges the universality of Western medical ideas in relation to the causes of and appropriate treatment for physical and mental illness.

The final reading for this chapter illustrates these dilemmas about cultural approaches to therapeutic intervention, at the same time revisiting many of the themes of Section 3 about children's resilience in the face of adversities.

Bhutanese refugees in a Nepalese camp. This photo was taken by a refugee child who wrote: 'These are friends playing nearby my hut. Now we have spent eight years in camp. My friends are here but it is not the place I call home.'

READING

Reading C is about children in a refugee camp in Nepal. It focuses on ethnic Nepalese families who have been forced to flee their homes in Bhutan. The children have experienced many dimensions of adversity. They are poor. They have been persecuted on the grounds of their ethnicity and sometimes witnessed the brutality of Bhutanese soldiers. They have lost their homes and familiar surroundings, been forced to travel with their families and make a new life in a refugee camp. We might expect these children to be suffering badly. But Rachel Hinton, an anthropologist, offers a very different account of these children's lives, based on twelve months as a participant observer in the refugee camps. This reading is an extract from a longer chapter in which Hinton asks about the kinds of intervention that are most effective to help these refugees. As you read through this extract, make a note of the ways in which children show resilience in the face of adversity, and ask yourself why they might be able to cope in some cases better than adults.

COMMENT

By almost any criteria, being a refugee is an adverse circumstance and certainly some children appear to miss the familiar landmarks and security of home. However, their reaction to these adverse circumstances is less predictable. Hinton is critical of approaches which assume these children are helpless victims, and of approaches based on individualistic Western approaches to intervention. She draws attention to the significance of extensive social networks within the refugee communities, especially the active role that children appear to play in supporting their parents.

SUMMARY OF SECTION 4

- Cultural studies of vulnerability and resilience suggest that risk and protective factors may be linked to specific contexts and sets of circumstances. Cultural beliefs about what counts as childhood adversity can affect children's abilities to cope with difficult situations.

- Western theories emphasize the effects of adversities on individuals, and the power of individual qualities to promote resilience. These theories give less attention to community processes for dealing with risk. Individual counselling or therapy is not always appropriate for all societies.

- Children can play an important role in supporting their parents' ability to cope with displacement, thus enabling them to cope with adversity themselves.

5 CONCLUSION

Vulnerability–resilience has proved a useful framework for academics and practitioners working with children at risk because it takes on board the variety of children's experiences and reactions to adversity. It also acknowledges a child's agency and active response to situations of adversity. It should not, however, detract from the recognition that in many circumstances children are especially vulnerable in the face of adversity, which can affect their physical and psychological well-being as well as their social adjustment. The fact that some children do cope even in the worst of circumstances requires a more sensitive understanding of the impact of adversities in children's lives. Issues of adversity, vulnerability and resilience will recur in the next three chapters of this book, which focus on poverty, ill-health and violence. All of these chapters discuss children's differing reactions to adversity and the interplay between external circumstances and individual characteristics. In Chapters 5 and 6, we will review approaches to intervention, including asking about situations where children are not just resilient in the face of adversity but actively engage in trying to change the social institutions that shape their lives.

REFERENCES

APFEL, R. AND SIMON, B. (1996) 'Psychosocial interventions for children of war: the value of a model of resiliency, medicine and global survival', http://www2.healthnet.org/MGS/Article3.html (accessed 29 May 2002).

BEARDSALL, L. and DUNN, J. (1992) 'Adversities in childhood: siblings' experiences, and their relations to self-esteem', *Journal of Child Psychology and Psychiatry*, **33**, pp. 349–59.

BIBBY, A. and BECKER, S. (2000) *Young Carers in their Own Words*, London, Turnaround Publisher Service.

BOYDEN, J. and MANN, G. (2000) 'Children's risk, resilience and coping in extreme situations', background paper to the Consultation on Children in Adversity, Oxford, 9–12 September 2000.

BRACKEN, P., GILLER, J. E. AND SUMMERFIELD, D. (1995) 'Psychological responses to war and atrocity: the limitations of current concepts', *Social Science and Medicine*, **40**(8), pp. 1073–82.

BURR, R. and MONTGOMERY, H. K. (2003) 'Children and rights' in WOODHEAD, M. and MONTGOMERY, H. K. (eds) *Understanding Childhood: an interdisciplinary approach*, Chichester, John Wiley and Sons Ltd/The Open University (Book 1 of the Open University course U212 *Childhood*).

CONNOLLY, P. (1998) *Racism, Gender Identities and Young Children: social relations in a multi-ethnic, inner city primary school*, London, Routledge.

DE BERRY, J. and BOYDEN, J. (2000) 'Children in adversity', *Forced Migration*, **9**, pp. 33–6.

ELDER, G. H. (1974) *Children of the Great Depression: social change in life experience*, Chicago, University of Chicago Press.

ELDER, G. H., MODELL, J. and PARKE, R. D. (1993) 'Studying children in a changing world' in ELDER, G. H., MODELL, J. and PARKE, R. D. (eds) *Children in Time and Place*, Cambridge, Cambridge University Press.

FERGUSSON, D. M., HORWOOD, L. J. and LYNSKEY, M. T. (1992) 'Family change, parental discord and early offending', *Journal of Child Psychology and Psychiatry*, **33**, pp. 1059–76.

FREUD, A., and DANN, S. (1951) 'An experiment in group upbringing', *Psychoanalytic Study of the Child*, **6**, pp. 127–68.

GREEN, L. (1999) 'Sexuality, sexual abuse and children's homes: oppression or protection?' in The Violence Against Children Study Group (eds) *Children, Child Abuse and Child Protection: placing children centrally*, Chichester, John Wiley & Sons.

KEHILY, M. J. and SWANN, J. (eds) (2003) *Children's Cultural Worlds*, Chichester, John Wiley and Sons Ltd/The Open University (Book 3 of the Open University course U212 *Childhood*).

MASTEN, A. S. (1994) 'Resilience in individual development: successful adaptation despite risk and adversity' in WANG, M. C. and GORDON, E. W. (eds), *Educational Resilience in Inner-city America*, Hillsdale, NJ, Lawrence Erlbaum.

MASTEN, A. S. (2001) 'Ordinary magic: resilience processes in development', *American Psychologist*, **56**(3), pp. 227–38.

MAYBIN, J. and WOODHEAD, M. (eds) (2003) *Childhoods in Context*, Chichester, John Wiley and Sons Ltd/The Open University (Book 2 of the Open University course U212 *Childhood*).

MORROW, V. (2003) 'Moving out of childhood' in MAYBIN, J. and WOODHEAD, M. (eds) *Childhoods in Context*, Chichester, John Wiley and Sons Ltd/The Open University (Book 2 of the Open University course U212 *Childhood*).

THE OPEN UNIVERSITY (2003) U212 *Childhood*, Video 1, Band 6, 'Being a Girl', Milton Keynes, The Open University.

RODGERS, B. and PRIOR, J. (1998) *Divorce and Separation: the outcomes for children*, York, Joseph Rowntree Foundation.

RUTTER, M. (1981, 2nd edn) *Maternal Deprivation Re-assessed*, Harmondsworth, Penguin Books.

RUTTER, M. (1987) 'Psychosocial resilience and protective mechanisms', *American Journal of Orthopsychiatry*, **57**, pp. 316–31.

SAVE THE CHILDREN (2001) *Disabled Children's Rights – a practical guide*, London, Save the Children.

SCHAFFER, H. R. (1996) *Social Development*, Oxford, Blackwell.

SCHAFFER, H. R. (2000) 'The early experience assumption: past, present and future', *International Journal of Behavioural Development*, **24**(1), pp. 5–14.

STAINTON ROGERS, W. (2003) 'Gendered childhoods' in WOODHEAD, M. and MONTGOMERY, H. (eds) (2003) *Understanding Childhood: an interdisciplinary approach*, Chichester, John Wiley and Sons Ltd/The Open University (Book 1 of the Open University course U212 *Childhood*).

STEPHENS, S. (1998) 'Reflections on environmental justice: children as victims and social actors' in WILLIAMS, C. (ed.) *Environmental Victims: new risks, new injustice*, London, Earthscan Publications.

UNITED NATIONS (1989) *United Nations Convention on the Rights of the Child*, New York, United Nations.

WADSWORTH, M. (1986) 'Evidence from three birth cohort studies for long-term and cross-generation effects on the development of children' in RICHARDS, M. and LIGHT, P. (eds) *Children of Social Worlds*, Cambridge, Polity Press.

WERNER, E. AND SMITH, R. (1982) *Vulnerable but Invincible*, New York, McGraw-Hill.

WOODHEAD, M. (1997) 'Psychology and the cultural construction of children's needs' in JAMES, A. and PROUT, A. (eds, 2nd edn) *Constructing and Reconstructing Childhood*, London, Falmer Press.

WOODHEAD, M. (1999) *Is There a Place for Work in Child Development?*, Stockholm, Save the Children.

READING A

Education as endless labor

Norma Field

For some two decades now, the Japanese media have reported the rising incidence of so-called adult diseases among school-aged children in Japan. A 1990 survey of grammar school children nationwide showed that 63.2 percent were suffering from high levels of blood cholesterol, 36.2 percent from ulcers, 22.1 percent from high blood pressure, and 21.4 percent from diabetes (Arita and Yamaoka, 1992:14). While these percentages are high, the symptoms themselves have become too familiar to shock. More freshly startling are the comments of a spokesperson for Aderansu, the leading artificial hair transplant manufacturers, that wigs are finding new customers among schoolchildren suffering from stress-related baldness attributable to the pressures of cram school attendance or bullying in their regular schools. Such reports, added to others detailing a new pervasiveness of eczema and chronic constipation, added to years of stories on school violence … are part of what lead me to believe that childhood itself is at risk in Japan today, and not because of war, disease, or malnutrition.

In thinking about the texture of the lives of children who suffer in these ways, I am led to the example of sports prodigies. We are all vaguely familiar with the texture of the lives led by sports prodigies and would-be sports prodigies in societies around the world, whether in Euroamerica, East Asia, or the former Eastern bloc: of how they relinquish the experience of childhood and adolescence, and of how their families willingly endure prolonged separation and financial hardship, no sacrifice being too great for the possibility of an Olympic medal or a touring contract. The early lives of musical prodigies suggest comparable structures of narrowly channeled self-expression and unremitting demands for discipline and performance. No child labor laws protect these young from the extractive industry for which they are the raw material, to be refined into spectacular commodities of however brief duration. Nor, presumably, do they need such laws, given that it is their 'choice' to dedicate themselves to these worthy goals.

There are no child labor laws to protect ordinary (at least, not yet demonstrably prodigious) Japanese two-year-olds from having to trace a path through countless mazes to acquire small-motor coordination, to match the same banal image – of strawberry, ball, shoe – in columns 1–4 with the one in column 5, from having to curb their sensibilities within the regime of the workbook before they can ride swings or wash their own faces – for of course, the point is neither merely to perfect small motor coordination nor to increase vocabulary per se, but to produce adults tolerant of joyless, repetitive tasks – in other words, disciplined workers.

There are also no child labor laws to protect the 50 percent of fourth through sixth graders in the capital region who attend cram schools from a routine of rushing home after school, grabbing dinners packed by their mothers, exchanging schoolbooks for cram school books, spending from 5 to 9 p.m. at the cram school (or going to more than one extra school if their mothers have chosen to have them specialize), perhaps staying on for private lessons until 11, and, when entrance exams are around the corner, getting home after midnight to tackle school homework, topped off with a touch of video game playing before going to sleep around 2 a.m. (Arita and Yamaoka, 1992:12). This, too, can be construed to be their choice, since these children know full well what it takes to get ahead and know, moreover, that the only way they will ever see friends is to go to cram school. The ideology of choice, nestled at the heart of liberalism, necessarily plays a complicated role in most societies. Its promise is compromised, if not altogether canceled, by refusal to acknowledge class, race, gender, and other forms of inequity on the one hand; on the other, it stunts social imagination by short-circuiting the impulse to question the proffered terms of choice. Whenever I hear that children like going to cram schools, or at least, that they do not mind it, I am reminded of the tactful caution with which it is necessary to treat statements that, to an outsider at least, seem to be affirmations by the oppressed of their conditions of oppression. At any rate, the recent statistics are suggestive of how the bodies of children speak even when their tongues do not.

The prevailing motifs in the march of Japanese educational progress are conveniently displayed in the writings of the prolific Ibuka Masaru, former chief executive officer and now honorary head of Sony Corporation and chair of the Conference on Culture and Education, a private group convened in the mid-1980s to advise then prime minister Nakasone. Ibuka's books bear such titles as *Why Age Zero? Life Is Decided at Age Zero* (1989) or *The Fetus Is a Genius. Education Begins before Birth* (1992). Ibuka insists that he is promoting techniques for the advancement of human character rather than recipes for smarter children … The spirit of capitalist progress is not only literally evident in the inclusion of advertisements for such devices as the 'Athleticot' (the crib that promotes infant development by providing monthly age-appropriate challenges), developed at the Organization for Child Development (headed by Ibuka), but in such chapter headings in the 1992 book as 'Even Age Zero Is Too Late,' which cancel the hope advanced but six years earlier that education might begin after a woman had actually seen her child ex utero.

The narrative of the progressively arduous journey of schooling can be clarified by referring to the model of the child prodigy once again. The prodigy is subjected to a punishing regimen where her marketable skills are concerned, but otherwise lavishly pampered. The children of averagely ambitious parents are handsomely rewarded to keep their noses to the bookish grindstone; they are at the least, especially the boys, outfitted with state-of-the-art video games …

Now, it is crucial to keep in mind that these pampered creatures are not prodigies but ordinary children to be found here, there, everywhere in Japan. (Indeed, health problems of the sort mentioned above and others are found evenly distributed in urban and rural areas.) It is the ordinary Japanese child who has become the raw material for the insatiable schooling industry, the ordinary child who at once toils and consumes, toils at consuming the products of this industry – cram schools, reference books, study guides, and above all, tests, tests, and more tests. To acknowledge the potential implied by, then abused, in this investment in the ordinary is a chilling exercise. For the prodigy model and the Japanese educational model should, and to some extent, do, have antithetical goals:

READING B **37**

for the former, the production of a relatively small number of individuals with remarkable, visible skills, who generate profit for a few others and themselves through the performance of those skills; for the latter, the production of an exceptionally competent society whose members work remarkably well but do not, should not, produce spectacle as individuals. In postwar Japanese education, the extraordinary investment in the ordinary has ended up generalizing the exploitative procedures designed to produce prodigies.

References

ARITA, M. and YAMAOKA, S. (1992) ' "Karoji" shokogun (the "overworthy child" syndrome)', *Asahi Journal*, March 20, pp. 11–16.

IBUKA, M. (1989) *Naze Zerosai Na No Ka: jinsei wa zerosai de kimarimasu* (Why age zero? Life is decided at age zero), Tokyo, Yojikaihatsu Kyokai.

IBUKA, M. (1992) *Taiji Wa Tensai Da* (The fetus is a genius), Tokyo, Yojikaihatsu Kyokai.

Source

FIELD, N. (1995) 'The child as labourer and consumer: the disappearance of childhood in contemporary Japan', in STEPHENS, S. (ed.) *Children and the Politics of Culture*, Princeton (NJ), Princeton University Press.

READING B

Vulnerable but invincible: a brief résumé of our findings

Emmy Werner and Ruth Smith

Our study group consisted of the children and grandchildren of immigrants who left the poverty of their Asian or European homelands to work for the sugar and pineapple plantations on the island of Kauai. Many intermarried with the local Hawaiians, who, oppressed by successive waves of newcomers, lost many lives and most of their land.

The children in our study had few material possessions, and most were raised by mothers who had not graduated from high school and by fathers who were semi- or unskilled laborers. They came of age during two and a half decades of unprecedented social change (1955–1979), which included statehood for Hawaii, the arrival of many newcomers from the U.S. mainland, and a prolonged and ill-fated war in Southeast Asia. During the first decade of their lives the children witnessed the assassination of one U.S. president, and during the second decade, the resignation, in disgrace, of another. In their teens they had access to contraceptive pills and mind-altering drugs, and they saw on television screens the space explorations that put man on the moon and his cameras within the range of other planets. Closer to home, they witnessed the undoing of the delicate balance of the island ecology that had evolved over millions of years by the rapid build-up of the tourist industry.

From an epidemiological point of view, these children were at high risk, since they were born and reared in chronic poverty, exposed to higher than average rates of prematurity and perinatal stress, and reared by mothers with little formal education. A combination of such social and biological variables correctly identified the majority of youth in this birth cohort who developed serious learning and behavior problems in childhood or adolescence.

Yet those in our [resilient high risk] index group (approximately one of ten in the cohort) managed to develop into competent and autonomous young adults who 'worked well, played well, loved well, and expected well.'

We contrasted their behavior characteristics and the features of their caregiving environment, from the perinatal period to the threshold of adulthood, with other high-risk children of the same age and sex who developed serious coping problems in the first and in the second decades of life.

Sex differences in vulnerability and resiliency

At birth, and throughout the first decade of life, more boys than girls were exposed to serious physical defects or illness requiring medical care, and more boys than girls had learning and behavior problems in the classroom and at home.

The physical immaturity of the boys, the more stringent expectations for male sex-role behavior in childhood, and the predominant feminine environment to which the boys were exposed, appeared to contribute both separately and in concert to a higher proportion of disordered behavior in childhood among the males than the females.

Trends were reversed in the second decade of life: The total number of boys with serious learning problems dropped, while the number of girls with serious behavior disorders rose. Boys seemed now more prepared for the demands of school and work, although they were still more often involved in antisocial and delinquent behavior. Girls were now confronted with social pressures and sex-role expectations that produced a higher rate of mental health problems in late adolescence and serious coping problems associated with teenage pregnancies and marriages ...

Related to this trend was the cumulative number of stressful life events reported by each sex. Boys with serious coping problems experienced more adversities than girls in *childhood*; girls with serious coping problems reported more stressful life events in *adolescence*. In spite of the biological and social pressures, which in this culture appear to make each sex more vulnerable at different times, more high-risk girls than high-risk boys grew into resilient young adults.

Coping patterns and sources of support among resilient children and youth

The resilient high-risk boys and girls had few serious illnesses in the first two decades of life and tended to recuperate quickly. Their mothers perceived them to be 'very active' and 'socially responsive' when they were infants, and independent observers noted their pronounced autonomy and positive social orientation when they were toddlers. Developmental examinations in the second year of life showed advanced self-help skills and adequate sensorimotor and language development for most of these children. In middle childhood the resilient boys and girls possessed adequate problem-solving and communication skills, and their perceptual-motor development was age-appropriate. Throughout childhood and adolescence they displayed both 'masculine' and 'feminine' interests and skills.

In late adolescence the resilient youth had a more internal locus of control [i.e. a sense of their own agency], a more positive self-concept, and a more nurturant, responsible, and achievement-oriented attitude toward life than peers who had developed serious coping problems. Their activities and interests were less sex-typed as well. At the threshold of adulthood, the resilient men and women had developed a sense of coherence in their lives and were able to draw on a number of informal sources of support. They also expressed a great desire to 'improve themselves,' i.e., toward continued psychological growth.

Among key factors in the caregiving environment that appeared to contribute to the resiliency and stress resistance of these high-risk children were: the age of the opposite-sex parent (younger mothers for resilient males, older fathers for resilient females); the number of children in the family (four or fewer); the spacing between the index child and the next-born sibling (more than 2 years); the number and type of alternate caretakers available to the mother within the household (father, grandparents, older siblings); the workload of the mother (including steady employment outside the household); the amount of attention given to the child by the primary caretaker(s) in infancy; the availability of a sibling as caretaker or confidant in childhood; structure and rules in the household in adolescence; the cohesiveness of the family; the presence of an informal multigenerational network of kin and friends in adolescence; and the cumulative number of chronic stressful life events in childhood and adolescence …

These families were poor by material standards, but a characteristically strong bond was forged between the infant and the primary caretaker during the first year of life. The physical robustness of the resilient children, their high activity level, and their social responsiveness were recognized by the caregivers and elicited a great deal of attention. There was little prolonged separation of the infants from their mothers and no prolonged bond disruption during the first year of life. The strong attachment that resulted appears to have been a secure base for the development of the advanced self-help skills and autonomy noted among these children in their second year of life.

Though many of their mothers worked for extended periods and were major contributors to family subsistence, the children had support from alternate caretakers, such as grandmothers or older sisters, to whom they became attached.

Many resilient children grew up in multiage households that included members of the grandparent generation. As older siblings departed from the household, the resilient girls took responsibility for the care of younger siblings. The employment of their mothers and the need for sibling caretaking seems to have contributed to a greater autonomy and sense of responsibility in the resilient girls, especially in households where the father was dead or otherwise permanently absent. Their competence was enhanced by a strong bond between the daughter and the other females in the family – sometimes across three generations (mother, grandmother, older sisters, or aunts).

Resilient boys, in turn, were often first born sons, lived in smaller families, and did not have to share their parents' attention with many additional children during the first decade of life. There were some males in their family who could serve as models for identification (fathers, older brothers, or uncles). There was structure and rules in the household, but space to explore in and less physical crowding. Last, but not least, there was an informal, multiage network of kin, peers, and elders who shared similar values and beliefs, and from whom the resilient youth sought counsel and support in times of crises and major role transitions.

These strong bonds were absent among families whose children had difficulties coping under duress. The lack of this emotional support was most devastating to children with a constitutional tendency toward withdrawal and passivity, with low activity levels, irregular sleeping and feeding habits, and a genetic background (i.e., parental psychoses, especially maternal schizophrenia) that made them more vulnerable to the influences of an adverse environment.

Most of these infants were perceived as retiring, passive, placid, or inactive in infancy by their mothers, and some had feeding and sleeping habits or a temper distressing to their primary caregiver. They experienced more prolonged bond disruptions during the first year of life. Mothers in these families worked sporadically outside the household, but there were few alternative caregivers in the home, such as fathers, grandparents, or older siblings. This lack of dependable substitute care appears to have been especially hard on the boys.

During childhood and adolescence, these youngsters were sick more often, more seriously, and more repeatedly than the resilient children, and they moved and changed schools more often as well. During the same period, they were exposed to more family discord and paternal absence (which took a greater toll among the boys), and to episodes of maternal mental illness (which took a greater toll among the girls).

By age 18 most of these youth had an external locus-of-control orientation and a low estimate of themselves. They felt that events happened to them as a result of luck, fate, or other factors beyond their control. Professional assistance sought from community agencies was considered of 'little help' to them.

Source

WERNER, E. and SMITH, R. (1982) *Vulnerable but Invincible*, New York, McGraw-Hill.

Seen but not heard: refugee children and models for intervention

Rachel Hinton

Since 1990, 87,000 men, women and children have fled from southern Bhutan to the Terai (lowland Nepal) … For adults who played significant social and economic roles in Bhutan, becoming a refugee has been a marginalizing experience. Their sense of abandonment is acute. In contrast, children's lifeworlds have been transplanted relatively intact into the crowded context of the refugee camp. While adults express feelings of abandonment, many of the children show greater concern with the material aspects of the camp environment.

This chapter discusses some hitherto unexplored social dynamics of camp interaction. It shows that when welfare intervention in the refugee camps focuses primarily on adults and seeks to identify vulnerable individuals or 'victims' for counselling, it overlooks the significant support role played by children, whose perceived position of vulnerability contributes to their being seen but not heard.

Concerned to provide a swift response to the needs of the refugees, policy-makers turned to traditional Western techniques of support. Many of these neglect the significant impact children have on the psychological and emotional worlds of adults. Despite high levels of community participation and involvement in aid programmes, the framework for interventions is rooted in Western notions of individualized and adult-centred counselling. In recent years this approach has been increasingly challenged (Ager, 1999). I extend this critique by reversing the focus of attention and flow of intervention from adults to children, highlighting the ways in which children often provide social support …

Reversing the focus of attention: children's agency in refugee camps

… The resilience of children and their ability to cope with physical displacement are best understood through an awareness of their lifeworlds, which are distinct from those of adults. Children spoke about losing their homeland in terms of the absence of familiar physical features of home: 'Now, we have no apple garden in the camp, my father doesn't get money from it. I like to eat apples, but we have no money to buy [here in the camp]. I always think of my apple orchard in Bhutan' (Purna, aged twelve). Many children did not block the reality of the present as one might have expected but integrated their new lives with their past ones. Some children described aspects of the changed social environment in positive terms: 'Here [in the camp] we are close to our friends. Here I can play everyday with my older brothers and sisters' (Sumitra, aged eight). The refugee environment brought children new networks of friends and social support.

In contrast to the adults, the refugee children were not always viewed as full social actors, but small events signalled that, far from being passive recipients of support, they were active in promoting cohesion within the social unit. The children I came to know were aware of their care-givers' emotions and used this knowledge to demand and gain attention. They found their own strategies both to provide support and to elicit it from others. These encompassed wider social circles than the nuclear family and included fictive and biological kin. This is not to imply that such strategies were salient in the children's consciousness; they were generally expressed in small gestures and actions such as the following (from my fieldnotes):

> Kaji [my five-year-old neighbour] came to me to ask for a flower for his mother. It was an interesting interaction which fulfilled two purposes: it ensured that I knew and showed approval of his action and his concern for his mother, and additionally it confirmed to him that I was aware of his mother's sadness. It seemed to be his way of taking control and initiating wider social support. Kaji regularly took flowers from my small plot and knew that I was happy for him to do so; he looked upon it as exchange for defending my garden when other children wanted to 'steal' the flowers, as he said, so there was no need for him to ask my permission. He was alerting my attention to his mother's suffering following his father's elopement with another woman.

The labelling of their parents through involvement in agency counselling also affected children in that it identified their care-givers as 'different', from other community members … The children, often without a full awareness of the history of the trauma suffered by adults, tended to internalize problems and to feel personally responsible for their parents' emotional state. Some lacked the tools and vocabulary to discuss the situation or express themselves fully. Coping with their care-givers became a paramount concern and often supplanted their own needs. One example of a child adopting such a role was five-year-old Kamal:

> Kamal regularly elicited caring behaviour. An acutely sensitive, small framed boy, he appeared constantly aware of his mother's psychological state. Frequently in the private forum of his own home he resorted to breastfeeding and behaviour patterns regarded as immature within his culture for a child of his age. In doing so he elicited an earlier maternal preoccupation from his mother which placed her back in a role that provided social value and unique utility. Interestingly this behaviour was infrequent when his mother was less depressed (as defined by self-reports). It appeared that Kamal was highly sensitive to his mother's state of mind.

Kamal's strategy of creating a role as a dependent child resulted from the recognition of the fulfilment this brought his mother. He emphasized and even created dependency and in so doing made salient his parent's value. Simultaneously he was aware of the private nature of this behaviour, and I never observed him playing this role in public space. Not surprisingly, children rarely provided a verbal explanation for this type of behaviour.

Indeed, it was difficult to determine the degree to which such behaviour was a result of conscious decision making. From conversations it was clear that children seldom explicitly considered themselves as supplying social support to their parents. However, on one occasion many months into fieldwork, sitting on the bamboo bunk in the privacy of my hut, thirteen-year-old Susma spoke with an unusual directness and coherence of analysis: 'Sometimes I play at being a child, I am grown up now, but my mother likes to have babies, and it makes her happy when I sit by her and she gives [spoon-feeds] me food.'

Another observed behaviour pattern was of the child's taking on parenting roles. Arati often played a parenting role with regard to her younger siblings that went beyond minding them to include behaviours that her mother usually performed. She was one of the few in the camp who extended such help into school hours: 'Mother is sick, there is no one else to help her; the others are too young. When I go to school she feels alone, so I do not like to attend. It is better that I stay at home; then there is no emptiness and loss.'

Where the children believed they were a cause of their parents' distress they were often less effective at providing support, as Bishnu (aged nine) explained:

> I don't know why mother is angry. Sometimes she sits all day, she doesn't even sit with the others, just inside the hut, without making the tea or cleaning the floors. I try to do the housework, but I think that she is cross with me – perhaps I have done a wrong deed or was bad in Bhutan. These days I stay at school and wait behind in the classroom …

Children's roles in community networks of support

Where external support is provided to children, the benefits are usually assumed to be an end in themselves. This narrow focus misses the opportunity to support children as a means of reaching certain vulnerable adults within the community. Children receive particular attention from extended kin and community members, and schooling gives them a valued position within the community.

The refugee children's priority and advantage was their resilience and speed at adapting to the new environment. The social structures and refugee context provided opportunities for building their confidence. Children were able to minimize the negative emotional effects of displacement by engaging in valued activities such as portraying their situation in paintings and playing on sports teams. Such activities and institutional support increased self-esteem, a mechanism for building a positive self-image that was closed to adults. Responsibilities were also given to children by the camp committee members, as Rajman, a health assistant, explained:

> The camp committee discussed this matter [a cholera epidemic] to find a solution. We realized that once one member of a hut had died it would not be long before the next would follow. So we decided to get the help of young boys and to ask them to go around the camp and advise people to go to hospital. After implementing that policy we found great changes. The people listened, and the numbers dying reduced substantially.

Requests to undertake work valued in the community gave children status and a feeling of self-worth.

In the Bhutanese case, while children's views appear to have been disregarded in public arenas, the young had a significant voice in private spaces, 'behind the plastic sheeting' (in the family hut). The significant influence of children in Bhutanese society had consequences across many domains. From listening to conversations it became clear that children were bringing home messages and ideas into the household that were both listened to and acted upon …

Conclusion

The perception among outsiders that Bhutanese refugee children in Nepal are abandoned victims is a stereotype reinforced by the international media. Children do not share adults' concepts of abandonment. In fact, many of the supportive relationships which children rely upon are more readily available in refugee camps. Parents, neighbours and teachers live and work close to them and have more time to devote to caring roles. Furthermore, the children themselves display a resilience that has remained largely invisible to policy-makers … The Bhutanese clearly consider children to have the skills required to take on the roles of community care-givers through both deliberate and unpremeditated actions. Notwithstanding children's critical stage of development and the potential long-term damage that may be produced by stress and trauma, their resilience and role in adding a 'protective' capacity should not be overlooked.

References

AGER, A. (1999) *Refugees: perspectives on the experience of forced migration*, London, Cassell.

Source

HINTON, R. (2000) 'Seen but not heard: refugee children and models for intervention' in PANTER-BRICK, C. and SMITH, M. (eds) *Abandoned Children*, Cambridge, Cambridge University Press.

Chapter 2

Children, poverty and social inequality

Heather Montgomery and Rachel Burr

CONTENTS

LEARNING OUTCOMES

When you have studied this chapter, you should be able to:

1 Define the concepts of relative and absolute poverty and relate these concepts to children's experiences.

2 Indicate some reasons why children continue to live in poverty in countries of both the North and the South.

3 Give examples of the differing effects of poverty on children.

4 Explore the relationship between poverty and social inequality within and between states.

5 Understand the inequalities within families, related to age and gender, that contribute to children's different experiences of poverty.

1 DEFINITIONS OF CHILD POVERTY

1.1 Absolute and relative poverty

This chapter is concerned with the different ways that poverty affects the lives of children throughout the world. It is also concerned with the relationship between poverty and social inequality on a global, national and family level. In particular, it will look at how poverty is defined, by whom, and how it is experienced by children. This first section will look at two different ways of understanding child poverty: through absolute and relative definitions. It will then go on to look at the impact of poverty on children's material, social and psychological well-being.

Allow about 15 minutes

ACTIVITY 1 **Definitions of poverty**

Read though these two descriptions of poverty, the first by an eleven-year-old girl in the UK, the second by a fourteen-year-old boy in Canada. How do they define poverty? What differences do you note between them?

Emma, eleven

Being poor is having no money and no house. Poverty means that you can't buy new clothes. Tramps and homeless people are the poorest. They get ill because they are out in the cold. People who are starving are the worst off.

(Children's Express, 2000)

Steven, fourteen

I live in a housing co-op ... The more well-off kids call it 'the Ghetto' and the kids that live in it are called 'Co-op Kids' and it is not very pleasant. When some of the kids in my class are going to a movie and ask me if I want to come, I have to say no because my mom doesn't have enough money. That makes me feel deprived ... We can't afford juice and most of the time I feel hungry because there is not a large enough selection of food in our house and I have to eat toast and crackers to keep feeling full. I can't invite my friends for dinner because we can only afford to have soup or one thing like salad, and the kids usually have soup, salad, and a main course with meat, and dessert.

(Baxter, 1993, p. 74)

COMMENT

In Emma's definition, poverty is about lacking the basics of food, clothes and shelter. It is therefore easy for her to point to those who are truly poor, such as tramps whose lack of such things is obvious. Steven gives a more nuanced version of how he understands poverty. For him, poverty is about being different, standing apart from his friends and feeling self-conscious about what he can and cannot afford. Steven struggles to hide his poverty and to fit in with friends. Being poor is a humiliating experience that affects every aspect of his life. Poverty has as great an impact on his emotional well-being as on his physical well-being. Although he talks about hunger, he also emphasizes the shame and stigma he feels about being poor.

These two viewpoints underline a very important distinction that exists when defining poverty – between *absolute* and *relative* poverty. In Emma's view, poverty is about the absolute lack of measurable resources, while Steven's experience of poverty is a comparative one – he sees himself as poor in relation to others in his society rather than in terms of absolute destitution. Steven's comment is also based on personal experiences whereas Emma, it appears, is observing what she sees around her.

Emma and Steven also differ on the effects of poverty. Emma comments on the very specific effects of poverty (such as not having a house) while Steven invokes more holistic concepts of well-being and psychological health. These distinctions lie at the heart of discussions of children's experiences of poverty and will be discussed in more detail in the following section.

Children playing in a back alley of a poor Oldham housing estate (UK).

READING

Reading A is from a short paper published by the United Nations Children's Fund's (UNICEF) research centre in Italy. It focuses on child poverty in richer nations and is intended for researchers and practitioners in the field of child poverty. It makes the point that different definitions of poverty have profound effects on the numbers of children who are considered poor. This is illustrated by two tables, the first looking at the number of children living in poverty when it is defined relatively and the second looking at the number of children who live in absolute poverty. Although you do not need to study the tables in very great detail, note the discrepancies between the two tables, especially in relation to the USA. As you read, think about the ideas of absolute and relative poverty – which do you think gives a better picture of child poverty? Why? Can you think of any limitations of using statistics to discuss child poverty?

COMMENT

This article shows clearly how definitions of child poverty affect the number of children claimed to be living in poverty. So by taking an absolute definition of child poverty (defined in the reading as 'the inability to purchase or consume a fixed minimum package of goods and services'), in 1995, 13.9 per cent of children in the USA lived in poverty. However, by taking a relative definition (defined as children living in households with an income below 50 per cent of the national average), in the same year 22.4 per cent of children in the USA lived in poverty. Defining poverty in absolute terms can be important in setting standards for the basic necessities of life needed by children. However, a relative definition of poverty gets closer to understanding issues of social inequality, an important theme which will be taken up in later sections of this chapter. It also shows how poverty is not just about a lack of material goods and services, but is also about a relationship to others in society. If you think back to Steven in Activity 1, he expressed this clearly: poverty for him involved feeling deprived, relative to those around him. The statistics from this reading also show that the two definitions are not mutually exclusive. It is possible to be poor in absolute terms and still experience poverty in relative terms.

Data such as those contained in this reading are very important because the ways in which poverty is defined will have an impact on governments' social welfare programmes and most significantly on who governments decide is eligible to receive state support. Yet these data also have limitations. They tell us nothing, for example, about whether poverty is a permanent or transitory experience in the lives of children. Neither do league tables look at the distribution of poverty within a country. We cannot tell, for instance, whether child poverty is more concentrated in urban or rural areas, or in certain parts of the country. Without knowing the different costs of living in different parts of the country, it is difficult to know how these figures translate into children's experiences. Tables such as these also do not tell us about children's different experiences of poverty within families.

Reading A is about the rich countries of the North but in poorer countries in the South, where children lack the basics to survive, it can be argued that absolute definitions of poverty are more appropriate. In 1995, the Copenhagen World Summit on Social Development aimed to look at poverty in all countries of the world and adopted the following definition of absolute poverty: 'a condition characterised by severe deprivation of basic human needs, including food, safe drinking water, sanitation facilities, health, shelter, education and information' (quoted in Gordon *et al.*, 2000, p. 9).

International agencies such as the World Bank and UNICEF have put a figure on absolute poverty, arguing for an 'international poverty line', which they define as US $1 per day per person, this being the minimum amount that purchases the goods and services deemed necessary for basic survival (UNICEF, 2000a, p. iv). Using this definition, there are between 600 million and 700 million children living in poverty worldwide. These children represent 40 per cent of all children in countries of the South (UNICEF, 2000a, p. 1).

This international definition of absolute poverty becomes problematic when it is applied within the world's richest nations, such as those in Reading A. It is difficult to argue that 13.9 per cent of American children are living in absolute poverty according to the World Summit on Social Development definition. While many children in the USA may be very poor indeed, few are starving or without fresh drinking water or live on less than a dollar a day. Therefore, in many countries of the North, it is more useful to view poverty in relative rather than absolute terms, often as a percentage of the average income and in relation to others in society. In the UK, for example, relative poverty is defined as having less than half the average household income (Gordon *et al.*, 2000). Using these figures, 14.3 million people, out of a total of 60 million, live in poverty in the UK, of which 4.4 million (out of a total of 11.3 million) are children (Gordon *et al.*, 2000, p. 9).

Children selling flowers to passing motorists on the streets of Dhaka, Bangladesh.

Understanding poverty relatively provides some information about the gap between the richest and the poorest in society. However, ideas about relative poverty go beyond this, encompassing issues such as social exclusion. As Reading A examines, and as Steven observes in Activity 1, poverty is not confined to a lack of money. It is also very much about experiencing humiliation, emotional stress and social exclusion. Poverty can affect children's emotional well-being and their ability to feel valued and involved with their peers. Although Steven sometimes goes hungry, he suggests that poverty, for him, is less about hunger, and more about his feelings of humiliation. The two quotes below from two sisters (Kelly, aged ten and Amy, aged thirteen) who live in Birmingham, UK emphasize the same point. Like Steven, they experience not only the material effects of poverty but also the social effects, such as not having the sorts of clothes that would enable them to fit in with their friends and prevent them being teased.

Kelly and Amy outside their house.

KELLY We haven't got that much money to, to get food and go shopping … the fridge is just bare. It's just horrible …

I'm worried about my mum, all of us are – because of all the things she's going through. She's got six kids, three bedrooms and six kids, it's just horrible … She's on tablets right now.

We look forward to go to school, because it's better at school, it's warm and it's got heaters and everything.

AMY [T]here's these kids, I weren't listening to them but they, it really got to me. I had these Airtech trainers … and, they went to me, 'Oh look what you're wearing … you ain't got named trousers and all that and named trainers… you ain't got nothing', and it just made me upset. And like Jenny sometimes, she comes up to me and she goes, oh you little tramp, and yeah it's not nice but I don't listen to them.

(The Open University, 2003)

1.2 Whose definition?

The examples of Kelly and Amy, as well as of Steven and Emma, draw attention to another important issue – who decides what counts as poverty? Official definitions have limited value if they do not take into account the experience of those most affected. For example, when researchers in India have asked women for their definitions of poverty, many have claimed that having an alcoholic husband is a form of poverty, not only because he is likely to earn less and spend the family money on alcohol, but also because he brings shame to his family. In other instances, poverty is defined differently. In many parts of Amazonia, it is having few or no kin. The poorest and most vulnerable group in many Amazonian societies are orphans, because they do not have the 'wealth' of many relatives. The non-material aspects of wealth and poverty are summarized by the

!Kung children in Namibia.

anthropologist Marshall Sahlins writing about the !Kung hunter-gatherers of the Kalahari desert: 'The world's most primitive people have few possessions, *but they are not poor*. Poverty is not a certain small amount of goods, nor is it just a relation between means and ends; above all it is a relation between people. Poverty is a social status' (Sahlins, 1988, p. 37).

This is further illustrated by the situation faced by Aboriginal Australians. For them, child poverty is defined as:

> ... the spiritual, psychological, emotional and cultural loss that has come with the failure to recognise the Aborigines' prior ownership of this land and the subsequent oppression of the Aboriginal people ... Therefore when we speak of the poverty of Aboriginal children we refer first to poverty that is broader than material poverty, although it includes this

Aboriginal family, Kalobidada outstation, Australia.

material poverty. It is the deprivation that is the … result of dislocation from their spiritual and economic base – the land.

(Choo, 1990, p. 32)

The next activity explores how poverty is understood by parents in the UK.

Allow about 30 minutes

ACTIVITY 2 **Necessities and luxuries**

In order to understand how different definitions of poverty relate to children's everyday lives, Gordon *et al.* (2000) conducted a survey among parents in the UK. These parents were given a list of items and asked whether or not they were necessities for children and whether they would consider children poor if they did not have them. These items related both to material items such as food, and to non-material things such as birthday treats. Some of the responses are summarized in Table 1 opposite. Read through them and note your own response as to whether or not you consider these items necessities and whether or not you would consider a child who did not have them to be poor. How do you justify your response?

COMMENT

Nearly all parents regarded food and clothes as necessities but many of their views of what constitutes poverty go beyond this. For example, 92 per cent believed that not being able to afford a celebration for a special occasion was a form of poverty while 53 per cent believed that not having enough money to invite a child's friends round to eat once a fortnight was also a sign of deprivation. Children's emotional ties with friends, as expressed through being able to invite them home for a meal, were seen as necessities by these parents. However, it is interesting to note that 47 per cent of parents disagreed, seeing treats such as these as luxuries rather than necessities (what they are seen as may depend on the child's age) .

Table 1 Necessities and 'necessities deprivation'.

Item	Percentage of parents regarding item as necessary
Food	
Fresh fruit or vegetables at least once a day	93
Three meals a day	91
Meat, fish or vegetarian equivalent at least twice a day	76
Clothes	
New, properly fitted, shoes	96
Warm, waterproof coat	95
A required school uniform*	88
At least 7 pairs of new underpants	84
At least 4 pairs of trousers	74
At least 4 jumpers/cardigans/sweatshirts	71
Some new, not second-hand, clothes	67
Participation and activities	
Celebrations on special occasions	92
Hobby or leisure activity*	88
School trip at least once a term*	73
Swimming at least once a month	71
Holiday away from home at least one week a year	63
Leisure equipment*	57
Friends round for tea/snack fortnightly*	53
Developmental	
Books of own	90
Play group at least once a week (pre-school age children)*	89
Educational games	84
Toys (e.g. dolls, teddies)	85
Construction toys	66
Bike: new/second-hand*	60
At least 50p a week for sweets	45
Computer suitable for schoolwork	38
Computer games	13
Environmental	
A bed and bedding for self	96
Bedroom for every child of different sex over 10 years*	76
Carpet in bedroom	75
Garden to play in	68
Base	*560*

* age-related items

Source: Gordon et al., 2000, p. 34.

This survey was conducted in the UK, and it may be that other European parents would regard the same list of necessities very differently. We also cannot tell from this table anything about class or ethnicity, or whether attitudes change according to the gender of the children under discussion. Outside countries of the North, much of this would seem very strange. For example, not all societies consider sharing a bed a sign of poverty, yet in the UK, 96 per cent of parents feel that a child's own bed is a necessity. If members of a different society (or even different groups within UK society) compiled this list it is likely that they would point to different things as essential to children's well-being.

However, the important thing about this list is that most parents feel that poverty goes beyond material basics. They point to ideas about children's quality of life and see poverty in terms of the damage it does to children's well-being and their relationships with others. It is clear therefore that the social environment informs people's ideas about poverty and that, for many people, poverty goes beyond ideas about quantifiable basics and concerns the quality of people's lives, which, while relative and contextual, is equally important to children's well-being.

It is also worth noting that just as some children may see themselves as poor, others may not, whatever their outward circumstances. For example, Vietnam is a very poor country, where the average yearly income for a family of four is $250 – well below the World Bank/UNICEF international poverty line of $1 a day per person. Yet the experiences of one boy, Luong, illustrate why a more complex understanding of poverty is needed.

Street children in Saigon, Vietnam.

I am sixteen years old. I moved to the city by myself five years ago to sell postcards, and I rent a room with a family that live by the river. Before then my mum died and my brother and I lived with my grandma, but she is old and struggled with money. I cannot see very well so I struggled in, and hated, school. Because of this I decided I was more use to my grandma if I left home. My brother goes to school and studies hard. My grandmother would like me to live at home and she sends me money to learn French, but I don't go to classes, I prefer to make as much money as I can and to have my freedom. If I get to eat twice a day, and hang out with friends I think life is OK. Some children are very poor and have nothing to eat, not like me I always have food to eat. When I get cold I ask people to buy me clothes and they do. Life is OK but I do get headaches.

(Adapted from Burr, 2000)

Clearly Luong experiences certain forms of poverty: he does not live with his family, and often eats at most twice a day. He does not have access to proper medical or optical treatment and is faced with a choice between education and earning money. However, Luong does not consider himself particularly poor, even though he has to beg for adequate clothing. This is because he is comparing his standard of living to that of other young people whom he knows. A full understanding of child poverty must include children's reactions and experiences of being poor, as much as external definitions, and must take into account issues such as shame or social exclusion as well as having enough to eat.

SUMMARY OF SECTION I

- Poverty can be understood and measured in two ways: absolute and relative.
- Absolute poverty is defined as the inability to purchase or consume a fixed minimum of goods and services in a given time.
- Relative poverty is defined in relation to general expectations of a society, taking into account issues such as social exclusion and deprivation.
- Child poverty can be seen in terms of a specific lack of material goods as well as more holistically, looking at ideas about well-being.
- It is not enough simply to measure and define poverty; we also need to understand how children and parents experience it.

2 THE CAUSES AND EFFECTS OF CHILD POVERTY

Throughout the world, poor children are disproportionately affected by armed conflict, environmental disasters and health issues such as HIV/AIDS (ILO, 2002). It is important therefore to acknowledge that while poverty has an impact on children individually, it also affects their families and communities and is usually linked to many other kinds of adversity, as Chapter 1 explained. In general, children who live in poverty have worse health, worse educational opportunities and worse access to services than wealthier children (UNICEF, 2000b). They are at greater risk from accidents, from living in polluted or inadequate housing and may also be developmentally delayed (CPAG, 2001). They are also likely to live in families where any unexpected or unplanned situation can prove disastrous. A child who becomes sick and needs medical care may mean that other children in the family cannot eat, or that the siblings have to drop out of school or take on more paid labour. This section will look at the multiple causes and effects of poverty, returning to ideas about social exclusion and humiliation and the links between poverty and other forms of adversity. We will begin with studies carried out in the UK.

2.1 Child poverty in the UK

READING

Reading B is an extract from Andrea Ashworth's memoir of growing up in Manchester in the early 1970s. Writing when she is in her late 20s, Ashworth remembers her feelings on moving back to Manchester from Canada at the age of eight, with her two younger sisters. Note the effects of poverty on her and examine the links between the forms of poverty she experienced and other adversities.

COMMENT

Ashworth's recollection of poverty reflects many of the themes of this chapter. She talks of the humiliations she felt at her poverty and also the sense that her family have fallen on hard times and lowered themselves socially. It is also apparent that the effects of poverty are multiple and reinforce each other. Andrea and her family live in a poor environment and her house is infested with fleas, which affects her both physically and emotionally. Her mother's depression also influences her and creates a difficult home environment. Food shopping involves having to buy only small quantities of the cheapest goods as well as the shame involved in having to return food her mother cannot afford.

So far in this chapter, children's understanding of poverty has been considered on an individual basis, and examples of children's experiences have been given in their own words. These have been used to show the impact that living in poverty has on individual children and to suggest the different ways that they respond to it. However, a focus on individual children does not indicate the scale of the problem nor the overall patterns and trends associated with living in poverty. For these, it is necessary to look at larger-scale studies carried out by organizations such as the Child Poverty Action Group (CPAG), a non-governmental organization based in the UK. Here are five major conclusions drawn by CPAG about the impact of poverty on children in the UK:

- Babies born to poorer families are more likely to be born prematurely and to be of low birth weight. The implications include a greater likelihood of impaired development and of particular chronic diseases later in life.

- Children in poorer families are more likely to experience illness with a greater risk of respiratory infection, gastro-enteritis, dental caries and tuberculosis.

- Children whose parents do unskilled work are five times more likely to die from accidents than children whose parents have professional occupations.

- Children living in temporary accommodation or poor quality social housing are at greater risk of fire ...

- Poverty in childhood can leave a long-term legacy. Children raised in poverty are, as adults, more likely to be unemployed, in low paid employment, are more likely to live in social housing, get in trouble with the police and are at greater risk of alcohol and drug abuse.

(CPAG, 2001, p. 1)

Other studies have combined both qualitative and quantitative research, looking at trends and issues among particular groups of children. Tess Ridge's study of school children in the UK is a particularly good example of this type of research (Ridge, 2002a). Taking a sample group of 40 school children whose parents were in receipt of income support (state benefit for low-paid or unemployed people), Ridge analyses both the patterns of

School children in a run-down area of inner-city Birmingham, UK.

poverty and children's individual experiences. In one part of the study she focuses on school uniforms, school trips, school meals and school projects, looking at how these relate to children's experiences of poverty and social exclusion.

Recall the comments made by Kelly and her sister in Section 1.1, especially about being teased for not wearing designer trainers. Having good enough clothes for school was also an issue for the children in Ridge's study. But children were also affected by missing out on costly school trips. School trips place an additional financial burden on poor parents. For children, missing out is not just about the trip itself. The social repercussions are long term, as fifteen-year-old Amy explained:

> 'Year 7 there was a French trip, it was one day and you stayed overnight on the ferry and most people went but I didn't go … I don't know it was a lot of money for one day … But even now my friends sometimes bring it up and I'm like "Oh I didn't go, I can't talk about it" ' (Amy, 15 years, two-parent family).
>
> (Ridge, 2002a, p. 76)

Some children commented on how their friends try to help them feel able to participate in school life, although this can also be humiliating. Eleven-year-old Sue talked about what happens when there is a school fair.

> 'Well say I cancel like if they are sort of having a school fair there or something. My friends … they are really good and they sort of like give me money and say "There, go and get something with this" ' (Sue, 11 years, lone-parent family).
>
> (Ridge, 2002a, p. 78)

One aspect of school life was a source of particular anxiety for the children in Ridge's study – free school meals.

> 'I don't [have free meals] because I realised when I was in Year 7 that the people who got free school meals were teased … I couldn't handle that as I was already getting teased enough so I don't get free school meals' (Nell, 17 years, two-parent family).
>
> (Ridge, 2002a, p. 82)

This research highlights the powerful social dimensions of poverty, and especially the importance of understanding how it feels from children's point of view. In a subsequent study, Ridge concluded:

> There is … a tension between those needs and concerns identified by children and those identified by adults. We may well not value the things that these children identify as important social needs, issues such as friendship and the maintenance of social relationships. However, these are important and critical areas in children's lives and in their social development.
>
> (Ridge, 2002b, p. 10)

Children in Kwaza Kehele squatter camp, Phillipi, Cape Town, South Africa.

2.2 Absolute poverty in Angola

Both Ashworth's personal account of poverty in Reading B and Ridge's study among school children in the UK show the links between poverty, social exclusion and other forms of adversity. In countries in the South, these links are even more apparent.

Allow about 10 minutes

ACTIVITY 3 Linda

Linda (not her real name) is fourteen years old and a refugee from Angola. She fled from fighting in her home town between the government and the UNITA rebels. When interviewed by the BBC in 2001 she had been living in a shack in the port city of Libito. Read through this account of her life and note down the ways that you feel she experiences poverty. How do you think this experience might affect her future expectations and experiences? How does her experience of poverty compare with Andrea Ashworth's experience detailed in Reading B?

> [Linda lives] in miserable poverty where clean water is rare, [and] makes do with 'filthy rags' for clothes.

> She describes an existence of appalling suffering: 'We're all dirty. If you can find water it's never clean, and I don't sleep well here.

> 'We have to lay out pieces of paper on the ground and lie on them.

> 'Sometimes we don't even have paper because rain comes in through our roof and everything gets soaked.'

Linda's poverty has taken its toll on her education.

She used to study before she was driven from her home, but now most of her time is taken up preparing food, keeping the shelter clean and caring for her six brothers and sisters.

Other opportunities for self-improvement are few. Linda explains: 'If you can find work, they hardly pay you anything.

'You can't afford clothes or shoes because they cost too much.'

(BBC News Online, 2001)

COMMENT

Linda's family lives in abject poverty. Although they have some money on which to survive and to eat, they have no access to clean drinking water and there is no money to spare. Any unexpected expense could have serious consequences for them. Linda has to take on a great deal of responsibility for her family, which means she cannot work to earn money or go to school. Her poverty therefore manifests itself by food insecurity, lack of adequate shelter, poor housing and lack of drinking water. However, the family's poverty also has less obvious effects. Linda is working hard and for long hours. She cannot sleep properly and is constantly worried about the future. Drinking dirty water is dangerous and it is only a matter of time before it makes her or her siblings ill. It is also highly probable that this will affect her future health and have long-term consequences. Linda does not go to school. She cannot therefore gain any qualifications that might improve her chances of getting a better job and increasing her longer-term financial security. Her siblings, in their turn, will have to work from an early age and forgo school. The effects of poverty therefore are manifold and encompass both the short and long term. They are also likely to be passed on through the generations, as it is hard to break out of the cycle of deprivation.

Although there are obvious differences between Linda's life in Libito and Andrea Ashworth's account of poverty in Manchester, there are also some very clear parallels. Both live on the margins of their society, both are taking risks with their health (both now and in the future), both suffer from financial insecurity and both feel the need to be responsible for their families. While Andrea is materially better off, both she and Linda are poor and socially excluded.

2.3 Cumulative causes of poverty: Thailand

So far we have concentrated on the ways poverty affects children, looking at the micro level of individual children's experiences and at the broader level of national trends. For the next example, we will concentrate on some of the causes of children's poverty, arguing that, like the effects of poverty, its causes are multiple, cumulative and have to be looked at on both a micro and a macro level. The inequitable distribution of resources on a global and local level and even within families is particularly important, and these will be discussed further in Section 3 of this chapter.

The slum village in which Lek's family lives, Thailand.

Allow about 15 minutes

A C T I V I T Y 4 Lek

Read the following story of a family living in Thailand. Lek is a thirteen-year-old girl and the story begins with her mother, Saew. As you read it, note down all the factors that exacerbated Lek's and her family's poverty.

> Saew is around forty years old. She was born and raised near Buriram in the northeast of Thailand, where her family are rice farmers. At twelve, she married Siphon. She gave birth to thirteen children of whom seven survived infancy, and only four are still living. The land that she farmed in her village became increasingly inadequate to support her family, and so her two eldest children left and went to a tourist resort to sell chewing-gum and other sweets in the streets. As they appeared to be making a reasonable living, she and Siphon took Lek to this resort and lived in a squatter community there. Saew started to work as a rubbish collector, going round the streets and picking up rubbish to sort out for re-sale. Although this did not provide a large income, she earned enough to rent a small piece of land in a local slum and build a house there. She continued to scavenge rubbish until she was hit by a car, an accident from which she never fully recovered. She could not walk properly or push her cart, and so she gave up this work.
>
> Lek and Saew's other children tried to continue collecting rubbish but it did not bring in enough money to cover Saew's medical bills and to pay the rent. Now they scavenge for scrap metal on a local rubbish tip

but this involves great risks, working among the rats, the filth and the infections that fester there, work which Lek hates. She is also often ill which means that she cannot always work. The family survives because when the children are not working on the rubbish heap, they beg from tourists, although this means running the risk of being arrested, or being fined, by the police.

(adapted from Montgomery, 2001)

COMMENT

Clearly Lek and her family are living in poverty but it is extremely hard to point to any single identifiable cause. Instead we have to look at the ways that multiple causes of poverty have an impact on the family. We could start by looking at the 'natural' causes of Lek's poverty. The downward spiral began when Lek's mother could no longer grow sufficient rice on her family's land and had to move away. But it is also worth remembering that 'natural' disasters may have social origins – silting up of rivers due to modern agricultural practices, deforestation, land enclosures and global warming may all contribute to flooding or to drought, while population pressure, over-farming and diversion of land to modern agribusiness may all contribute to crop failure.

Ill health also contributed to the family's poverty. Saew's accident was partially responsible for her family's poverty, both through limiting her earning capacities and through diverting scarce resources to pay for medical care.

There are also social causes of Lek's poverty. Neither she nor her family have much education or access to school, which would improve their ability to earn. There is also a lack of legal and adequately paid earning opportunities, forcing the children into illegal or dangerous employment that is much more insecure. The lack of state-funded social security payments also plays a part in keeping Lek's family poor.

Issues concerning the global distribution of wealth are also important. Children in some parts of the world never have to do the badly paid, dangerous, illegal jobs that Lek and her siblings have to take on in order to survive.

The final point to make about this scenario is to note how tightly bound up children are in their parents' circumstances. Lek would not be poor if her parents were not. Therefore child poverty is very dependent on adult poverty, even though it may have different, and sometimes worse, effects on children than it does on adults.

Figure 1 shows the multiple links between these various forms of poverty very clearly, illustrating the different factors in Lek's family's poverty and the interconnections between them. The diagram shows the complexity of the causes and effects of poverty and the ways in which they reinforce each other.

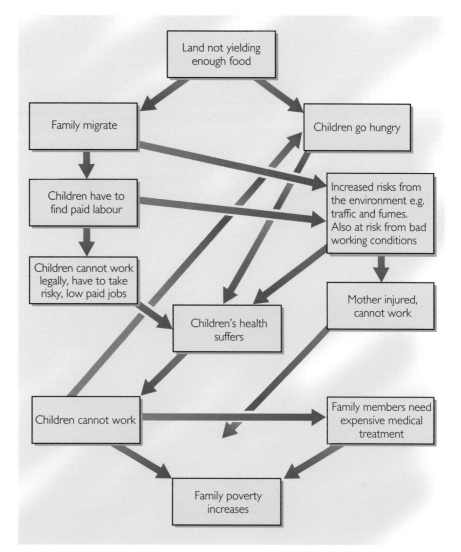

Figure 1 Flow chart showing the multiple causes of poverty in Lek's family, and the relationships between them.

SUMMARY OF SECTION 2

- Poverty is intertwined with other forms of adversity.
- Poverty has an impact on a children's health, their well-being and their access to resources.
- Many factors contribute to children living in poverty, including ill health, social inequalities, environmental damage and 'natural' causes.

3 POVERTY AND SOCIAL INEQUALITY

So far this chapter has concentrated mainly on children's own experiences of poverty. It has examined absolute and relative poverty and focused on the idea that poverty is not only about material aspects but also about the relationship between those who are poor and those who are not. As Reading A made clear, relative definitions of poverty are closely tied to social inequality. In this section we will explore the links between poverty and social inequality at three levels: between countries, within countries, and within families and communities.

3.1 Social inequality between countries

The contemporary world is characterized by vast disparities between rich and poor countries, and these differences inevitably have an impact on the lives of children within these countries. According to UNICEF, 10 per cent of the people in the world possess 90 per cent of the world's wealth. 'Poverty has been described as the new face of apartheid: millions of people living in wretched conditions side by side with those who enjoy unprecedented prosperity' (UNICEF, 2000a, p. 44).

These disparities are growing worse. UNICEF quotes the *Human Development Report* (a report produced by the United Nations Development Programme – UNDP), which estimates that, in 1997, the poorest fifth 'obtained only 1 per cent of global income – half the share they controlled in 1960' (UNICEF, 2000a, p. 44). In 1996, the *Human Development Report* noted that of the total global wealth of $23 trillion generated, only $5 trillion was generated by countries in the South, even though they have nearly 80 per cent of the world's population. Furthermore, the poor are getting poorer in absolute terms as well as relative terms. The real income of the world's poorest 5 per cent fell by an estimated one quarter over the period 1988–93.

Figure 2
Global income disparities are widening. (from UNICEF, 2002a).

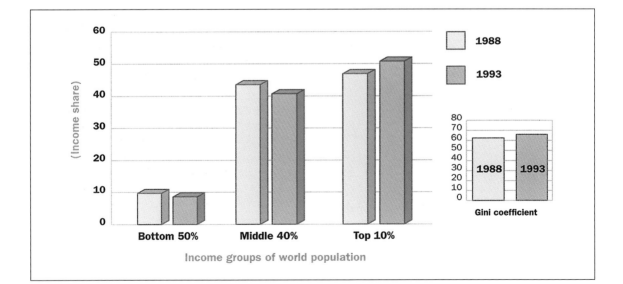

Children with HIV/ AIDS being cared for at Nazareth House, an AIDS hospice in Cape Town, South Africa.

The reasons for these global inequalities are multiple and there are many macro-economic factors that affect children's well-being. For example, the European Union imposes high import duties on goods from countries of the South, while allowing free trade within its borders. Therefore goods from the South appear expensive in European markets and it is difficult for those countries to compete with European manufacturers and producers who do not have to pay these import duties. In other cases, many governments place higher priorities on arms and military spending than they do on children's welfare. Countries in sub-Saharan Africa with extremely high infant mortality rates also tend to have high per capita military expenditure. In contrast, the governments of countries such as Costa Rica, Panama and Haiti have abolished their armies altogether, arguing that poor, small countries such as theirs cannot support large military expenditure.

In many other areas also, the inequality between countries affects children's lives directly. Despite fears of refugees and migrants in Europe, it is the poor countries of Africa and Asia who accommodate 90 per cent of the world's refugees, struggling to provide food and shelter, when their own countries are already suffering shortages. The HIV/AIDS pandemic has also hit sub-Saharan Africa harder than other countries, killing millions of children, creating a generation of 'AIDS orphans', and seriously reducing adult productivity. With so many adults unable to work, taxes cannot be raised, basic services cannot be staffed and children suffer both directly and indirectly. The Report of the Director General of the International Labour Organization (ILO) succinctly sums up the links between poverty, HIV/AIDS and the detrimental effects on children:

> HIV/AIDS has a direct impact on children's participation in the workforce. Prolonged periods of illness and eventual death in the family cause dramatic cuts in income and loss of assets. Even before one or both of their parents die of AIDS-related illnesses, children, especially girls, are likely to have to take on a heavier workload within the household, including domestic chores and caring for siblings and sick adults. This can compromise their schooling and their health. Both boys and girls may be obliged to seek income-earning opportunities to make up for the lost adult income and to help pay medical expenses. Children are also likely to be called upon to compensate for the loss of women's labour in farming tasks. Increased migration as a consequence of HIV/ AIDS, by both boys and girls, from rural settings to urban areas swells the ranks of children in the urban informal economy. The presence of children on the street and their need for money, food, shelter and companionship all increase their chances of being drawn into casual sexual relationships or into commercial sexual exploitation. This, in turn, increases the risk of their becoming infected with HIV and thus the circle from being affected to becoming infected is completed.

(ILO, 2002, p. 42)

The impact of structural adjustment programmes

One influence on global inequalities in child poverty deserves particular attention – the structural adjustment programmes (SAPs) that, it is argued, have served to increase rather than reduce child poverty. As poor countries attempt to improve their overall standards of living and increase their gross national product, they often follow certain Northern-derived (and sometimes enforced) strategies that emphasize debt repayment and export programmes at the cost of social welfare provision. SAPs are imposed on a country as a condition of its borrowing money from the World Bank. Such policies are part of a neo-liberal economic strategy, which is pursued by the World Bank and most countries of the North, meaning that economic growth is seen as the key to social progress. The strategy is founded on the belief that governments should not interfere with market forces, which are seen as the best way to improve a country's prosperity.

Box 1 The World Bank

The World Bank was set up in 1944 to loan money to less developed countries so that they could develop the infrastructure to compete openly on the global market. At its inception, it was seen as a way to bring prosperity to a world that had recently been shaken by war. It was believed that by contributing to a world central bank governments would enable poorer countries to borrow in an orderly way, avoiding the boom and bust cycles of the past. In many respects such ideals appear to be very straightforward and noble, yet the work of the World Bank remains controversial.

In order to qualify for loans from the World Bank, countries have to agree to implement particular economic policies – SAPs. Policies imposed under structural adjustment programmes focus on the repayment of foreign debt, the balancing of national budgets (so that governments do not spend more than they can produce) and the promotion of the free market. In practice, these policies mean that governments have to agree to allow foreign corporations to repatriate profits, they have to balance the national budget by cutting social spending and selling off publicly owned assets through privatization and they have to devalue the currency so that exports are cheaper for other countries to buy. This can have devastating, if unintended, consequences for poor children. In particular, it can affect their health and nutrition. When state subsidies on food are removed or reduced, prices increase, so that the poor, especially the urban poor dependent on the cash economy, are unable to buy enough to eat. The diversion of food production to cash crops for export reduces the food available locally, and the scarcity further increases prices. Local currency is devalued to make exports more competitive on the world market, but at the cost of increasing the price of imports such as vehicle fuel and essential drugs needed for vaccination and other preventive health campaigns.

The goal of structural adjustment programmes is not to target the poor or to make them suffer, whatever the results. Instead, they are aimed at starting 'trickle-down' economic growth. The expectation is that the overall

Children washing at a comunal tap in a shanty town in El Salvador.

economic situation of the country will improve and that wealth will trickle down to the very poorest, raising their standards of living along with everyone else's. However, in reality, this does not always happen. In El Salvador, for example, SAPs have focused on dealing with inflation rather than creating new jobs or revitalizing the economy. These policies have kept up interest rates, which affects many sectors, but especially housing, leading to a serious housing shortage. SAPs have also emphasized producing a flexible labour market, but this has meant that jobs are precarious and income uncertain. Health services and water distribution are due to be privatized. All these have a devastating impact on children who suffer as their parents do not have stable jobs, cannot feed them properly and are forced to live in poor-quality housing in bad neighbourhoods (Moreno, 2000).

Allow about 10 minutes

A C T I V I T Y 5 SAPs in Vietnam

In the 1990s, Vietnam implemented SAPs in order to help it change from a centrally planned economy, under communist rule, to a free market economy, based on free trade, decentralization and private enterprise. After several years, Vietnam achieved impressive rates of growth in terms of its gross domestic product. From what you have read in this chapter so far about SAPs, what do you think the positive effects on children might be? What negative effects might these policies have?

COMMENT

An overall growth rate, caused by the imposition of SAPs, will benefit some children. Children whose families have been successful in the new enterprise culture will benefit as their parents have more income, which they may choose to spend on the family. Overall growth also means that the government has more money, which it may decide to invest in social welfare provision, better health services or education for children. Some economists would argue that this increased wealth will 'trickle down' and have an impact on poorer children's lives.

However, this has not always been the case in Vietnam. While some families are better off, there is limited evidence of a trickle-down effect. Indeed, Vietnam, like other countries following SAPs, has introduced charges for health and pre-school services, putting them out of the reach of many poor children. It has attempted to invest in health care, but this has often been in large hospitals in city centres rather than in rural primary health care centres that target the poorest and more marginalized people. Finally, as more people saw an opportunity to earn money in the new system, an increasing number of children dropped out of school in order to work and boost their own and their family's income (see Pham Thi Lan, 2000).

SAPs place much emphasis on the repayment of foreign debt. It is unsurprising, therefore, that those countries in which SAPs have had the most detrimental effects are also those countries that are most heavily indebted in the first place. These countries are known as Heavily Indebted Poor Countries (HIPCs). They have the world's worst human development indicators: half the citizens are living below the poverty line of $1 income a day, and average life expectancy is 10 years less than in the Southern countries as a whole (UNICEF, 2000b). Although there is now some debt relief for certain poor countries, Burdon (2000) explains why children in particular suffer when countries are heavily indebted.

Children bear the highest cost of the debt tragedy for they are most vulnerable to the effects of debilitated health services in indebted countries. In the education sector, lack of investment consigns children, particularly girls, to lives trapped by poverty.

HIPC countries suffer some of the worst levels of deprivation in the developing world. Here about 3.4 million children (almost 20 per cent) will die before they turn five. Life expectancy is 51 years, which is 26 years less than life expectancy in the industrialised countries. Around 47 million children are not in school, and these numbers are growing, rather than declining. Based on current trends, by 2015 HIPC countries will not meet the international development goal to reduce child mortality by two thirds. In fact the gap between trend and target represents two million *additional* child deaths.

The picture is similarly bleak in education. Oxfam estimates that, based on current trends, by 2015 over 75 million children will remain out of school; and the majority of these children will be in HIPC countries.

(Burdon, 2000, p. 28)

More recently, due to criticism of SAPs and the acknowledgement of the effects that they have on children, there has been a shift in emphasis away from externally imposed SAPs towards 'Partnerships for Poverty Reduction'. Countries receiving aid agree, with the help of European donor countries, to try to halve the proportion of people living in poverty by 2015, while committing themselves to 'good governance'. This means that they promise to support a democratic system, the rule of law, a free press and to sign up to and enforce international conventions. In return, European governments have agreed to make a long-term commitment to recipient countries and to show greater flexibility over the terms on which they lend money, if the recipient countries put the systems into place that best protect children. While these goals are ambitious and dependent on the mutual trust and commitment of each partner, such partnerships do provide an alternative to the heavy-handed implementation of SAPs in previous decades.

3.2 Social inequality within countries

The second level of social inequality this section looks at is inequality within countries.

> Growing economic disparities and poverty characterize not simply the state system, but the global social order. In other words, it is no longer enough to think only in terms of rich and poor *states*; we need to consider *groups or classes* of rich and poor people which cut across state boundaries. Of course, if we group populations by territorial states, we find that the North/South disparity remains a central facet of the global order ... such territorial categorization serves to mask, and even mystify, the much more significant global social distribution of inequality ... While there is an indisputable concentration of poverty in the geographic South there is also growing wealth among certain classes in the geographic South, just as there is growing poverty among certain classes in the geographic North.
>
> (Thomas, 1997, pp. 2–3)

Research from the United Nations University, published in 1999, looked at income distribution and social inequality in 77 countries since the 1950s. It found that 45 of these countries witnessed rising inequality, with only 16 showing an improvement in equality (UNICEF, 2000a, p. 44). Again, these macro-economic figures may seem very far removed from the experiences of actual children but they do have an effect on children's lives and need to be understood in order to get a clear picture of how poverty affects children. Just as not all children in the North are wealthy, so not all children in the South are poor. Taking overall figures of poverty for a country obscures the differentials in income levels and access to resources within a country. In the Côte d'Ivoire, for example, overall school enrolment among girls (one indicator of increasing wealth) has risen since 1985, except among the very poorest families where it has decreased (UNICEF, 2000a).

Taking overall figures also makes it difficult to establish differences in children's experiences of poverty. For example, there are differences in poverty between rural and urban areas. In the example of Lek quoted in

Activity 4 (Section 2.3), her family struggled in both the countryside and the city, in the former from low yields from their land and in the latter due to the difficulties in finding and keeping work and from the effects of a poor environment where they were exposed to risks from the traffic. The family's attempts to overcome poverty involved migration and exchanging one type of poverty for another. It was also part of a much wider pattern seen in many countries, where many people from rural areas are migrating to cities to find work, thereby putting great pressure on resources in the city while leaving the agricultural heartland of many countries to be run by those who stay behind. The people left behind in rural areas are often women, girls and older people, while those who go to the city are younger men and boys, so the effects of migration can have important demographic consequences for a country.

READING

Now read Reading C about poor and rich children in Brazil. The author compares the childhoods of the urban middle and upper classes with those children of the favela (slum). What differences do you note between the two? Are there similar discrepancies in your own community?

COMMENT

Brazil is a society of extremes with a highly unequal distribution of wealth. Pockets of absolute poverty exist side by side with a wealthy middle class. In this extract, Goldstein is making the point that poverty and social inequality do not just affect the material goods that children own or have

Children working on a rubbish dump in Jao Persao, Brazil.

an impact on their feelings of social exclusion. She claims that social inequality changes the very nature of their childhood. Because of their poverty, slum children are conceptualized differently from rich children, they are treated differently, even by their own families, and are valued significantly less. The social inequality of Brazilian society, and that of many South American countries, is vast but, as the chapter has implied, poor children in rich countries throughout the world are systematically undervalued, put in worse accommodation, placed at greater risk of ill health and disease and do not have the same opportunities as their richer counterparts.

A fairer distribution of wealth and resources remains, however, politically controversial and sometimes unenforceable. Many countries do not have systems for redistributing wealth, such as tax, or if they do, corruption is rife. In other countries, there are economic and political arguments against raising taxes to pay for improved welfare systems. Yet many governments have tried to alleviate child poverty. For example, in 2000 the UK government announced a target to abolish child poverty in 20 years, and to halve it by 2010 (UK Parliament, 2000). The government has set up a series of anti-poverty programmes such as Sure Start in England (the Scottish equivalent is called Starting Well), which provide integrated services for families with young children, such as home visiting, expanded day care and health education (see Chapter 5 for more details about this). It has also launched schemes such as the Working Families tax credit, which guarantees a minimum income for working families.

Children in a Swedish nursery.

Nevertheless, there is evidence that the solution to child poverty lies not in overall economic growth but in greater social equality and in a political willingness to create a fairer and more equitable society. The USA is the richest country in the world and yet it has the second largest percentage of children who live in relative poverty (around 22.4 per cent according to the UNICEF league table in Reading A – it is topped only by Mexico, in which 26.6 per cent of children live in poverty). The USA is also a country that has very wide disparities of income between rich and poor. In contrast, countries in the European Union that have the smallest gap between richest and poorest, such as the Scandinavian countries, are also those with the lowest levels of child poverty. In Sweden, for example, the child poverty rate is approximately 5 per cent. However, this commitment to social justice, equality and provision of services to the poor comes at a price. Sweden has very high levels of taxation, as does most of continental Europe, averaging around 50 per cent. In the UK, in contrast, public spending as a share of national income is around 40 per cent. Successive governments in the UK have prioritized tax cuts and therefore spending on child welfare has been given lower priority. As the Child Poverty Action Group has pointed out, ending child poverty and cutting income tax rates are mutually exclusive; child poverty cannot be tackled if there is no money to pay for it and no redistribution of wealth.

Box 2   The children's budget in South Africa

Some governments have recognized the inequalities within their societies and acknowledged that social inequality has a particularly devastating effect on children. South Africa, in particular, has instituted a children's budget, looking at how government economic policies directly affect children. South Africa is the first country in the world to do this, examining the effects of governmental policies, not on the level of families or communities but on children themselves. The children's budget is not a separate budget with certain funds earmarked for children; rather it is an overall attempt to see what resources have been allocated to improving children's welfare and making sure that children's needs are taken into account in every budgetary decision. Shirley Robinson, one of the advocates of the children's budget in South Africa, explains:

> The Children's Budget is a first step towards evaluating what government is spending on children in South Africa. To 'mainstream' children in policy dialogue and encourage a 'child-centred' development strategy, monitoring expenditure on budgetary programmes is necessary. The Children's Budget is a base-line study that provides information that will support the policy-making and advocacy efforts of children's rights advocates. It will also help these groups track specified indicators on government spending targeting children, thereby monitoring whether government is meeting its policy commitments to children in South Africa.

(Biersteker and Robinson, 1997, pp. 15–16)

South Africa has made a commitment to improving social justice and equality for children. It has set aside funds to do so and put in place systems of measuring and monitoring children's poverty. Despite the economic difficulties of the country, the government has acknowledged children as a priority and set up a system whereby its commitment to their welfare can be tested.

Finally, as discussed in Chapter 1, one of the major differentials within countries is based on ethnicity. For many children throughout the world, poverty, social exclusion and ethnicity are closely linked. In the UK and the USA, minority children are significantly more likely to live in poverty than their white counterparts. In the USA, '16% of white children are "officially poor" ', while for Hispanic and African-American children, the figure is 40 per cent (University of Minnesota, 2002). In the UK also, there are major discrepancies in income between ethnic groups, with Pakistani and Bangladeshi families having a poverty rate four times that of white people. Children of ethnic minorities tend to live in poorer areas, have worse schooling, poorer access to health care, and poorer access to state benefits. If they do not speak the majority language they may not be able to access

Homeless family sign in for a free meal in Daytona Beach, Florida.

these services, even if they do exist (CRE, 2002). Children from ethnic minorities are more likely to experience multiple forms of social exclusion and deprivation. In the UK, for example, Afro-Caribbean boys are six times more likely to be excluded from school than white boys, and they have worse exam results (CRE, 2002). In other countries, too, this pattern is repeated. In Brazil, and throughout South America, children of African heritage tend to be poorer and live in worse conditions than white children.

3.3 Social inequality within families

The final level of inequality this section examines is that of inequality within families. Many policies that are designed to tackle child poverty do so on a familial level, attempting to raise children out of poverty by ensuring that their parents have enough money and opportunities to enable them to fulfil their children's needs. Yet this strategy is problematic. Poverty levels are traditionally measured in terms of income levels per household, and child poverty levels are extrapolated from that, but this tells us nothing about the distribution of wealth among individual household members. It is possible that even when family income is high, it is not shared equally between all members of the family and different family members may have different standards of living. Hidden poverty can exist in apparently affluent families, and where this is the case the distribution of wealth is most often weighted against women and children and in favour of male household members. When women and children do not work or have no control over or access to money, or other resources, and are reliant on the male head of household, then they may experience poverty. In other instances, when a family is poor, hard decisions have to be made as to distribution of resources.

Allow about 10 minutes

ACTIVITY 6   **Marlene**

Read the vignette below concerning nine-year-old Marlene from El Salvador. List all the effects that you think that living in poverty have on her. Do you think that she has the same experiences of poverty as her siblings?

> In La Libertad, El Salvador, nine-year-old Marlene is already used to going without food as her family struggles to make ends meet. Marlene gets up at 6 am and does housework until 11 or 12. In the afternoon she studies a little and takes care of her little brother, Tomasito. Both her parents are working more these days because what her father makes does not stretch far enough. Marlene has learned to run the house, prepare the corn and cook. They only eat twice a day. At night, they just drink coffee. On the days when there is not enough food to go round, Marlene and her little sister Jessica do not eat. Tomasito always eats.
>
> (Save the Children, 1995, p. 21)

COMMENT

We are told little about Marlene's family, but from this small piece it is obvious that she does have different experiences of poverty from her siblings. Because she is older, she takes on a great deal of responsibility in the home, which means that she cannot go to school regularly. She has to take responsibility for her younger siblings as well as for looking after the house, which she does because she is older than them. Therefore, while all her family are likely to suffer from the effects of poverty, Marlene is especially vulnerable to ill health because she has a poor diet and works so hard. It is also apparent that when food goes short, she and her sister go without while her brother does not. Whether this is because of her gender or her age, it is difficult to know. Nevertheless, priority is given to her younger brother. Poverty therefore exacerbates the age and gender inequalities in her community.

Given that children are not a single category and that childhood experience needs to be disaggregated by age and gender (among other things), it is not surprising that girls and boys have very different experiences of poverty. On a global scale, more girls than boys miss out on school. Some studies suggest that three in ten girls do not go to school compared with only one in ten boys. Most studies show that girls begin working at home at a younger age than their brothers, and that they work more hours per day than boys. The vast majority of girls who work at home work between four and sixteen hours a day, work which is not counted by economists because it is unpaid and unrecognized (CRIN, 2000, p. 24). We have seen previously some of the links between HIV/AIDS and general childhood poverty but even here, there is a startling gender division. The HIV infection rates of girls between the ages of fifteen and nineteen are significantly higher than boys in the same age group. In Uganda, for example, the ratio of girls to boys in this age group who are infected with HIV is six to one. In Zambia and Malawi the girl-to-boy infection ratio in that age group is five to one (ILO, 2002). The issue of gender discrimination in terms of health care will be taken up again in the next chapter.

Cultural expectations about girls' and boys' relative contributions to the family will also affect poverty rates within families. Amongst working children in Thailand, for example, girls are expected to hand over most, if not all, of their wages to their parents whereas it is expected that boys will keep some back for their own personal expenses. Furthermore, studies of child prostitution in Thailand have shown that it is mostly girls who work in the sex industry and that the majority of these girls do so in order to support their families. Often parents are paid in advance for their daughters' services and even when girls are given money directly by clients or by brothel owners, they send most of it back to their parents (Phongpaichit, 1982). This pattern is true throughout much of the world – where boys and girls both work, girls' work is lower paid, less skilled and affords less occupational mobility.

In Nepal, both age and gender affect a child's experience of poverty. Older children may be sent away to work in carpet factories leaving younger children at home to work in agriculture. Maita Sungh Waiba, a boy of about fourteen working in a carpet factory in Kathmandu, told researchers from ActionAid about his family: '[My father and brother] will have to work more now that I've gone: ploughing, digging and looking after the animals' (Johnson, Hill and Ivan-Smith, 1995, p. 62).

Buddhi Maya Tamung, a twelve-year-old girl also working in a carpet factory in Kathmandu, concurred with this but felt that gender inequalities would mean a greater burden placed on her sister: 'My sister will have to do my work in the village now. Perhaps she might have to spend more time collecting fodder and fuelwood because I am not there. I don't think my brother will be affected very much' (Johnson, Hill and Ivan-Smith, 1995, p. 62).

Child carpet weavers in Kathmandu, Nepal.

Girls in Nepal generally do not inherit land (although they do inherit cattle and jewellery). They cannot perform rituals at their parents' funerals and

because they marry out of their communities and live with their husbands and need dowries to take with them, they are often not considered as good an investment as boys. It is unsurprising therefore that fewer resources are devoted to them and that they are more likely to experience worse poverty within the family than boys.

Age also affects children's experiences of poverty. For example, because of international pressure, countries such as Pakistan have forbidden children under the age of fourteen to work. However, poor families cannot afford to have non-productive children and therefore offer their children in illegal arrangements to sweatshops and carpet weaving factories. The conditions in these places are often worse than in the legal sector and therefore younger children become more vulnerable to abuse and exploitation than their older siblings who are able to work legally (Save the Children, 1995).

Birth order too is important. An older child is likely to be treated differently from younger ones. Sometimes the older child is expected to go to work to support the younger ones and carry a heavier burden of responsibility for the family. In Rwanda, after the genocide, children formed households together, after their parents died. In many cases the burden fell on the oldest children, and in particular on the eldest girl, who felt a special responsibility as the head of the next generation. Over 75 per cent of child-headed households in Rwanda are headed by girls under eighteen. One such person is Habasa, a seventeen year old who must look after her younger brothers and sisters as well as her own baby.

> Interviewer: 'As the oldest in your family, what do you worry about most?'
>
> 'Looking after the children. You know I am still very young and I cannot manage. But I have no alternative, I have got to do what I am supposed to do.'
>
> […]
>
> Interviewer: 'Habasa, you are a family of five, how do you share the workload?'
>
> 'We take turns, cooking, fetching water, cleaning etc. The little boy lives with us, he helps whenever he can mending broken things and fetching water. The younger ones don't do much. We teach them a few tasks. At weekends we go to church and my sisters earn a bit of pocket money performing dances and songs at various places, for example at weddings.'
>
> (BBC World Service, 2002)

Poverty and inequality are closely linked and, as this section has shown, poverty has different effects on children, according to their gender, their ethnicity, their age or whether they are the eldest or youngest child. How a child responds to poverty, as Chapter 1 discussed, will depend on individual factors of resilience, as well as on the social and cultural circumstances in which a child finds him or herself.

- Poverty and social inequality are intrinsically linked.
- Social inequalities can be found between nations, within nations and within families.
- Inequalities between countries have been getting worse since the 1960s.
- Structural adjustment programmes have had a negative effect on children's lives in countries of the South because they emphasize debt repayment and exports at the expense of social services that benefit children.
- Within countries the gaps between richer and poorer have become greater.
- Within families, girls and boys often have different experiences of poverty, as do younger and older children.

4 CONCLUSION

The relationship between children and poverty is complex and, as this chapter shows, it cannot be understood in isolation from other causes and effects of adversity such as ill health. The number of children living in poverty worldwide is extremely high and while the majority of these children live in the South, there are also pockets of deprivation in the wealthy countries of the North. The distinction between relative and absolute poverty is helpful in understanding children's experiences of poverty and the impact it has on them, because it acknowledges that cultural expectations about standards of living are important. However, by looking at poverty not only in relative or absolute terms, but in terms of inequality, it is possible to see that at the heart of discussions about poverty lies the issue of social justice. Inequalities exist between countries, within countries and within families and these inequalities are critical both in understanding children's experience of poverty and in formulating policies that might alleviate their poverty.

REFERENCES

BAXTER, S. (1993) *A Child is Not a Toy,* Vancouver (Canada), New Star Books Limited.

BBC NEWS ONLINE (2001) 'A sheet of paper for a bed', http://news.bbc.co.uk/1/hi/world/africa/1186527.stm (last accessed 29 January 2003).

BBC WORLD SERVICE (2002) *Children of Conflict: child headed households,* http://www.bbc.co.uk/worldservice/people/features/childrensrights/childrenofconflict/headtxt.shtml#04 (last accessed 29 January 2003).

BIERSTEKER, L. AND ROBINSON, S. (1997) 'Children and the budget', in ROBINSON, S. and BIERSTEKER, L. (eds) *First Call: the South African children's budget,* Cape Town, IDASA.

BURDON, T. (2000) 'A clear case of relief', *Child Rights Information Network Newsletter,* **13**, p. 28.

BURR, R. (2000) unpublished field-notes for doctoral thesis, London, Brunel University.

CHILD POVERTY ACTION GROUP (CPAG) (2001) *An End In Sight? Tackling child poverty in the UK. Background briefing and summary,* London, Child Poverty Action Group.

CHILD RIGHTS INFORMATION NETWORK (CRIN) (2000) 'Factfile', *Child Rights Information Network Newsletter,* **13**, p. 28.

CHOO, C. (1990) *Aboriginal Child Poverty,* Melbourne, Brotherhood of St Laurence.

CHILDREN'S EXPRESS (UK) (2000) 'Vicious trap that pins you to a life of misery', first published in the *Newcastle Evening Chronicle,* 27 July 2000, http://www.childrens-express.org/dynamic/public/d503187.htm (accessed 28 June 2002).

COMMISSION FOR RACIAL EQUALITY (CRE) (2002) *Disadvantage and Discrimination in Britain Today – the facts,* http://www.cre.gov.uk/duty/duty_facts.html (accessed 15 September 2002).

GORDON, D., LEVITAS, R., PANTAZIS, D., PAYNE, S., TOWNSEND, P., ADELMAN, L., ASHWORTH, K., MIDDLETON, S., BRADSHAW, J. AND WILLIAMS, J. (2000) *Poverty and Social Exclusion in Britain,* York, Joseph Rowntree Foundation.

INTERNATIONAL LABOUR ORGANIZATION (ILO) (2002) *A Future without Child Labour; Report of the Director-General 2002,* Geneva, ILO, p. 42.

JOHNSON, V., HILL, J. AND IVAN-SMITH, E. (1995) *Listening to Smaller Voices: children in an environment of change,* London, ActionAid UK.

MONTGOMERY, H. K. (2001) *Modern Babylon? Prostituting children in Thailand.* Oxford, Berghahn Books.

MORENO, R. (2000) 'Zero interest for El Salvador's children', *Child Rights Information Network Newsletter,* **13**, p. 28.

THE OPEN UNIVERSITY (2003) U212 *Childhood,* Video 4, Band 2, 'Kelly and her sisters', Milton Keynes, The Open University.

PHAM THI LAN (2000) 'When children are the losers', *Child Rights Information Network Newsletter*, **13**, p. 28.

PHONGPAICHIT, P. (1982) *From Peasant Girls to Bangkok Masseuses,* Geneva, ILO.

RIDGE, T. (2002a) *Childhood Poverty and Social Exclusion: from a child's perspective*, Bristol, Policy Press.

RIDGE, T. (2002b) '"Fitting in" and "joining in", addressing the needs of children in poverty', paper given at the Politics of Childhood Conference, Hull, 10–12 September 2002.

SAHLINS, M. (1988) *Stone Age Economics*, London, Routledge.

SAVE THE CHILDREN (1995) *Towards a Children's Agenda*, London, Save the Children, p. 21.

THOMAS, C. (1997) 'Globalization and the South', in THOMAS, C. and WILKIN, P. (eds) *Globalization and the South*, London, Macmillan Press.

UK PARLIAMENT, HOUSE OF COMMONS (2000) Budget statement by Chancellor of the Exchequer, House of Commons Hansard, 21 March 2000, Col. 865.

UNICEF (2000a) *Poverty Reduction Begins with Children,* New York, UNICEF.

UNICEF (2000b) *State of the World's Children*, New York, UNICEF.

UNIVERSITY OF MINNESOTA HUMAN RIGHTS RESOURCES CENTER (2002) *Imagine a Country*, http://hrusa.org/hrmaterials/hreduseries/TB1a/Section2/imagine_a_countryH1.html (accessed 15 September 2002).

Ending child poverty

UNICEF

By the middle of the century that has just ended, the world's richest nations were confident that poverty would be overcome by a combination of economic growth and welfare spending. A prediction that poverty would still afflict significant numbers of their children in the 21st century would not have been believed. Today [article published in 2000], despite a doubling and redoubling of national incomes in most nations since 1950, a significant percentage of their children are still living in families so materially poor that normal health and growth are at risk. And as the [league tables on pp. 82–3 of child poverty] show, a far larger proportion remain in the twilight world of relative poverty; their physical needs may be minimally catered for, but they are painfully excluded from the activities and advantages that are considered normal by their peers.

Such statistics represent the unnecessary suffering and deprivation of millions of individual children. They also represent a failure to hold faith with the developed world's ideal of equality of opportunity. For no matter how many individual and anecdotal exceptions there may be, the fact remains that the children of the poor simply do not have the same opportunities as the children of the non-poor. Whether measured by physical and mental development, health and survival rates, educational achievement or job prospects, incomes or life expectancies, those who spend their childhood in poverty of income and expectation are at a marked and measurable disadvantage.

[Poverty represents] a threat to the quality of life of *all* citizens in those nations with high rates of child poverty. For while it is true that many poor families make sacrifices to give their children the best possible start in life, the broader picture shows that those who grow up in poverty are more likely to have learning difficulties, to drop out of school, to resort to drugs, to commit crimes, to be out of work, to become pregnant at too early an age, and to live lives that perpetuate poverty and disadvantage into succeeding generations. In other words, many of the most serious problems facing today's advanced industrialized nations have roots in the denial and deprivation that mark the childhoods of so many of their future citizens.

Child poverty therefore confronts the industrialized world with a test both of its ideals and of its capacity to resolve many of its most intractable social problems.

It is a test that cannot easily be avoided by arguments about individual responsibility. No one would argue that being born into poverty is the fault of the child. It is merely the lottery of birth. And it is fundamental to shared concepts of progress and civilisation that an accident of birth should not be allowed to circumscribe the quality of life. The poverty-bar may not be written into the laws and institutions of the land; but it is written into both the statistical chances and the everyday realities of millions of children who happen to be born into the poorest strata of our societies.

The new century has opened with a renewal of interest in the issue of poverty within the borders of the world's richest nations. In the European Union, heads of government have called for specific targets to be established as part of an effort to 'make a decisive impact on the eradication of poverty'. In the United States, official poverty lines are being reviewed for the first time in over 30 years. In France, the Prime Minister's Conseil d'Analyse Économique has focused national attention on poverty and social exclusion. In the Republic of Ireland, specific targets and programmes have been announced for a ten-year anti-poverty effort. In the United Kingdom, the government has committed itself to halving child poverty in ten years and eradicating it in twenty.

In part, this new interest appears to be driven by the ethical imperative that poverty, and particularly child poverty, is a stain on the record of today's advanced nations – and one that should not have been allowed to seep into the 21st century. But in part, also, the renewal of interest is born of a growing recognition that many of the other problems confronting today's industrial societies – from drug abuse and crime to educational underachievement and alienation from common values – are strongly associated with the poverty-amid-prosperity that afflicts a significant proportion of their populations. [...]

Defining poverty

Poverty in the world's rich nations has long been seen as the enemy that must inevitably surrender to the combination of economic growth and welfare spending. The deep-rooted social and psychological dimensions of the problem have, for the most part, been seen as secondary problems that would yield once the economic problem had been overcome. More recent interest in the issue has been marked by a humbler understanding of poverty's complexity, and of the inter-relationships between its economic and social dimensions. Increasingly, poverty of expectation and poverty of opportunity are being recognised as forces to be reckoned with in their own right rather than as mere camp-followers of low income ...

Even with the focus narrowed to income-poverty, measurement remains a complex issue. And underlying all attempts at measurement is a fundamental problem of definition. Is poverty to be defined as an absolute condition – the inability to purchase or consume a fixed minimum package of goods and services? Or is it to be defined as a relative state – the falling behind, by more than a certain degree, from the average income and life-style enjoyed by the rest of the society in which one lives?

This [article] opts for the latter concept. The poverty measured and analysed [here] is the poverty of those whose 'resources (material, cultural, and social) are so limited as to exclude them from the minimum acceptable way of life in the Member States in which they live'. This definition, adopted by the European Union in 1984, is today the most commonly used definition in the industrialized world. For practical purposes, it is usually interpreted as 'those whose incomes fall below half of the average income (as measured by the median) for the nation in which they live'.

In other words, it is a measure of *relative* poverty.

In the United States, an alternative approach holds sway. Here, the official poverty line is set in dollars and represents the annual income required to allow a family of a given size to purchase the range of goods and services that are seen as constituting the minimum acceptable way of life in America. Originally drawn in the 1960s as a battle line in President Johnson's 'War on Poverty', the dollar figure was arrived at by taking the cost of an adequate diet and multiplying by three (in line with the fact that food accounted for one third of average household expenditure). For almost forty years, this figure has been adjusted to reflect only changing prices rather than changing perceptions of what constitutes a minimum acceptable American way of life.

It is therefore intended as a measure of *absolute* poverty. [...]

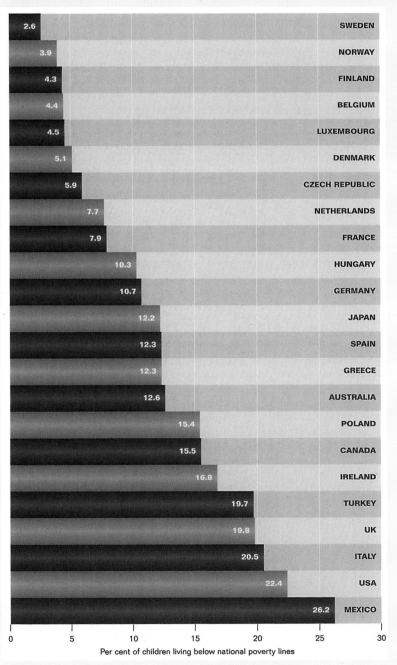

Figure 1
The Child Poverty League. The table shows the percentage of children defined as living in 'relative' poverty, defined as households with income below 50 per cent of the national median.

	Per cent
SWEDEN	2.6
NORWAY	3.9
FINLAND	4.3
BELGIUM	4.4
LUXEMBOURG	4.5
DENMARK	5.1
CZECH REPUBLIC	5.9
NETHERLANDS	7.7
FRANCE	7.9
HUNGARY	10.3
GERMANY	10.7
JAPAN	12.2
SPAIN	12.3
GREECE	12.3
AUSTRALIA	12.6
POLAND	15.4
CANADA	15.5
IRELAND	16.8
TURKEY	19.7
UK	19.8
ITALY	20.5
USA	22.4
MEXICO	26.2

Per cent of children living below national poverty lines

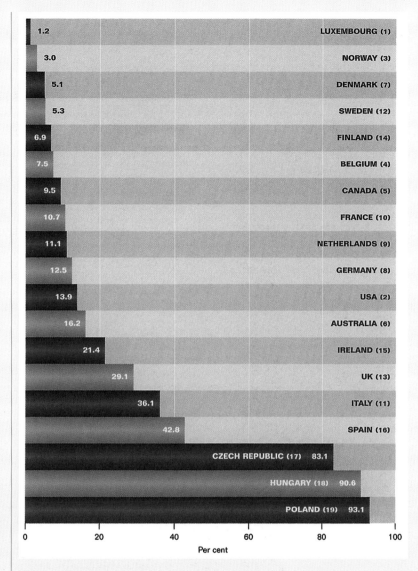

Figure 2 'Absolute' child poverty. The table shows the percentage of children living in households with incomes below the US official poverty line converted into national currencies (with purchasing power parity exchange rates). GNP per capita ranks are given in brackets (GNP values are in purchasing power parity terms and relate to the same years as the poverty data).

Figure 1 shows the percentage of children living below the relative poverty line in 23 nations of the OECD [Organisation for Economic Co-operation and Development]. Figure 2 shows the percentage of children living below the equivalent of the US official poverty line (translated into each national currency and adjusted to take into account national prices). For the latter table, data are available for 19 countries only.

The difference comes into a particularly sharp focus when we compare the placings of the United States and of the three former communist countries admitted to the OECD in the 1990s. In the relative league table, the Czech Republic is placed seventh with fewer than 6 per cent of its children below the poverty line. The United States is in next-to-bottom place with over 22 per cent of its children in poverty. When we turn to the league table based on poverty defined as an 'absolute' (the equivalent of the US poverty line), we find that the three former-communist states have fallen to the bottom of the rankings with over 80 per cent of their children below the poverty line – a proportion approximately twice that of any other OECD nation. The United States, on the other hand, rises to the middle of the table with a child poverty rate of just under 14 per cent – about the same as Germany or the Netherlands.

It might be argued, therefore, that the concept of relative child poverty is merely measuring inequality. In support of this view, it could be said that the low levels of child poverty revealed in the Czech Republic or Hungary are attributable to nothing more than a degree of income equality, and that this is in itself no more than a passing legacy of the communism that also bequeathed so much misery and pollution before being overthrown by the popular will. Conversely, the supposedly high level of child poverty in the United States might be said to reveal nothing more than the higher degree of income inequality which is what provides the incentives to make the United States what it is – the richest country on earth.

Counter-argument

The use of a relative definition of child poverty can, however, be just as vigorously defended.

The current review of the poverty line in the United States is being driven, in part, by the fact that over the last 40 years great changes have occurred in American society and in Americans' perceptions and expectations of what constitutes a minimum acceptable way of life (changes can to some extent be captured in the fact that food now accounts for considerably less than one third of average household expenditure). This, by implication, is an admission that the poverty line ought to change as society becomes wealthier. This conceded, it can be argued that the necessary relationship between poverty lines and rising national wealth ought to be maintained in a way that is consistent and dependable, rather than arbitrary and uncertain.

It can further be argued that it is relative poverty which most accurately reflects the equality of opportunity that has long been the boast and battle-cry of the industrialized nations. No matter how complicated the debate about the relationships between poverty in childhood and prospects in later life ... few would seriously maintain that the sons and daughters of the poor have the same opportunities as the sons and daughters of the rich.

But perhaps the most important argument is that it is the level of relative poverty that most accurately captures what it is that we should be concerned about. Once economic development has progressed beyond a certain minimum level, the rub of the poverty problem – from the point of view of both the poor individual and of the societies in which they live – is not so much the effects of poverty in any absolute form but the effects of the contrast, daily perceived, between the lives of the poor and the lives of those around them. For practical purposes, the problem of poverty in the industrialized nations today is a problem of *relative* poverty.

As for the argument that such an emphasis on relative incomes runs counter to the need for incentives, it can be argued that, whatever the intricacies of this long-running debate, nations such as Sweden, Norway and Finland contrive to be among the most egalitarian and yet among the wealthiest countries in the world. The top six places in both child poverty league tables – relative and absolute – are occupied by the same six northern European countries all of which combine a high degree of economic development with a reasonable degree of equity.

Finally, there is the essentially ethical argument that clearly underlies the European Union definition of poverty cited above, and that is enshrined in the United Nations Convention on the Rights of the Child which provides for the right to 'a standard of living adequate for physical, mental, spiritual, moral and social development' (Article 27).

It is a definition not dissimilar to one articulated by an American economist nearly half a century ago:

> 'People are poverty-stricken when their income, even if adequate for survival, falls markedly behind that of the community. Then they cannot have what the larger community regards as the minimum necessary for decency; and they cannot wholly escape, therefore, the judgement of the larger community that they are indecent. They are degraded, for, in a literal sense, they live outside the grades or categories which the community regards as respectable.'

J. K. Galbraith, *The Affluent Society* (1958)

Reference

GALBRAITH, J. K. (1958) *The Affluent Society*, Boston, Houghton Mifflin Company.

Source

UNICEF Innocenti Research Centre, Florence, Italy, *Innocenti Report Card* No. 1, June 2000, 'A league table of child poverty in rich nations', United Nations Children's Fund, pp. 3–9.

Once in a house on fire

Andrea Ashworth

We clambered on to the bus with all our belongings, then waved goodbye to Auntie Vera, who soon shrank to a funny-sad smudge. The green world withered, and a grimier one shot up. Blocks of curved towers loomed, with shirts and stockings dripping out of the windows. The Bull Ring, our mother called it, crammed with skinheads and pensioners and dark-eyed families flown in from far away. We gaped at smashed glass and graffiti shrieking Fuck Off Wogs, Paki Scum Go Home.

'Don't worry,' our mother muttered when we wondered what the flats looked like inside, 'we'll not end up anywhere like this.'

Lost black ladies, boys in turbans, bald men dangling fags, all gazed into the clouds or down on to the pavement. I imagined living with them, everyone baked in at the windows like currants in a concrete cake.

'Don't you worry.' Our mother turned her back on the high-rise estates and fixed her eyes on the road ahead. 'We're not that bloody desperate!'

Everything we owned was stuffed into our single surviving suitcase and a pile of plastic bags whose handles gouged our fingers, making raspberries of the fingertips. We got off the bus in the centre of Chorlton and dragged our things down strange streets. When the strap of the suitcase snapped off, we had to shove it over the pavestones, stiffening our backs so as not to seem common, while its hinges screeched and its flowery sides bulged like a fat lady with bellyache.

'Seventy-two, Denton Road.' Our mother muttered her way down the shabby street. We would be staying with Auntie Jackie, the lady who used to live next door to us on Thornton Road when we were little. We scoured doorways for what was to be our future.

Door-window-door-window-door-window-door, with the odd house boarded up. There were no spaces between them, unlike the ones at Auntie Vera's, which were built out of blond stone and clumped in twos. Here, the sky stood still, over streets blessed with nothing that could be called a garden: splurges of dusty hedge and the odd clump of dandelions. Our eyes dived into front room after front room.

'Enough nosing,' our mother panted, pausing in her wrestle with the suitcase to prise our gazes away from bedraggled curtains and twitching sooty nets. Chorlton would be posh, she had promised, while we were packing at Auntie Vera's.

'Where do they keep the trees?' Sarah asked, sparking giggles that slumped into silence. We followed our mother's frown down the road full of lamp-posts, where there were no leafy branches swaying against slate greys and brown brick. My eyes fell back to earth, snagging on dog turds and gutted fag packets. Flaps of newspaper strewed busty ladies along the broken pavement.

'Here we go.' Our mother halted. 'Seventy-flamin'-two!'

Black paint flaked off a door whose window panes had been smashed into glass webs. Someone had stuck them together with Sellotape, which had rotted to the colour of wee. We hauled our things through the whingeing wrought-iron gate.

'It'll only be making do, mind,' our mother whispered after ringing the bell. 'Just for the time being.' [...]

Grubbing around in her purse, our mother came up with pocket money to keep Laurie, Sarah and me out of her hair. On top of pennies for sweets, she sent us to buy a tennis ball and a rainbow box of chalk to go with the skipping ropes that Auntie Vera had given us, with handles that used to be bobbins, shuttling cotton in old mill-buildings. She lined us up after breakfast, to give out the rules about where was safe to play and where was bloody well not. Mostly we stayed in the square opposite the house, watching grown-ups step in and out of the red telephone box – some laughing, some whispering, some shouting – while we kept our distance so that no one would think we were noseys. I hopscotched myself stupid and skipped with Laurie and Sarah, until local kids crowded around. Then I bounced my ball against the wall in snazzy arcs, whistling, while my little sisters carried on with their hops, skips and jumps.

'Where you lot from, then?' Kids with sticky jumpers sized us up in our old-fashioned cardigans, swirly buttons fastened up to our necks. Our mother had scolded us into woollens that made our movements stiff, like robots: 'I'm not having you traipsing about looking poor.'

'We've just come from Rawtenstall.' I spoke for the three of us. 'And before that we lived in Vancouver – it's this place in a corner of Canada, across the Atlantic Ocean.'

We stood in the centre of the scruffy kids' circle, letting them mull over our cardies and Canada, giving them a go of our ropes with the bobbin handles. They squinted at our sharp 't's, the rasp of our aitches and the way that our 'g's rang at the end of words like having and singing and running, where theirs had fallen off.

'Think yer posh, don't yer?'

Running clear of the accusation, Laurie and I beat them at tag and spurted the odd loud 'Oi' although we knew we would have to pay for it over the baked beans at tea-time. Our mother would let out an end-of-her-tether sigh at our shameless flaming antics, our screaming like banshees and acting proper common for all the world to witness.

Tucked up with my book on the settee, I could be free of my little sisters for half an hour before tea every day. I would study my mother's face over the pages, swallowing guilt at the cash she had stumped up the day she took me, just me, to John Menzies, where I picked out a prize for passing my Eleven-Plus exam. She stood over me with her snakeskin purse, while I lurked along the bookshelves, gripping my hands behind my, back. 'Go on, Andy, love!' Her smile never wavered, although the cost mounted up – and up and up and up – as I slid out The Twins at Saint Clare's, the complete set by Enid Blyton, then hurried, clutching them against my chest, to the cash till.

I read them to death, one by one, then one by one again, dreaming of a boarding school brimming with brainy girls. I saw myself plucked up and plopped into Saint Clare's, in the light of my affinity for spelling and sums, but squirmed at the ruse I would have to pull to get into such a school. Since I hadn't been blessed with rich parents, I would have to pretend that there were no parents at all. If you were an orphan, it seemed to me, pity would persuade people to spot your talents instead of your clothes and shoes, and no one would mind if you had no money.

'Can't we do anything about them?' I fought back tears in front of my mother when welts sprang up along my arms and burrowed, burning, into my neck. The fleas on Auntie Jackie's cats seemed to ignore everyone else, making a meal of me.

'What can we do?' My mother dabbed pink calamine lotion, chalky and cool, over the livid flea bites. 'They're your Auntie Jackie's pride and joy, those cats. And it won't be much longer now, Andy – don't be whingeing.'

As if to show just how soon we would find our own house, our mother slept on a spindly folding bed next to the mattress where Laurie and I huddled with our Sarah on the floor. It was magical, lying low, hearing her breathing above our heads. A slight squeak sang out when she turned over in the night, sighing. A car might glide by, shooting light through the crack in the curtains, up the wall in a wave. Otherwise silence pressed in, purple-black, coloured by crying. Our mother sobbed through her knuckles.

I wanted to cry too, to keep her company, but I had too much grub grinning inside. Auntie Jackie packed us to bed full of pizzas and glistening vinegary chips: Auntie Vera thought fried food was wicked, but Auntie Jackie swore it was sacrilege to eat potatoes unless they'd been chopped into chunky fingers and plunged in bubbling gold lard. […]

'Absolutely brassic, we are'. Our mother composed the shopping list in perfect handwriting, on the back of an envelope from Norweb. It was like a poem, except that 'loaves' meant flimsy, thin-sliced white bread, 'margarine' meant watery, petrol-tasting stuff, and 'milk' came not in bottles or cartons but in boxes of powder that left lumps, no matter how long you whisked it in water with a fork. Fastening all the press studs on our anoraks, we braced ourselves against icy wind and rain. A mile-and-a-half's walk lay between us and Kwik Save on Dickenson Road. Four miles there and back, if you counted a detour to the freezer-food emporium, where pounds performed miracles for people even poorer than ourselves. Ladies with no stockings leaned into icy chests to pull out fish fingers and so-called beefburgers in bumper bags. Everybody knew that they shrivelled to a cardboardy pulp after the fat and water had melted under the grill, but at 69p a dozen nobody seemed to care.

'Tot it up for us, Andy.' My mother compared the amount in her purse with the figure I tugged out of the trolley, after adding the prices of packets and cans. We went through our cash-out routine, putting items back on the shelf to bring the total into line.

'Right, how much is it now?'

I subtracted a pot of jam, a jar of pickled onions and two packets of Rich Tea. My mother made a calculation in her own head, then put the jam next to the till to be checked out, bidding goodbye to the onions and biscuits, pursing her lips against our heartbroken looks.

Source

ASHWORTH, A. (1998) *Once in a House on Fire*, London, Picador, pp. 101–15.

Nothing bad intended: child discipline, punishment, and survival in a shantytown in Rio de Janeiro, Brazil

Donna M. Goldstein

Childhood is a privilege of the rich

> In the early evening, along the beachfront in a city in Northeast Brazil, people are out strolling. A well-dressed white man of the upper class and his son, probably about the age of seven or eight, decide to stop and have their shoes shined by a dark-skinned boy, shoeless and not more than seven or eight years old himself. I was close enough to hear the father instructing his son how to speak to the other boy, how to demand a certain polish to be done in a certain way at a certain price. The father insisted that the job, both the shine and the orchestration of behavior between his son and the shoe-shine boy, be done to perfection. The shoe-shine boy was keen to show off his dexterity and did not need any instruction about what to do. At the end of the shine, the young son paid the shoe-shine boy with his father's money, and the shoe-shine boy, happy to have earned a few coins, walked off down the beach in search of new customers. The man and his son continued strolling along. (from author's field notes, 1988)

This scene, witnessed during an extended field visit in 1988, captures well the fact that childhood is lived and experienced differently by the disparate classes that characterize Brazilian urban culture. Indeed, in Brazil childhood is a privilege of the rich and practically nonexistent for the poor. [...]

In an age in which class analyses are passé, perhaps it is pointless to call attention to the fact that the condition of Brazil's poor children is a direct result of the highly unequal aspects of Brazilian society – aspects that stem from colonialism, slavery, unequal trade relations, and a rigid class and race system. Yet, these legacies have served to create the contemporary masks of domination, and one of the results has been a shortened childhood for much of Brazil's urban poor. [...]

Class and the notion of childhood in Brazil

It bears repeating that childhood in Brazil is a privilege of the rich and is practically nonexistent for the poor. This fact is particularly marked in the urban centers, where the middle and upper classes customarily employ domestic help in the form of cooks, nannies, and housecleaners, generally from neighboring favelas or lower-class neighborhoods. The relationship of this domestic help within Brazilian middle- and upper-class households is a key one: their relationship borders, in terms of actual wages, on domestic slavery, but in terms of intimacy and affective nature, it may have the feel of being a quasi-family member. This construction fits easily into what James Scott (1989) has termed the 'euphemization of power relations.' The children of the wealthy learn at an early age how to 'treat' the maid, and this includes ordering her to do various tasks for them. One of the many results of this relationship is that the children of the wealthy are indulged and spoiled, being catered to daily by their parents and the servants in their midst. At the same time, the children of the poor, often accompanying their mothers who are domestic servants in the homes of the rich, are not treated as children in that social milieu. Contardo Calligaris (1991) recounts, for example, how he was always surprised that the domestic worker would serve food to her employers and their children before serving food to her own child, without regard to the age of her child. This etiquette, an obvious leftover of slave relations, is ubiquitous and denies poor children the privileges that they might otherwise receive merely for being children. In this example, poor children learn early on that their needs are secondary to those of the rich. In contrast, the children of the upper classes are superprivileged: they are welcomed at social functions and generously accepted and appreciated in the public sphere, such as at restaurants and shops, certainly more than their counterparts are in comparative settings in western Europe and the United States.

In the favela, children are expected to be productive and to begin working at a very young age. By the age of five or six, children are participating in various chores, such as cleaning, washing clothes and dishes, sweeping, and taking care of younger siblings. By the age of nine or ten, young girls are often taking primary care of their baby siblings. Girls, especially, are frequently sent out as domestic workers or as wageless helpers. Favela children may accompany their parent to the home of a rich person, where they will aid in all of the tasks their parent is involved in. In contrast, the children of the rich are usually prohibited from entering the kitchen. There is absolutely no encouragement or value placed on learning to clean or cook since these are tasks carried out by the domestic help. Because these tasks are taken care of by the domestic help, it is a class marker to be inept at these tasks. Moreover, there is a disturbing discourse, sometimes heard among domestic workers in the favela, which at times speaks more lovingly of the children of their *patroa* (employer) than about their own children. The existence of this discourse is perhaps explicable in terms of Albert Memmi's analysis (1965) of the colonized mind: he describes the psychological process of the damage that is done to those who are colonized and that is embedded in their desire sometimes to emulate the colonizer (or dominant class), to prefer their company, and to find them more beautiful and their habits more respectable than people of their own family or class. Indeed, the favelados prefer, to some extent, the way of being of the children of their employers to that of their own children. Additionally, it seems that the love of the domestic worker for the employer's children has something to do with the differing standards of behavior for middle- and upper-class children and lower-class children. Middle- and upper-class children can be loved and adored as children, while lower-class children are hastened into becoming adults in order to survive.

Children learn the manners of their parents. Middle- and upper-class children never need to learn any kitchen skills, for example, but they must learn how to eat using a knife and fork correctly and how to behave at the table. [...] The favela child may never learn to eat with a knife and fork, since a spoon is more commonly used for eating beans and rice, the daily fare of the poor. More importantly, children of both classes are taught by adults of their class the survival skills that their backgrounds require – child discipline and punishment included. Just as knowing the appropriate table manners is part of a small tradition passed on from adult to child, the favela mother knows intuitively that in order for her own children to survive, toughness, obedience, subservience, and street smarts are necessary; otherwise, the child can end up dead. It is important to learn these survival strategies at an early age – by five or six years old. But from the perspective of the domestic worker, the children of the employer do not need to learn the same skills that her children do. They can be pampered, spoiled, and infantilized, and such treatment would not harm or alter their survival capabilities.

Rich children must adhere to the habits and regulations of their class or be 'excluded from the life of that class.' They can be more childlike and be so for longer periods of time, since it is part of their class training to be spoiled and even helpless. In contrast, the younger children in a typical favela household are often parented by their older siblings, since their parents are out working so much of the time. They cannot afford to be childlike, spoiled, or helpless. There is thus collusion at the societal, household, and individual levels in creating these two distinct forms of childhood.

References

CALLIGARIS, CONTARDO. 1991. *Hello Brasil! Notas de um psicanalista europeu viajando ao Brasil.* São Paulo: Escuta.

MEMMI, ALBERT. 1965. *The Colonizer and the Colonized.* Boston: Beacon Press.

SCOTT, JAMES. 1989. 'Prestige As the Public Discourse of Domination' *Cultural Critique* 12 (Spring): 146–66.

Source

GOLDSTEIN, D. M. (1998) 'Nothing bad intended: child discipline, punishment, and survival in a shantytown in Rio de Janeiro, Brazil', in Scheper-Hughes, N. and Sargent, C. (eds) *Small Wars: the cultural politics of childhood*, Berkeley and Los Angeles, University of California Press, pp. 389–95.

Chapter 3

Achieving health for children

Catherine Panter-Brick

CONTENTS

When you have studied this chapter, you should be able to:

1 Recognize why child health matters and identify the goals set for the improvement of children's health.

2 Evaluate critically definitions of health and appraise why views regarding the treatment of ill health vary across cultures.

3 Recognize why children still suffer from preventable malnutrition and curable diseases.

4 Examine how social inequalities affects children's health.

5 Discuss the health consequences of discrimination against children on ethnic, gender, or other grounds.

1 CHILD HEALTH MATTERS

This chapter will discuss some of the major health issues for children and the steps taken on their behalf to achieve good health. The focus will be mostly on the poorest countries of the world, and especially on children under five. Why this focus? Is it because young children are particularly vulnerable, dying in huge numbers when conditions are adverse to health? Is it because they die unnecessarily of largely preventable malnutrition and curable infectious diseases? The answer to both these questions is undoubtedly 'yes'. Note that a quarter of all deaths in the world occur among children under five, such that:

> Nearly 11 million children still die each year before their fifth birthday, often from readily preventable causes. An estimated 150 million children are malnourished.

> (UNICEF, 2001, p. 4)

These statistics are a startling reminder of the failures to ensure children's health. In this context, it is important to realize that international legislation is already in place for the purposes of giving all children *rights* to health care. Significantly, the issues of children's survival and access to proper health care are no longer just a matter of charitable humanitarian concern: they are enshrined in law, through the United Nations Convention on the Rights of the Child (UNCRC). Children's rights to health and health services are now a matter of legal responsibility for the states that ratified the Convention.

> Article 6
> 1. States Parties recognize that every child has the inherent right to life.
> 2. States Parties shall ensure to the maximum extent possible the survival and development of the child.
> …
> Article 24
> 1. States Parties recognize the right of the child to the enjoyment of the highest attainable standard of health and to facilities for the treatment of illness and rehabilitation of health.

> (UNCRC, cited in Child Rights Information Network, 2002)

Box I WHO and UNICEF

The World Health Organization (WHO) and the United Nations Children's Fund (UNICEF) are major international bodies that monitor and promote health issues on a global scale. These organizations collect systematic information about health and health inequalities – the relative chance to live, die and fall sick – across geographic areas and socio-economic groups. They also design and promote large-scale health interventions (the eradication of smallpox in the 1980s is the best example of a successful worldwide campaign). Both produce annual reports, with the WHO focusing on selected health problems and UNICEF producing *The State of the World's Children*, which gives an up-to-date review of health statistics, identifies key aspects of children's lives or issues for special consideration and reports on the progress of specific health intervention.

Logo of the World Health Organization.

Logo of the United Nations Children's Fund.

Providing children with a meal each day is a high priority for this early childhood centre in rural India.

Despite such a clear agenda in matters of child health, the lives of many children are brutish and short, particularly for the poor. Improving children's health may well be a universal mandate, but the implementation of health programmes at the local level can be difficult. Many obstacles still frustrate what should be a straightforward course of action – feeding children in cases of malnutrition, vaccinating or treating common infections, as well as providing a healthy environment and appropriate care. One such obstacle is the complex relationship between poverty and ill health. This has already been mentioned in Chapter 2, 'Children, poverty and social inequality', and is highlighted in this statement:

> Just as low income is a contributing factor to poor health and malnutrition, so poor health and malnutrition are key reasons for the persistence of poverty.

> (UNICEF, 2001, p. 19)

It is of course well known that underlying poverty frustrates efforts to achieve good health. Yet most health programmes advocate quite specific interventions, focusing, for example, on severe malnutrition or specific infectious diseases, without tackling poverty *per se*.

This chapter will look in detail at these and other challenges to achieving good health for children. Some of the major reasons why child health is such an important issue will be explored in greater detail in the rest of this section. Section 2 will then consider some influential definitions of child health, as well as a range of cultural views about the causes and treatment of illness. Section 3 will review international progress in achieving child health, drawing attention to some of the reasons why death rates amongst children remain hugely unequal across both nations and local communities. It will also consider the significance of gender in shaping survival and health prospects. Finally, Section 4 considers the social context of malnutrition and obesity and looks at issues surrounding the effectiveness of child health interventions. Basic health solutions may be readily available, but may not always be welcomed or applied. This section analyses some of the complex reasons why so-called 'magic bullets' don't always reach their targets, taking vaccination programmes and oral rehydration salts as examples.

1.1 Critical issues for children

Allow about 10 minutes

ACTIVITY 1   **A special focus on children**

Why do you think that matters of child health are important? Make a list of possible reasons why child health should be of particular concern to adults. Are concerns for children's health different from those about adults' health?

COMMENT

It has been argued that children should get 'first call' or top priority in matters of health care and health interventions. There are many reasons for this and your list should illustrate why children's health is an important issue for governments, families and communities. Your points might reflect a range of medical, social, moral and political concerns. These might include:

1 The sheer scale of child deaths and ill health.

2 The greater vulnerability of children to neglect, malnutrition and disease.

3 The consequences of ill health during the critical period of life when children are growing and developing.

4 The emotional significance of child mortality, disability and ill health to parents and communities.

5 The moral responsibility on the part of adults to care for children who cannot fend for themselves.

6 The economic and social loss of individuals as human capital.

7 The greater scope for effective interventions to save or improve the lives of children, in combating risks to health.

We will now look at these points in more detail.

Figure 1
Consequences of malnutrition and its intergenerational aspects (adapted from ACC/SCN, 2000, cited in UNEP, UNICEF and WHO, 2002).

We have already touched on the first two points in the list above. Children are particularly vulnerable to neglect, malnutrition and disease in the first five years of life – when a quarter of all deaths across the globe occur. There is also plenty of evidence that episodes of ill health affect future development. For example, a malnourished infant can be listless and have slow social and cognitive development, which affects school performance and opportunities for education. The child will be less able to resist infections and will show retarded growth, which can affect work performance and future income. These effects can also damage the next generation. For example, when a malnourished girl becomes an adult, she will be more likely to have low birth-weight babies and, given her short stature and small hips, suffer complications from childbirth. The vulnerability of children and the manifold consequences of early child malnutrition throughout the life-cycle are illustrated in Figure 1.

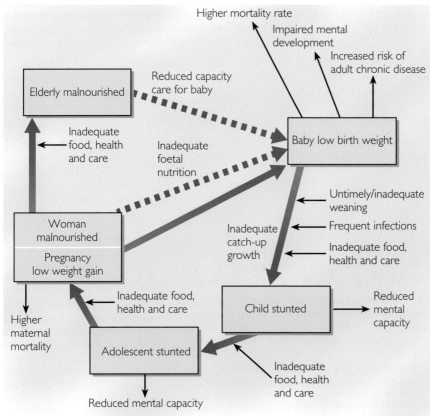

Points 4 and 5 on our list are about the emotional, moral or religious significance of death, illness and disability for parents who assume the responsibility of care, and the perceived failure in not providing protection and care for children. Death, disability or illness of children also entails an economic and social loss of individuals as workforce or 'human capital' for society at large. Children's health, therefore, is not simply the concern and responsibility of individual parents, but of communities and society on a national and international scale.

The final point on our list emphasizes another respect in which health issues for children merit attention. Consider the ten leading causes of disability and premature mortality worldwide in 1990: lower respiratory infections, diarrhoeal diseases, perinatal conditions, depression, ischaemic heart disease, cerebrovascular disease, tuberculosis, measles, road traffic crashes and congenital abnormalities (Dabis *et al.*, 2002). Five of these are primarily or exclusively childhood diseases (the first three listed, plus measles and congenital abnormalities). Several of these diseases – respiratory infections, diarrhoeal diseases and measles – are readily prevented or treated in healthy children. However, many young children have reduced resistance to infections as a result of mild but chronic malnutrition. This is illustrated in Figure 2, which shows the main causes of death amongst children under five: malnutrition underlies most causes of deaths, with the two biggest killer diseases being acute respiratory infections (for example, pneumonia) and diarrhoea. Among the various possible forms of malnutrition, chronic mild-to-moderate under-nutrition is a largely 'silent and invisible emergency, exacting a terrible toll on children and their families' (Bellamy, 1998, p. 1). It is silent and invisible because it commands less attention than severe under-nutrition in famine situations, yet it is a real emergency, because it is implicated in more than half of all child deaths worldwide. The fact that these deaths are preventable makes them a blatant violation of children's rights.

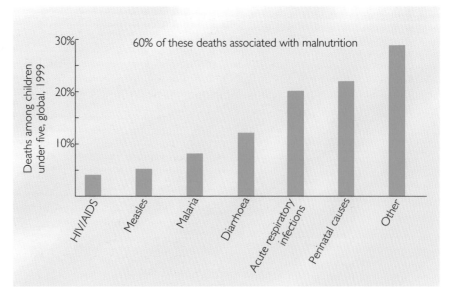

Figure 2
Causes of child
mortality (adapted from
World Bank, 2002).

Sections 3 and 4 will look at these issues in greater detail, asking why achieving health for children remains such an elusive goal. But first we need to consider what exactly is meant by 'health' and 'ill-health'.

SUMMARY OF SECTION I

- Children have rights to health and their access to good health is a matter of responsibility for families, communities and society.
- Over 25 per cent of all deaths in the world occur among children under five years of age.
- Children are particularly vulnerable to the leading causes of deaths and disability worldwide. Many common childhood illnesses are preventable and include curable conditions such as respiratory infections, diarrhoea and malnutrition.

2 WHAT KIND OF HEALTH?

2.1 What is health?

Allow about 10 minutes

Health is a state of complete physical, mental and social well-being, and not merely the absence of disease and infirmity (WHO, 1992, quoted in Lewis, 2001).

A C T I V I T Y 2 **Concepts of good health**

Health and ill health are tricky concepts to define – try it for yourself! Write down what you think constitutes good health in children. Then think about the definition of health given by the World Health Organization (WHO) – reproduced here in the margin – in relation to situations you know. What do you understand by 'a state of well-being'?

C O M M E N T

In the first instance, you might have thought of the obvious and clinically measurable physical signs of child health, such as a lack of diseases and disability as well as a steady pattern of physical growth and development. Being physically well is an important start to being healthy, but there are other aspects to good health in children. You might have thought of the quality of children's home life, and how far children feel secure and raised with love. Such ideas of being well in an emotional and social sense are harder to appraise but are important for healthy development. They call for a broader definition of health, to take into account social and mental as well as physical ideas of wellness.

The WHO definition captures the idea that health is a holistic concept encompassing mental, physical and social dimensions. This definition, first promoted in 1948, has been significant in broadening a vision of health beyond the idea of mere physical survival. It also promoted a positive concept of health, rather than making a negative statement about the absence of physical infirmity.

Children near Kathmandu, Nepal.

The definition has been criticized for being idealistic and unrealistic. Lewis is concerned that this definition 'puts health beyond everyone's reach' (Lewis, 2001, p. 59). It would be difficult for anyone to be truly healthy by this definition and extremely hard work to stay that way. It would seem that the state of complete physical, mental and social well-being corresponds more closely to 'happiness' than 'health'. However, the distinction between these two concepts is crucial: only health is a universal human right (Saracci, 1997).

The definition is also difficult to put into practice. For example, how does one evaluate the 'social' dimension of health? If social well-being means social adjustment, then it would strongly depend upon the values promoted by a particular culture – ideas about social well-being tend to be controlled by dominant groups in society, who uphold a particular norm of social adjustment. A good example here relates to diagnoses of child hyperactivity: whether a lively child's behaviour is seen as normal, boisterous or pathological depends in part on what is expected or indeed found disrupting at home, at school or in wider society (Woodhead, 1995).

Despite these complexities, it is worth noting that a holistic definition resonates with understandings about health in many cultures. For example, the Huli, who live in Papua New Guinea, have no single word for 'health', but characterize health as the absence of disease, resilience (to illness) and social effectiveness (the attraction of wealth and influence). The Huli hold protective rituals to resist illnesses and malign influences, and perceive efforts to promote a good physique as entwined with efforts to attract wealth and social distinction. The converse of a person with 'good skin' is said to be *ibatari*: 'a shabby, sickly, impoverished recluse'. For the Huli, as emphasized by anthropologist Stephen Frankel, 'health is as much a social as a physical state' (Frankel, 1986, p. 55). This brings the Huli notions close to the WHO definition of health.

Although the WHO promotes a broad definition of health, much of the child health data collected by state and international organizations focuses on a narrow range of indicators for disease, such as malnutrition and mortality amongst the under fives. In practice, promoting health is often still equated with ensuring physical health and survival. For some, this emphasis seems justified, given the high child mortality statistics across the globe (Tilford, 1995). Others have argued that priorities in terms of physical survival should be considerably shifted to broader issues about child development and quality of life (Myers, 1992). (This issue will be examined further in Chapter 5.) Epilepsy, for example, appeared to be a relatively unimportant priority for children's health when diseases were ranked according to their impact on infant or child mortality (because it rarely killed).

Huli boy, Tari Valley, Papua New Guinea. Concepts of health among the Huli are holistic and cover notions such as the absence of disease, resilience and social effectiveness.

When the World Bank introduced a new ranking system for diseases (the Disability-Adjusted Life Year, or DALY), which measured the disabling potential of diseases, epilepsy was recognized as one of the ten most important diseases among all five to fourteen year olds in developing countries, leading to school withdrawal, social isolation and inability to find work.

2.2 Views about ill health

Ways of understanding ill health are formed as much by cultural ideas as by diagnoses of a physical condition. In contemporary Western cultures, ideas about ill health emphasize a biomedical approach to children's health. The biomedical model sees a healthy body functioning like a machine with all the constituent parts in good working order. However, many non-Western medical systems focus on the personal, spiritual or social experiences of illness rather than the 'faulty' part of the machine. And where Western biomedicine tends to demarcate between the physical and mental causes of ill health, other explanatory systems may not. It follows that views about ill health and appropriate treatment can be very different across cultures, as the rest of this section illustrates.

With respect to the physical dimension of well-being, society plays an important role in defining what is 'healthy' and 'not healthy' in light of ideas of what is 'normal' in society. A dramatic example of a cultural redefinition of normality is the belief that red urine signals sexual maturity in adolescent boys – the equivalent of menstruation in girls – among the Bozo tribe of Mali. Red urine is caused by a parasitic infection (schistosomiasis) that

Mother with one-year-old child, Nigeria. Many people think the diarrhoea their children suffer from is a consequence of teething.

begins in childhood and becomes progressively heavier, causing internal bleeding around the time of adolescence. Because this affects the whole community, however, it is perceived by the Bozo as normal – so much so that it is celebrated as a rite of passage (Dettwyler, 1998). Another example of local definitions of normality is 'teething diarrhoea'. In a study of market women in Nigeria, 71 per cent of mothers perceived that diarrhoea was caused by teething – a normal sign of growth and development accompanying the milestone of tooth eruption (Ene-Obong *et al.*, 2000). In both instances, what would be defined in Western medicine as a symptom of disease and ill health is reclassified as a normal part of healthy child development. Such beliefs have major implications for the management of disease: in Nigeria, mothers did not share the biomedical explanations of diarrhoea being caused by poor personal and environmental hygiene practices, nor did they seek prevention or treatment, as they believed there was nothing anybody could do about it. Achieving good health for these children therefore entails understanding local and biomedical definitions about health and ill health and reconciling any significant disparities of views.

When it comes to the mental dimension of ill health, the distinction between being mentally well and mentally ill is far from clear-cut, and therefore a matter of interpretation both for medicine and for society. Different cultures may come to espouse very different worldviews about mental health and illnesses. The difficult cultural demarcation between healthy and disturbed behaviour in lively, active children has already been mentioned. Another example would relate to young people reported to be 'hearing voices'. This is a characteristic symptom of schizophrenia in Western diagnoses, yet hearing voices is normal for shamans (spiritual healers) when they enter a trance during rituals. In Inuit and Amazonian societies, or indeed any society with a belief in the spirit world (as in the Hmong, featured in Reading A), a child hearing voices may well be trained as a shaman and invested with a large amount of ritual authority, rather than be treated as ill.

At the end of Section 2.1, it was mentioned that epilepsy is now recognized as a major disease affecting children throughout the world, following a better understanding of its disabling effects. Childhood epilepsy offers a particularly good example of the power of cultural beliefs regarding childhood illnesses. In Western medicine, epilepsy is understood as a neurological disorder caused by a chemical imbalance in the brain. In other cultures it is viewed very differently. The next reading gives an account of a Hmong family's experience of epilepsy in North America.

Hmong girls in Xieng Khang province, Laos. Many Hmong became refugees during the Vietnam War (1965–75) and emigrated to the USA.

READING

Reading A is from a book, *The Spirit Catches You and You Fall Down*, by Anne Fadiman. Fadiman describes the experiences of Lia Lee, a Hmong girl, and her parents Foua and Nao Kao, who had settled in Merced County, California after several years in a refugee camp in Thailand, following the communist take-over of their country.

The Hmong are a group from Laos in South East Asia. The period described in Fadiman's book is the early 1980s, when almost all Hmong living in America had, like Lia's parents, recently arrived as refugees. The spiritual beliefs Fadiman writes about, including views on the causes of epilepsy, were prevalent among the Hmong at that time. These beliefs emphasised epilepsy's spiritual origins rather than its physical causes (a spirit is known as a *dab* and the ceremony to fix a soul in a person and prevent a *dab* from taking it is called a *hu plig*). Such beliefs are still common among the older generation of Hmong refugees in North America, though younger Hmong (especially Christian converts) are more likely today to subscribe to more Western beliefs or to a combination of the two.

As you read the extract, make notes on the traditional Hmong views of illness and compare them with your own views. What do you think might be the implications of these beliefs for treating Lia's condition?

COMMENT

Ideas about illness are intricately bound up in cultural beliefs, so that different people have profoundly different explanations of the causes and effects of illness. As Fadiman emphasized elsewhere in her book, Lia's parents and her doctors had noted the same symptoms, but the doctors would have been surprised to hear that they were caused by soul loss, and

Lia's parents would have been surprised to hear that they were caused by an electro-chemical storm inside their daughter's head (Fadiman, 1997, p. 2).

The fact that Western medical treatment focuses especially on the physical symptoms and physical causes of epilepsy may prove frustrating to people who have grown up in a different cultural tradition and are informed by different healthcare principles.

Foua and Nao Kao Lee do not necessarily reject Western medical intervention and recognize that it may have saved their children's lives in the refugee camp. However, while they recognize that Western medicine may be able to treat the symptoms of their daughter's illness, they do not think it can do anything about its causes. Fundamentally, they have very different ideas about the causes of illness and do not share a Western biomedical model that sees epilepsy in terms of brain dysfunction and neurological disorder. Indeed, they do not even share the idea that epilepsy is a problem or a disorder, seeing it as a gift and a vocation. The doctors they consulted perceived epilepsy very differently, focusing entirely on its debilitating physical aspects.

Such differences in worldviews matter when it comes to treating children's ill health. If the physical, mental and social significance of these different worldviews are not reconciled, diagnoses may be contested, treatment may be interrupted and distrust or tension may arise between doctors, parents and children.

This was shown in Lia's case. While both her parents and doctors wanted the best available care for her, the differences in worldviews and understandings of health proved insurmountable. Lia had a number of seizures and the Lees eventually lost faith in the doctors who treated her and the medicine they provided. They did not give their daughter her prescribed medicine and eventually Lia was taken into foster care against her parents' wishes. Her epileptic seizures became increasingly severe, leaving Lia severely brain damaged. At this point, Western medical care could offer her nothing more and she was taken back by her parents, who continued, unsuccessfully, try to heal her. In the end neither Western medicine nor traditional Hmong soul-calling techniques could do anything to remedy the damage that epileptic fits were doing to Lia.

SUMMARY OF SECTION 2

- The World Health Organization promotes a holistic view of health that covers physical, mental and social dimensions.

- Notions of health and ill health are culturally interpreted. Worldviews about ill health matter because they shape people's views about the appropriateness of different kinds of treatment.

- Western medicine favours a biomedical model that sees the body functioning like a machine: all parts should be in good working order. It tends to separate the mental and physical causes of ill health.

- Medical systems that focus on the biological causation of disease and biomedical treatment often clash with approaches that take a more holistic view. Achieving good health for children entails reconciling disparities in worldviews.

3 WHY DOES ILL HEALTH PERSIST?

3.1 Unfulfilled promises?

This section will look in detail at some of the reasons why good health for children is still not assured worldwide, despite unprecedented international attention on the necessity for implementing health interventions that give priority to the interests of children.

The 1989 UN Convention on the Rights of the Child was a milestone in the promotion of child health because it secured international consensus for a new rights-based approach to promoting the interests of children (see Chapter 5, Section 4, 'Ensuring children's rights'). This was followed by the World Summit for Children in 1990, organized by the United Nations, at which world leaders agreed to realize seven major goals towards improving child survival, development and quality of life by 2000. These goals were:

Reduce by one-third the infant and under-five mortality rates.

Reduce by half the maternal mortality rates in pregnancy or childbirth.

Reduce by half severe and moderate under-five malnutrition.

Provide universal access to safe drinking water and to sanitation.

Provide universal access to basic education.

Reduce the adult illiteracy rate.

Improve the protection of children in especially difficult circumstances.

This was an ambitious agenda, calling for action at national and international levels. Ten years later, a follow-up summit (The Millennium Summit of 2000) endorsed these goals and also set further objectives such as specific campaigns for malaria and HIV/AIDS control. The Millennium Summit also reviewed the achievements of the previous decade, looking at which targets had been reached and which remained unfulfilled promises. It provided a 'child health balance sheet', which assessed how far the goals set in 1990 had been achieved. Table 1 lists some major items on the balance sheet. You will see that specific goals regarding the international agenda on child health have been clearly specified but, despite the progress made, have not been fully achieved. The unfulfilled promises of the 1990 World Summit are vividly portrayed in the next reading.

READING

Read Reading B, 'Birth and broken promises', which is an extract from *The State of the World's Children*, UNICEF's annual publication that looks at issues concerning the health and welfare of children in every country in the world. This extract takes one West African child, Ayodele, as representative of children in the South generally. As you read, compare the changes in Ayodele's life with those promised by the 1990 World Summit. Which goals have been met and which have not been? Can you think of reasons why targets might not have been met?

Table 1   Child health balance sheet.

Goal	Gains	Unfinished business
Infant and under-five mortality: reduction by one-third in infant mortality and under-five mortality rate.	More than 60 countries achieved the under-five mortality rate goal. At the global level the under-five mortality rate declined by 11 per cent.	Under-five mortality rates increased in 14 countries (nine of them in Sub-Saharan Africa) and were unchanged in 11 others. Serious disparities remain in under-five mortality rates within countries: by income level, urban versus rural and among minority groups.
Measles: reduction by 95 per cent in deaths and 90 per cent in cases by 1995 as a major step to global eradication.	Worldwide reported measles incidence declined by almost 40 per cent between 1990 and 1999.	In 14 countries, measles vaccination coverage is less than 50 per cent.
Acute respiratory infections (ARI): reduction of deaths by one-third in children under five.	ARI case management has improved at the health centre level. The effectiveness of HIB and pneumococcus vaccines is established.	ARI remains one of the greatest causes of death among children. Vertical, single-focus ARI programmes seem to have had little impact.
Deaths due to diarrhoea: reduction by 50 per cent.	This goal was achieved globally, according to WHO estimates.	Diarrhoea remains one of the major causes of death among children.

Source: adapted from *We the Children*, UNICEF, 2001.

COMMENT

This extract makes for pessimistic reading, suggesting that few of the goals of the World Summit have been met for Ayodele's family. Ayodele has experienced the death of her siblings, food insecurities and lack of immunization. She has also not been able to realize her full potential in terms of schooling and the reading implies that she is not much better off in 2000 than an equivalent ten year old would have been in 1990. Although the extract does not give reasons why this might be so, it is obvious that Ayodele and her siblings live in poverty and this has significantly affected their health. The reading also implicates global inequalities, as children are ill, malnourished or dying in large numbers in certain parts of the world only.

The rest of Section 3 will look at the effects of inequalities on children's health at global, local and familial levels. It follows a similar format to Chapter 2 by looking first at inequalities between countries, then within countries and finally within families and communities.

Mariam, an eleven-year-old girl from Burkina Faso, prepares food for her family. Despite the goals set in the World Summit, the lives of many girls such as Mariam have not improved significantly since 1990.

3.2 Global inequalities

The story of Ayodele in Reading B clearly shows that the risks of ill health are strikingly different across the globe. The important question is why a clear international agenda and top-level commitment to children should not have yielded more effective results. Explanations for this failure to achieve clearly set goals in matters of child health were offered by UNICEF in its book, *We the Children* (2001). This stark end-of-decade review drew attention to many of the global inequalities summarized in Chapter 2, Section 3.1, 'Social inequalities between countries'. The authors stressed that despite unprecedented global prosperity, half of humanity remains desperately impoverished, and half of the 1.2 billion people forced to survive on less than $1 per day are children (that is about 600 million children experience absolute and persistent poverty). UNICEF concluded that 'chronic poverty remains the greatest obstacle to fulfilling the rights of children' (UNICEF, 2001, p. 5). These economic inequalities are in turn closely linked to health inequalities.

One of the clearest ways to illustrate global child health inequalities is through data on child mortality. The number of deaths for the age group 0–5 years of age (per thousand live births) is known as the under-five mortality rate (U5MR), while the number of deaths for 0–1 year olds is referred to as the infant mortality rate (IMR). Such mortality rates are considered very sensitive indicators of the health of nations and overall development, including the adequacy of public health services, as well as being a yardstick for measuring poverty. Figure 3 compares U5MR in 1990 and 2000, for different regions of the world.

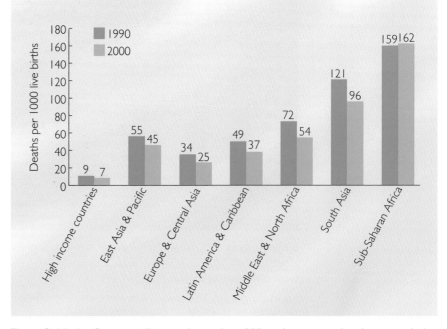

Figure 3 Under-five mortality rate by region. Although progress has been made in some regions since 1990, the rates in areas such as Sub-Saharan Africa have shown little improvement (adapted from World Bank, 2002).

Figure 3 illustrates the continuing inequalities in children's survival prospects between different regions of world. While most regions have made progress in reducing mortality rates, Sub-Saharan Africa is a notable exception. Under-five mortality rates were already markedly higher than any other region in 1990 and they have actually increased during the decade. This is due to the impact of armed conflict, to a long-term economic decline and to the weakness of health services and their reduced use by poor people after the introduction of user charges and health privatization under the structural adjustment programmes discussed in Chapter 2 (see also Costello, 2001). Added to these factors, the impact of AIDS has had a devastating effect on under-five mortality rates in Sub-Saharan Africa. As UNICEF maintained:

> Sub-Saharan Africa is the epicentre of the HIV/AIDS pandemic. It has just 10 per cent of the world's population but 70 per cent of the world's people with HIV/AIDS, 80 per cent of AIDS deaths and 90 per cent of AIDS orphans. In stark contrast to children everywhere else, today's southern African children are likely to live shorter lives than their grandparents.

(UNICEF, 2001, p. 10)

South Bugunda province, Uganda. Pupils who have lost their parents to AIDS raise their hands.

In contrast, some countries have managed a substantial reduction in child mortality. Bangladesh is one of the poorest 49 countries of the world, but unlike the countries within Sub-Saharan Africa, it has achieved reductions in child mortality. The under-five mortality rate declined from 136 per thousand live births in 1990 to 83 per thousand in 2000 (World Bank, 2002). The reason for this is simple: there was a national commitment to invest in basic social services that would directly benefit mothers and children. Thus in 1999, 26 per cent of the national budget was spent on social services, boosting adult literacy and primary school enrolment (UNICEF, 2001, p. 5). This is compared to the 12 to 14 per cent of national budgets usually allocated to basic social services by countries in the South. However, the infrastructure of health services in Bangladesh is still very restricted, especially for poor communities, as the example in Box 2 shows.

One final example is Cuba, whose 'revolutionary approach' to health and health services resulted in excellent health outcomes in the midst of a severe economic crisis exacerbated by economic blockade by the USA (Chomsky, 2000). Cuba's infant and under-five mortality rates are only nine per thousand and ten per thousand respectively (1997 data). These are the lowest rates in Latin America (in Brazil, for instance, the IMR is 45 per thousand), rates on a par with those of the world's wealthiest countries (in the USA, the IMR is eight per thousand). Thus male and female life expectancies at birth are similar in Cuba and in the United States, despite a nine-fold difference in per capita gross domestic product (GDP). According to Chomsky, Cuba's approach:

> has created an egalitarian society in which the entire population is guaranteed access to food, employment, and education. In addition, the government has rebuilt a health-care delivery system aimed at both public and preventive health *and* at universally accessible, high-tech, hospital-based care.

(Chomsky, 2000, p. 335)

The Cuban example shows that excellent health outcomes are possible even with limited material resources. It also shows that a government-level commitment to social equality (as in Cuba's national health service) goes further than a government-level guarantee of universal access to health services (as in the UK). Cuba has grasped health issues in a unique way, yet its example is sidelined by mainstream studies of health and economic growth which prefer to focus on 'development' in terms of GNP and structural adjustment.

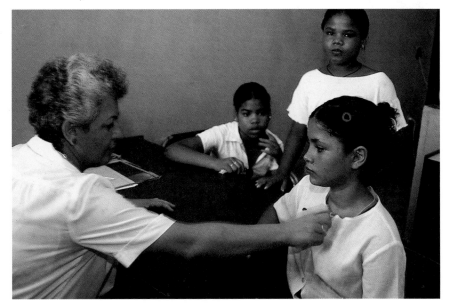

Primary health centre, Havana, Cuba.

Box 2 Child health issues at a mother and baby hospital in Bangladesh

Chittagong is a rapidly growing city in one of the poorest countries in the world. The population is estimated to be about four million, including surrounding villages. Nearly 50 per cent are children, many living in overcrowded shanties, with poor sanitation and an inadequate water supply. Many mothers are malnourished themselves. Chittagong Shishu Ma (Mother and Baby) Hospital is the only specialist hospital serving poor communities, with only 200 beds. There is also a general hospital in the city with just 50 paediatric beds.

Most patients at the hospital are babies and children under five. Most are suffering from easily preventable diseases, such as diarrhoea and respiratory tract infections.

One of the mothers at the hospital describes how her child became ill:

> My son first got a cold, and this developed into a severe respiratory problem. He became sick when he was fourteen days old. He had a cough which grew worse each day, he was breathless and had a fever. So I came to the hospital initially, and took the medicine he was prescribed, and took him home for treatment. His fever persisted, and his respiratory problems became severe, so I brought him again to the hospital, and this time he was admitted.

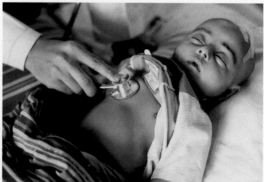

The director of the hospital explains that these conditions could be treated by small neighbourhood health clinics and by health visitors, but these are still not widely available. So parents bring sick children to the hospital, if they seek medical help at all.

> The diarrhoea comes as an epidemic during the monsoon, and the pressure on this hospital is so much, that we cannot cope. Sometimes we have to put two children in one bed, and sometimes we have to put children on the floor. There are people who lack sanitation, and any sort of health attention … For example, the parents are so poor, they cannot afford to lose work and take them to hospitals, and there is no system for home visits for these children … So they are left uncared for.

(The Open University, 2003)

3.3 Differences within nations

We live in a polarized world characterized by significant disparities both across nations and across groups within a nation, as already highlighted in Chapter 2. Within-nation health differentials are significant both in developing countries such as Brazil – one of the economic success stories of Latin America – and in countries such as the United States – where child health varies significantly according to ethnic group and relative wealth or deprivation. Thus, in the United States over three-quarters of children with HIV/AIDS are from minority ethnic communities. These children may also be disadvantaged by factors such as poverty, inadequate housing, lack of access to basic welfare services and a struggle with the dominant language. There are pockets of urban deprivation, such as in Harlem (an inner-city community in upper Manhattan, New York, where 96 per cent of residents are black and 41 per cent live below the poverty line), where the likelihood of a male child surviving beyond the age of 40 is actually lower than in Bangladesh (McCord and Freeman, 1990).

These examples emphasize the point that children's health often has a socio-political dimension. Countries where the income differentials between rich and poor are large tend to have worse health than countries in which such differences are small. Inequality is 'bad' for national health, because social and material inequalities generally go hand in hand with poor investment in human resources, including education and health services. According to Wilkinson:

> Countries in which the income differences between rich and poor are larger (meaning more or deeper relative poverty) tend to have worse health than countries in which the differences are smaller. It is … the most egalitarian rather than the richest developed countries which have the best health.

(Wilkinson, 1996, pp. 75–76)

Social inequalities structure not only access to health care and experience of mortality, but also exposure to environmental factors and thereby risk of ill health. As children are still growing and developing, the impact of radiation, lead poisoning or toxic waste is particularly severe. As discussed briefly in Chapter 1, children from minority ethnic groups are particularly vulnerable to health problems such as lead poisoning and radioactivity. These children often live in neighbourhoods where the environment is poor and traffic heavy, placing them at risk both from traffic fumes and accidents. Research in the United States has shown that African-American children are two to three times more likely than white children to suffer from lead poisoning (Stephens, 1998). Moreover, toxic waste dumps and landfill sites tend to be placed in poorer areas, where the majority of the population are members of minority ethnic groups. The health problems caused by such pollution are so pronounced that some commentators coined the phrase 'environmental racism' to describe the ways African-American and Native American children are especially affected (Stephens, 1998).

The effects of social inequality on child health can also be seen in the UK. In 1980 a report into health inequalities, *The Black Report* (Black, 1980), showed major social class differences in the health and well-being of children in their early years of life. Babies born to parents in unskilled manual occupations (class V) were two to three times more likely to die in the first year of life than those born to professional parents (class I). Throughout childhood, deaths from accidents, from respiratory diseases and, to a lesser extent, from infectious diseases showed the steepest class gradients. Referring to children under fourteen, *The Black Report* stated:

> Accidents, which are by far the biggest single cause of childhood deaths (30 per cent of the total), continue to show the sharpest class gradient. Boys in class V have a ten times greater chance of dying from fire, falls or drowning than those in class I. The corresponding ratio of deaths caused to youthful pedestrians by motor vehicles is more than 7 to 1.

> (Black, 1980, p. 45)

Twenty years after the Black Report, health differentials linked to poverty are a key government concern in the UK. The Department of the Environment, Transport and the Regions has stressed that 'the life expectancy of a boy born into the bottom social class is over nine years less than a boy born into the most affluent social class' (2001). In 2002, the first-ever national health inequalities targets were published with the goal of reducing social class inequalities in infant mortality by 10 per cent in England by 2010 (Department of Health, 2002). Planned interventions include:

- smoking control
- improved uptake and continuation of breast feeding
- parental support by health visitors and community nurses
- reduced poverty
- improved maternal mental health
- better access to antenatal, paediatric and neonatal intensive health care.

Note that reducing health inequalities in the UK is not reflected in a very large fall in the actual number of deaths, because infant mortality rates are already low.

Allow about 10 minutes

A C T I V I T Y 3   Danielle

Read through the case study below about Danielle. List the connections that you see between poverty and ill health. What difference would it make if Danielle had been born into a wealthier family?

> In January 1995, a six-week-old baby, Danielle, came out of hospital in London, UK for the second time since her birth. The first visit was for a chest infection when she was a few days old. The second was for a severe bout of diarrhoea. Danielle lives in a damp, two-bedroom flat that is home to three adults and three children … According to the doctor, the early illness will leave Danielle with lung defects which will make her prone to bronchitis and asthma throughout her life. 'The stigma of deprivation forced upon her as a child will continue into adult life – she will forever carry the mark of poverty.'

> (Save the Children, 1995, p. 21)

COMMENT

The links between social inequality and ill health are striking in Danielle's case. Her poverty means that she was born into cramped conditions in a damp flat, which has had a direct impact on her health, both now and in the future. The damp has damaged her lungs; if she continues to live in the flat, the damage will be exacerbated on a daily basis.

Poor children are often trapped in situations that lead to significant health problems. They are more likely to live in sub-standard housing and suffer from respiratory infections such as asthma and tuberculosis, more likely to have dental problems and gastro-enteritis and they are more at risk from accidents than children in wealthier families.

3.4 Health inequalities within families

Another aspect of the complex relationship between il -health and poverty is enacted within families at the household level; this too has dramatic consequences for children.

People who live in poverty have to allocate their scarce resources and find themselves obliged to establish priorities regarding access to health care or access to nutritious food. Research has shown that discrimination against children within a household occurs between siblings of different age, gender, birth order or perceived health/disability (Panter-Brick, 1998). The importance of social inequalities at the household level has already been highlighted in Chapter 2, Section 3.3, 'Social inequalities within families'. Gender inequalities are amongst the most striking and significant for child health.

Three children of the same age in rural Nepal. The one on the left has severe protein-energy malnutrition, largely due to maternal neglect (he is the last-born son in a household of six children). The girl in the middle is an only child whose mother cannot have any more children. The one to the right is a boy whose father has a steady income.

In many parts of the world, but particularly in South Asia, girls have significantly higher rates of malnutrition, reduced access to health care services and greater rates of mortality. In India and China, they are particularly at risk of being aborted before birth on the grounds of their gender. The increased availability of pre-natal screening has meant that parents can know the sex of their child long before it is born. In India, where there is a strong preference for boys, as well as concern over dowries that must accompany a daughter's marriage, the results of these tests have been dramatic:

> In one of the first hospitals to offer low-cost tests, a study by a Bombay women's organisation between 1979 and 1982 found that of 8,000 women who came from all over India, 7,999 wanted an abortion if the test revealed a female child. Many advertisements set the costs of the sex tests and abortions against the future costs of a daughter, including that of her dowry, with slogans such as 'better 500 rupees now than 50,000 rupees later on'.

(Croll, 2000, p. 95)

At the root of gender discrimination lie beliefs about female inferiority and the realization of unequal opportunities for girls and adult women. It is worth noting that this discrimination can be at the hands of women themselves, for example, where women are the primary care-givers who allocate food at meal times. The consequences of this discrimination in countries such as India or Pakistan are seen in the significantly higher rates of malnutrition among girl children, their reduced access to health care services and their greater rates of mortality. Improving girls' health therefore means more than the mere provision of food and health care. To be truly effective, projects must promote gender equality and attempt to raise the status of women. One of the most consistent findings in development policy is the correlation between levels of female education and infant mortality. The better educated the mothers, the higher the chances of survival for children.

Allow about 10 minutes

A C T I V I T Y 4   **Sex preferences in China**

Read through the following passage, which discusses the traditional preference for sons in China. It also refers to China's 'one child' per family policy, introduced in 1980 to curb population growth. What do you think the effects of these views on the health of girls might be?

> 'May you have many sons' has long been a common felicitation and references to sons or a son as the 'greatest of blessings' punctuate everyday language and ceremonial occasions, such as weddings. Customarily each generation has been exhorted anew to have a son and continue the family line, so that the greatest of unfilial acts has been the failure to produce a son and the most venomous of curses has been: 'May you die without sons.' Although such phrases are less likely to be openly articulated in present-day China, prestige and stature are still linked to sons and it is often said that the birth of a son causes a house 'to grow by three feet'. In contemporary China, with its stringent birth-control and single-child policies, the quest for sons has

been magnified with the result that, in the absence of sons, the birth of a daughter not only remains a disappointment but more than ever before means a 'lost opportunity' for a son.

(Croll, 2000, p. 71)

COMMENT

In some instances, girls' health and survival have been immediately imperilled the moment their sex is discovered. The maintenance of family life and the performance of ceremonial duties can only be carried out by sons in traditional Chinese society, which means that girls are fundamentally less important to their families. Although pre-natal tests are banned in China, many families do arrange for ultrasound tests to see if they are carrying a girl and abort the baby if they can. Therefore, even before she is born, a girl's survival is considerably more precarious than a boy's. Under the 'one child' policy, parents cannot try for a son after a girl is born so the girl is doubly unwelcome. If the pregnancy does go to term, a girl may be less well looked after than a boy. As in India, studies have shown that she is likely to be breast fed for shorter periods than a boy, less likely to be taken to hospital when ill, less likely to be given extra food and is more at risk from abandonment (Croll, 2000). In some state-run orphanages, over 90 per cent of the children are girls, abandoned by their parents in the hope of having another child, this time a boy. Gender inequality thus has a profound effect on the survival and health of girls in China (and elsewhere). Systematic discrimination affects their health and life chances, before birth and throughout their lives. Finally, note that Croll is writing about the period up to 2000. Social attitudes and practices towards girls are changing, in China as elsewhere.

Five generations of the Yang family, China. Many grand parents have only one grandchild. These children are known as 'little emperors' because they are so indulged.

- Specific goals regarding the international agenda on child health have been clearly specified, and so too have the shortfalls of the strategy.

- Global inequalities between nations, within nations and within families remain, although the general picture is one of improvement.

- Infant and child mortality rates are significant social indicators of general poverty and under-development. The poorest countries of the world are the countries with the highest rates of under-five mortality.

- There is a socio-political dimension to children's health. Within nations, there are significant differences in child health as poverty affects access to health care, exposure to environmental pollutants and the risk of accidents.

- Within families, there exists further discrimination against children – well documented in the case of gender – and this affects their health.

4 ACHIEVING HEALTH IN PRACTICE

To summarize the arguments in this chapter so far, specific global campaigns are in place to improve the health of children, backed by international organizations such as the United Nations. They show many tangible successes, but also disappointment in reducing inequalities in children's health status. We have seen that chronic poverty combined with economic, social and health inequalities are the main obstacles to fulfilling an international mandate to give first call to the interests and to the rights of children.

Significantly, UNICEF has argued that the task of achieving good health for children is a feasible and affordable proposition. 'Compared to what the world spends on armaments or luxury consumer items, the resources needed to provide for the basic needs of children are modest' (UNICEF, 2001 p. 6). It has been said that the task could be accomplished within a decade at a cost of $25 billion a year – 'half the amount that is spent on cigarettes in Europe for one year or about the same amount as the proposed new Hong Kong airport' (Grant, 1993, cited in Tilford, 1995, p. 253). This would require political will and a rethinking of priorities, as many governments spend much more on arms, for example, than they do on social development.

However, effective intervention is not simply a matter of channelling more money to systems of health care but of finding ways to intervene in effective and efficient ways. There are pertinent criticisms about health interventions, which must be taken into account when efforts are made to improve children's health. The first critique is that top-down interventions need a better understanding of community practices and beliefs at the local level. Why is this really important? Recall the arguments in Section 2 on concepts of ill health and how these affect recourse to medical treatment or satisfaction with the medical care provided. It is apparent that top-down interventions are unlikely to be sustained if they are not shaped to match people's own understandings of health and illness as well as people's own priorities regarding health-seeking and livelihood-sustaining behaviours. The availability of a 'cure' for specific diseases is no guarantee that people will use it, and making more food available is no guarantee that people will channel it to their small children. The second critique is that top-down interventions may well reduce deaths from a specific cause, but may do little to improve quality of life overall. It is argued that a life saved must be a sustainable life. These arguments will be developed by looking at three specific case studies on local and global interventions in child malnutrition, breast feeding and diarrhoea.

4.1 The social context of child malnutrition

According to the WHO, 60 per cent of deaths among children under five are linked to malnutrition (see Figure 2, page 98, which draws on WHO data). Malnutrition also has devastating consequences for children's development (in terms of impaired intellect, poor resistance to infections, stunted growth, sapped productivity and risk of complications in childbirth). We now turn to examine some of the complex reasons why malnutrition exists and persists in local communities. We begin by taking one specific example of child malnutrition from anthropological research in Mali. Then we turn to a different expression of malnutrition, namely child obesity. The point to emphasize is that in order to be truly effective, global interventions to combat malnutrition must be sensitive to local cultural practices of families and communities.

READING

Read Reading C, 'Cases of malnutrition in Mali', which is an extract from Katherine Dettwyler's paper on one of the poorest countries in the world. The rural community she studied in 1989 lacked electricity, sewage treatment and waste disposal services. However, this account is more concerned with the social correlates of malnutrition and the links between community practices and children's ill-health. As you read the extract, note particularly the reason why the twins Fatoumata and Oumou suffer from malnutrition despite there being enough money to buy food within the household. Write down what you think the causes of malnutrition are in the case of these twins.

COMMENT

In this article, Dettwyler emphasizes that malnutrition has no single, identifiable cause. Instead it must be understood as part and parcel of aspects of community life, namely issues regarding the status of women and cultural rules about child care practices. Although the community is very poor, Aminata's family is relatively well-off. However, Aminata cannot gain access to resources because of her low status in the household and the stigma of being an unmarried mother. It is only when one twin dies and the other is sent away that she is able to gain status through marriage and to provide better care for her other children. It is easy to look upon Aminata as callous, and indeed, this is what Dettwyler does when she first encounters her. For Dettwyler, it is clear that feeding good food to children will solve the problem of malnutrition and ensure healthy growth (as the photograph she included in her book, and that is reproduced here, is meant to show). Aminata feels much less powerful; when pressed regarding the causes of her children's ill-health, she invokes a more fatalistic belief that Allah will take the children when their turn comes.

This reading also makes another important point. A main issue in this example is the mother's access to resources, rather than a lack of household resources *per se*. Access to resources (that is, entitlement) is powerfully shaped by the social relations prevailing between and within families in a local community. The result of social inequality and differential entitlement to resources can have major implications for the health of children within families. Dettwyler provides a stark example where discrimination against children begins with discrimination against the mother on the basis of her social status and age, a discrimination that could extend further to children on the basis of their birth order or gender. These are important root causes of health inequality operating at a local level, which have critical consequences for children.

Aminata's twins, Oumou and Fatoumata, with Dettwyler's own daughter Miranda. The children are exactly the same age, but have achieved strikingly different physical heights, largely as a result of living in different environments. The twins only reach up to Miranda's chest. Fatoumata, who had been more seriously ill with measles, is even shorter than Oumou.

Reading C also illustrates significant cross-cultural differences in the way individual parents and communities understand the significance of a child's ill health – differences related to ideas about children and their roles in society. This point is critical, in that it cannot be assumed that a Western-led intervention and a community in Mali share the same priorities in matters of child health. In affluent societies, a focus on child survival, growth and nutrition is seen as self-evident and sufficient in itself; in the face of poverty, disease or malnutrition, the cultural imperative is to save children's lives. By contrast, many other societies find such emphasis on child survival misplaced, in the absence of an alleviation of poverty and an improvement in quality of life. This has been highlighted as a conflict of worldviews regarding children in society and regarding priorities to ensure individual survival or sustainable livelihoods (Cassidy, 1987). When it comes to feeding young children, this contrast of worldviews has been expressed as the 'needs versus contribution' rules. While some people feed children according to biological *needs* for growth and physical development, others allocate food according to real or perceived, actual or future *contribution* in society (Engle and Nieves, 1993).

Obesity is a growing problem for children in the North.

Malnutrition is not only an issue for poor countries like Mali. It affects children in the richest countries of the world, most noticeably through obesity. There is a social dimension to understanding obesity too: rates of over-nutrition also mirror lifestyle choices and cultural values. Obesity rates are rising among younger children and adolescents, linked to low levels of physical activity and a diet of fast foods. The issue of child obesity has been most widely discussed in relation to the United States, the UK and China. In Britain, 8 per cent of boys and 7 per cent of girls – about 550,000 children – are now officially obese. Four to fifteen year olds watch an average of two to three hours of television every day, and have on average only one hour a week of physical education allocated in the school curriculum. Although the nature and amount of childhood physical activity that would confer lasting cardiovascular fitness and protection against coronary heart disease, diabetes, osteoporosis and obesity are still under debate, it is clear that

British children are not getting enough exercise (Panter-Brick, 2002). Thus efforts to increase physical activity in schools and local communities are a focus of current interventions in the UK, as in China. China is currently facing an 'epidemic' of child obesity. In urban centres like Beijing, where couples are strongly discouraged from having more than one child and where four grandparents might have only one grandchild, the health consequences of over-indulging children – known as 'little emperors' – are striking: there are plentiful treats in the form of Western 'junk food' and sugary drinks, coupled with increased sedentary behaviours associated with home video games and transport by motor car. Child malnutrition in China, far from being a consequence of parental powerlessness to secure good resources as seen in Mali, arises out of parental indulgence for children at a time of a strictly enforced policy for population control.

It is also known that obesity is a particular problem for the poor, partly because they are less able to afford a varied, nutritious diet and come to rely on cheap 'fast foods'. Perhaps, counter-intuitively, obesity affects mostly the poor who live in the richest countries as well as people experiencing a nutritional 'transition' in rapidly modernizing countries such as Brazil and South Africa. There is increased evidence of a particular genetic susceptibility for obesity – making some children and adults particularly efficient at depositing fat. Children raised in very poor conditions who have this genetic make-up – advantageous under conditions of adversity – become caught in a 'fat trap' when (fat-laden) foods become plentiful and physical activity for subsistence is reduced in conditions of rapid socio-economic development.

Thus, rather surprising associations have been found between nutritional deprivation in early life (even foetal life) and obesity in later life. For instance, studies of the Dutch famine of 1944 to 1945 (due to an embargo by the Nazi occupation) noted a high prevalence of obesity in adult men who had been exposed to under-nutrition during the first half of their mother's pregnancy (suggesting a developmental response that prioritized the deposition of fat, which led to obesity when later food sources became plentiful). The risk of obesity was less for those exposed to under-nutrition in the last trimester of pregnancy and the first few months of life. The association between under-nutrition at critical periods of development and later obesity is a particular concern in countries in the South where maternal child malnutrition exists alongside rapid changes in socio-economic conditions (Martorell *et al.*, 2000). Indeed, stunted growth in childhood has been associated with being overweight later in life in countries as diverse as Russia, Brazil, South Africa and China (Popkin *et al.*, 1996).

Of further concern are the associations reported between poor environments (appraised by failure to gain weight in foetal life and early infant life) and the risks in later life of cardiovascular diseases. Barker (1994) noted that the geographical areas in Britain with the highest rates of death from cardiovascular disease also featured the highest rates of infant mortality in previous generations, suggesting long-term health consequences for those who survived infancy. While these associations are under further investigation, it is clear that early nutritional experiences have long-lasting health outcomes.

4.2 Difficult choices

In this section we turn to debates about breast feeding versus formula feeding. This debate offers another example of the ways in which health interventions need to be understood in social, cultural and commercial contexts.

Lack of breast milk can lead to malnutrition in infants. There are many reasons why formula feeding is particularly damaging to children in the South. Water to mix with the formula is more likely to be contaminated and some parents may under or over-dilute the formula. It is very hard in impoverished conditions to sterilize bottles, dishes and spoons properly. Formula milk is also an expensive substitute for breast milk. The link between child malnutrition and bottle feeding is so significant that some governments have passed laws against the use of bottled or formula milk. In 1977, the government of Papua New Guinea legislated that baby bottles were only available by prescription, while in 1980, the Nicaraguan government limited the sale of infant milk formulas and insisted that warning labels be placed on all infant formula products (Scheper-Hughes, 1993).

For reasons ranging from worldwide marketing of commercial products to the fact that more women have to take on paid labour outside the home and are therefore a long way from their children, breast feeding is on the wane throughout the world. As migration increases from the rural areas to the cities and paid labour takes over from agriculture, it is often very difficult for women to continue to breast feed. In Brazil, for example, the numbers of babies breast fed for any significant period declined from 96 per cent in 1940 to less than 40 per cent in 1975. It has since declined even further (Scheper-Hughes, 1993).

Nancy Scheper-Hughes interviewed many mothers in the slums of north eastern Brazil, looking at why the children were fed on bottled milk rather than breast milk. The mothers were clear about why their children's health suffered:

> When asked what it is that infants need most to survive the first and most precarious year of life, Alto women invariably answered that it was *food*, pure and simple: 'Can it be that mothers of ten, twelve, even sixteen children don't know what a child needs to survive? Of course we know! … Babies need food to live. Most older babies require at least two cans [four hundred grams each] of powdered milk a week. But people here can afford only one can, and so the babies are fed mostly on water. Soon their blood turns to water as well. Money would solve all our problems.

> (Scheper-Hughes, 1993, p. 313)

It is important, however, to emphasize that babies are not dying because their mothers do not know how to feed them properly. Poor Brazilian mothers gave several kinds of explanations for infant deaths. They were well aware that poverty forces them into making difficult choices, such as going to work and leaving children behind without proper food or supervision, or not having nutritious food to give as supplementary food. There was an important wider socio-political aspect to their poverty – such as the lack of support given by government or health authorities, the lack of provision of clean water and waste disposal, the lack of employment opportunities offering a living wage. Scheper-Hughes emphasized the deadly consequences of marketing powdered milk – an expensive substitute for breast milk, which precipitates infant diarrhoea when made up with contaminated water, and leads to infant malnutrition when diluted to make supplies last longer. Yet gifts of powdered milk became an important cement of social relationships – for instance a father might make the baby a gift of powdered milk, signalling commitment in what are often transient relationships. For reasons ranging from worldwide marketing of commercial products to the working out of crucial social relationships in adverse environments, breast feeding rates are declining. And as Nancy Scheper-Hughes concluded, the consequences are nothing but deadly.

4.3 Are magic bullets enough?

We have seen that mortality, disability and illness caused by malnutrition and infectious diseases are greatly exacerbated by poverty and social inequality. This is why critiques of health care interventions have emphasized that availability of medical treatment cannot guarantee the eradication of preventable and curable conditions. A medical technological breakthrough might prepare the ground for a 'miracle cure', or 'magic bullet' intervention, but this alone would not address other important causes of child deaths and neither would it respond to community concerns that may undermine the success of an intervention. This is well illustrated by debates surrounding vaccination of young children in the UK.

Allow 10 minutes

ACTIVITY 5 **MMR vaccination in the UK**

Measles is a disease that can have devastating consequences for children, causing blindness, mental health problems and death. There is a highly effective vaccine against it, conferring life-long immunity, currently taken as part of a triple vaccination against measles, mumps and rubella (the MMR vaccine). It was recently claimed that MMR vaccination led to bowel problems, infections and autism in young children, and some families believe the vaccine is to blame for the onset of autism in their otherwise healthy children. Many parents in the UK have been reluctant to have their children vaccinated with MMR despite vigorous reassurance by the National Health Service about the safety and importance of this triple vaccine. Why do you think that some people hesitate or refuse to have their children vaccinated? How do you think the government or health services could better promote vaccination?

COMMENT

Childhood infectious diseases in the UK have been largely conquered. Few individuals die of measles or smallpox, diphtheria or any other disease that would have been fatal even 50 years ago. At the same time, childhood autism is on the rise (affecting one in 166 British children under the age of eight – a ten-fold increase since 1988) and the reasons for this have yet to be explained. Thus UK parents may not appreciate the potentially devastating consequences of children contracting measles, giving greater weight to the possible (but unproven) risk of childhood autism. Because parents do not perceive the gravity of the risk of measles, they are reluctant to expose their children to the well-publicized but unconfirmed risk of autism. Parents are told by the medical establishment that the claimed links between MMR and autism are without foundation, but may be suspicious of this information; they may rely on other (non-medical) sources of information, trusting their own judgement rather than the 'official' information presented to them. Many have opted to pay for single doses of vaccination rather than the triple vaccine available on the NHS. Single vaccinations are actively discouraged in the UK, while the MMR vaccine is profitable both to drug companies and to doctors who receive extra funds if they achieve near 90 per cent vaccination coverage in their practices.

Non-compliance on the part of parents has posed a great dilemma for the government and health services in the UK. Because the measles virus is so infectious, 93 per cent of all children must be vaccinated against it in order to avoid the threat of a measles epidemic in the UK. This target is not currently (2003) being met in many areas. The UK Department of Health therefore needs to persuade parents that its advice is unbiased – when its main objective seems to be preserving public confidence rather than investigating suspected adverse consequences – and that its advice concerns the good health of all children, without sacrificing the well-being of a few. It appears that if the government and health services lose the trust of parents on this issue, and if vaccination rates fall further, a younger generation of UK children will be exposed to the threat of measles.

What this example illustrates is that 'magic bullets' can be highly effective technological interventions, but making them available within health services cannot constitute the be-all and end-all of an intervention. Technological breakthroughs alone are not sufficient. To eradicate childhood infectious diseases also requires the confidence of parents to ensure full community participation. This necessitates trustworthy information and sensitive communication on the part of the officials in power, in addition to the provision of health infrastructure and social development. Thus MMR serves as a reminder that in affluent societies well-informed parents may reject a procedure hailed as a highly effective cure for a killer disease. Non-compliance with a 'magic bullet' treatment can follow from a lack of trust in the information presented to parents. In the next example you will see how information given about treatment for diarrhoea was discounted by Huli mothers in Papua New Guinea, because they doubted that it could be really appropriate in light of their own understanding and experience of the disease.

The case of diarrhoea illustrates particularly well some of the complexities of health care intervention. The symptoms of diarrhoea can be treated with an extremely low-cost intervention, namely oral rehydration salts (ORS are a water solution of salt and sugar, providing essential water and electrolytes for the body to combat dehydration). Diarrhoea kills by dehydration: the body cannot retain enough fluids and the child dies. ORS restore the necessary salts to the cells of the body, enabling the cells to retain water and the child to stay hydrated. The treatment is very cheap (about 6 pence per pack of ORS) and has been promoted worldwide in a campaign to reduce deaths from dehydration. However, careful anthropological studies have shown that ORS are no 'magic bullet' cure. Their effectiveness depends to a very large extent on a parent's willingness to administer them as part of rehydration therapy.

This point was well argued by Frankel and Lehman, who monitored the success of an ORS treatment programme among the Huli people of highland Papua New Guinea (Frankel and Lehman, 1984). Huli mothers initially complied very well with this programme, and diarrhoea-specific mortality fell significantly. However, mothers began showing less compliance. To understand why, the authors undertook a careful evaluation of the Huli's beliefs and practices regarding diarrhoeal disease.

The Huli understood an illness episode at different levels. First, they sought a pragmatic explanation in terms of immediate causes, to address the question 'how did this illness occur?' Second, they asked the critical question 'why me?' or 'why did this particular child become ill at this time?', seeking more complex explanations drawing on wider social and religious issues. What is significant is that the type of explanation influenced their choice of treatment (foods given or withdrawn, the use of spells, prayer readings and other healing ceremonies). When their child became ill, mothers tried Western medicine alongside other traditional treatments. But they expressed increasing dissatisfaction with ORS, eventually coming to health posts only if children with diarrhoea also had other symptoms such as fever, for which Western treatment was perceived to be very effective.

Dissatisfaction occurred because Western biomedical explanations and courses of treatment seemed irrelevant in the case of diarrhoea when mothers did not share the biomedical explanatory model. They had real difficulty getting sick children to drink an adequate quantity of ORS, or even plain water. Mothers said that their children refused to drink the solution, finding its taste unpleasant, or that the fluid made the diarrhoea worse over the next few days. In fact, a mother's first requirement for diarrhoea treatment was the control of its symptoms. She would attempt to dry the child's stool – by withholding fluids and by offering dry, firm, solid foods such as taro or plantain scorched in fire. In contrast, the ORS provided did not block the flow of diarrhoea: it only prevented dehydration. The Huli initially tried ORS given the proven efficacy of other health post treatments. But since they did not embrace the concept of rehydration in their own understanding of diarrhoea treatment, it was not surprising to find that people were becoming sceptical of ORS efficacy. When a child had dry skin and a very runny stool, Huli mothers were reluctant to follow the advice to 'give the child lots of water'.

ORS interventions are 'magic bullet' interventions because they save lives in preventing deaths from diarrhoea. They have been improved in recent years, in that public health specialists made available a food-based Oral Rehydration Treatment that contains not just salt and glucose (to address dehydration), but also cereal such as rice (to control runny stools and alleviate the symptoms of diarrhoea). However, these programmes do not address the causes of diarrhoea. If children 'saved' from diarrhoea die a few weeks or months later from malnutrition or infection, then has the intervention actually been successful? Thus the case of diarrhoea well illustrates that a single top-down intervention (known as selective, vertical intervention) may well save lives (from diarrhoea) but does little to improve the quality of lives (in terms of access to water or sanitation, and in terms of reducing mortality and morbidity from other causes). The implementation of low-cost technology might well have seemed an efficient campaign in the eyes of officials at the World Health Organization, but it was far from sufficient to make a lasting impact on the lives of children at the local level. What would be more effective would be to provide clean water, proper sewage, etc. (a package of primary health care also known as comprehensive, horizontal intervention).

This argument points to major limitations of health care interventions having a lasting impact on quality of life. One of the key goals of the 1990 World Summit for Children, reducing by 50 per cent childhood deaths from diarrhoeal diseases, was achieved during the 1990s – thereby saving as many as a million children's lives (UNICEF, 2001, p. 3). Yet diarrhoea remains one of the major causes of childhood death, even though the means for saving children is known: promotion of ORS and/or home fluids, use of increased fluid, continued feeding at home and improved sanitation, to name but a few. It has been emphasized that in order to achieve a real reduction in child mortality and sustainable improvements in quality of life, attention needs to be focused not just on the availability of ORS but on the environmental and social factors that underlie childhood diseases. Thus with respect to diarrhoea, the most successful child health programmes have used ORS treatment as one strategy among other parallel and complementary interventions. They have tackled the problem of the children's limited access to water and sanitation and tried to improve children's long-term prospects for good health. The case has been made loud and clear for more integrated environmental and social management when designing interventions.

SUMMARY OF SECTION 4

- Efficient investment in basic social services is the key to effective health interventions.

- Top-down interventions are unlikely to be effective if they are insensitive to local priorities in matters of child health. The former often place the emphasis on saving lives, while local communities may put their priority on sustainable lives or quality of life.

- Malnutrition persists as it mirrors practices in local communities and global society. Children are denied good nutrition when care-givers are relatively powerless in securing access to resources. Infants are denied breast milk, with deadly consequences for their survival, when very poor communities are tempted by the commercial promotion of formula foods. Heavy reliance on cheap fast foods is one reason why obesity rates are rising, particularly among the poor.

- Many killer diseases are contracted because children lack adequate sanitation, food and health care. Specific interventions limited to the eradication or control of a single disease may well reduce deaths from a specific cause, but they often fail to address the underlying causes – those which are embedded in poverty.

- The success of interventions lies not just in designing a highly effective or 'magic' technological cure, but in improving key aspects of the social and environmental management of ill health.

5 CONCLUSION

This chapter has emphasized that successful health interventions go beyond top-down interventions promoting the mere survival of children, aiming instead to achieve a sustainable quality of life. Achieving good health for children – a fulfilment of their basic human right – is a particularly critical commitment to uphold in a world that can already do so much to combat mortality, illness and disability but is still characterized by significant poverty, social inequalities and discrimination in matters of health. Specific global campaigns are already in place to improve the health of children. They are backed by international organizations such as the United Nations, which already know a great deal about the kind of action needed to meet children's needs, realize their rights and guarantee their well-being and opportunities in life. Achieving health in practice requires looking for ways to integrate global health campaigns with effective investment in social services, as well as finding ways to elicit stronger community participation through grounding health interventions in a thorough understanding of local situations.

REFERENCES

ADMINISTRATIVE COMMITTEE ON COORDINATION/SUB-COMMITTEE ON NUTRITION (ACC/SCN) (2000) 'Low birthweight: report of a meeting in Dhaka', Bangladesh on 14–17 June 1999, Pojda, J. and Kelly, L. (eds) *Nutrition Policy Paper*, **18**, Geneva, 2000.

BARKER, D. (1994) *Mothers, Babies, and Disease in Later Life*, London, BMJ Publishing Group.

BELLAMY, C. (1998) 'Foreword' in *State of the World's Children*, New York, The United Nations Children's Fund (UNICEF).

BLACK, D. (1980) *Inequalities in Health*, London, Penguin.

CASSIDY, C. (1987) 'World-view conflict about toddler malnutrition: change agent dilemmas' in SCHEPER-HUGHES, N. (ED.) *Child Survival*, Reidel, Dordrecht.

CHILD RIGHTS INFORMATION NETWORK (CRIN) (2002) *Convention on the Rights of the Child* [online], http://www.crin.org/docs/resources/treaties/uncrc.htm (accessed 30 January 2003).

CHOMSKY, A. (2000) 'The threat of a good example' in KIM, J., MILEN, J., IRWIN, A. and GERSHMAN, J. (eds) *Dying for Growth: global inequality and the health of the poor*, Monroe, Common Courage Press.

COSTELLO, A. (2001) 'Reducing global inequalities in child health', *Archives of Disease in Childhood*, **84**, pp. 98–102.

CROLL, E. (2000) *Endangered Daughters*, London, Routledge.

DABIS, F., ORNE-GLIEMANN, J., PEREZ, F., LEROY, V., NEWELL, M. L., COUTSOUDIS, A. and COOVADIA, H. (2002) 'Improving child health: the role of research', *British Medical Journal*, **324**, pp. 1444–7.

DEPARTMENT OF HEALTH (2002) *The NHS Plan: a plan for investment, a plan for reform*, London, The Stationery Office.

DEPARTMENT OF THE ENVIRONMENT, TRANSPORT AND THE REGIONS (2001) *Achieving a Better Quality of Life*, London, Department of the Environment, Transport and the Regions.

DETTWYLER, K. (1998) 'The biocultural approach in nutritional anthropology: case studies of malnutrition in Mali' in BROWN, P. (ed.) *Understanding and Applying Medical Anthropology*, London and Toronto, Mayfield Publishing Company.

ENE-OBONG, H. N., IROEGBU, C. U. and UWAEGBUTE, A. C. (2000) 'Perceived causes and management of diarrhoea in young children by market women in Enugu State, Nigeria', *Journal of Health and Population Nutrition*, **18**(2), pp. 97–102.

ENGLE, P. and NIEVES, I. (1993) 'Intra-household food distribution among Guatemalan families in a supplementary feeding program: behavior patterns', *Social Science and Medicine*, **36**, pp. 1605–12.

FRANKEL, S. (1986) *The Huli Response to Illness*, Cambridge, Cambridge University Press.

FRANKEL, S. and LEHMAN, D. (1984) 'Oral rehydration therapy: combining anthropological and epidemiological approaches in the evaluation of a Papua New Guinea programme', *Journal of Tropical Medicine and Hygiene*, **87**, pp. 137–42.

GRANT, J. P. (1993) *The State of the World's Children*, Oxford, Oxford University Press.

LEWIS, G. (2001) 'Health: an elusive concept' in MACBETH, H. and SHETTY, P. (eds) *Health and Ethnicity*, London, Taylor and Francis.

McCORD, C. and H. FREEMAN (1990) 'Excess mortality in Harlem', *The New England Journal of Medicine,* **322**(3), pp. 173–77.

MARTORELL, R., KETTEL KHAN, L., HUGHES, M. L. and GRUMMER-STAWN, L. M. (2000). 'Overweight and obesity in preschool children from developing countries', *International Journal of Obesity*, **24**, pp. 959–67.

MYERS, R. (1992) *The Twelve Who Survive*, London, Routledge.

PANTER-BRICK, C. (1998) 'Biological anthropology and child health: context, process and outcome' in PANTER-BRICK, C. (ed.) *Biosocial Perspectives on Children*, Cambridge, Cambridge University Press.

PANTER-BRICK, C. (2002) 'The anthropology of physical activity' in RIDDOCH, C. and McKENNA, J. (eds) *Perspectives on Health and Exercise*, Basingstoke, Palgrave Macmillan.

POPKIN, B., RICHARDS, M. and MONTEIRO, C. (1996) 'Stunting is associated with overweight in children of four nations that are undergoing the nutrition transition', *Journal of Nutrition*, **126**, pp. 3009–16.

SAVE THE CHILDREN (1995) *Towards a Children's Agenda*, London, Save the Children.

SARACCI, R. (1997) 'The World Health Organization needs to reconsider its definition of health', *British Medical Journal*, **314**, pp. 1409–10.

SCHEPER-HUGHES, N. (1993) *Death Without Weeping*, Berkeley, University of California Press.

STEPHENS, S. (1998) 'Reflections on environmental justice: children as victims and actors' in WILLIAMS, C. (ed.) *Environmental Victims: new risks, new injustices*, London, Earthscan Publications.

THE OPEN UNIVERSITY (2003) U212 *Childhood*, Audio 7, Band 3, 'Chittagong Children's Hospital', Milton Keynes, The Open University.

TILFORD, S. (1995) 'Promoting the health of the world's children' in FATCHETT, A. (ed.) *Childhood to Adolescence – Caring for Health*, London, Balliere Tindall.

UNITED NATIONS CHILDREN'S FUND (UNICEF) (2001) *We the Children*, New York, UNICEF.

UNITED NATIONS CHILDREN'S FUND (UNICEF) (2002) *State of the World's Children*, New York, UNICEF.

UNITED NATIONS ENVIRONMENT PROGRAMME (UNEP), UNITED NATIONS CHILDREN'S FUND (UNICEF) and WORLD HEALTH ORGANIZATION (WHO) (2002) *Children in the New Millennium: environmental impact on health*, Nairobi, New York and Geneva, UNEP, UNICEF and WHO.

WORLD HEALTH ORGANIZATION (WHO) (1992) *Basic Documents*, 39th edition, Geneva, WHO.

WILKINSON, R. G. (1996) *Unhealthy Societies: the afflictions of inequality*, London, Routledge.

WOODHEAD, M. (1995) 'Disturbing behaviour in young children' in BARNES P. (ed.) *Personal, Social and Emotional Development of Children*, Oxford, Blackwell/The Open University.

WORLD BANK *(2002) World Development Indicators Database* [online], http://www.developmentgoals.org (accessed 4 November 2002).

READING A

The spirit catches you and you fall down

Anne Fadiman

Although the Hmong believe that illness can be caused by a variety of sources – including eating the wrong food, drinking contaminated water, being affected by a change in the weather, failing to ejaculate completely during sexual intercourse, neglecting to make offerings to one's ancestors, being punished for one's ancestors' transgressions, being cursed, being hit by a whirlwind, having a stone implanted in one's body by an evil spirit master, having one's blood sucked by a *dab* bumping into a *dab* who lives in a tree or a stream, digging a well in a *dab's* living place, catching sight of a dwarf female *dab* who eats earthworms, having a *dab* sit on one's chest while one is sleeping, doing one's laundry in a lake inhabited by a dragon, pointing one's finger at the full moon, touching a newborn mouse, killing a large snake, urinating on a rock that looks like a tiger, urinating on or kicking a benevolent house spirit, or having bird droppings fall on one's head – by far the most common cause of illness is soul loss. Although the Hmong do not agree on just how many souls people have (estimates range from one to thirty-two; the Lees believe there is only one), there is a general consensus that whatever the number, it is the life-soul, whose presence is necessary for health and happiness, that tends to get lost. A life-soul can become separated from its body through anger, grief, fear, curiosity, or wanderlust. The life-souls of newborn babies are especially prone to disappearance; since they are so small, so vulnerable, and so precariously poised between the realm of the unseen, from which they have just traveled, and the realm of the living. Babies' souls may wander away, drawn by bright colors, sweet sounds, or fragrant smells; they may leave if a baby is sad, lonely, or insufficiently loved by its parents; they may be frightened away by a sudden loud noise; or they may be stolen by a *dab*. Some Hmong are careful never to say aloud that a baby is pretty, lest a *dab* be listening. Hmong babies are often dressed in intricately embroidered hats (Foua made several for Lia) which, when seen from a heavenly perspective, might fool a predatory *dab* into thinking the child was a flower. They spend much of their time swaddled against their mothers' backs in cloth carriers called *nyias* (Foua made Lia several of these too) that have been embroidered with soul retaining motifs, such as the pigpen, which symbolizes enclosure. They may wear silver necklaces fastened with soul-shackling locks. When babies or small children go on an outing, their parents may call loudly to their souls before the family returns home, to make sure that none remain behind. Hmong families in Merced can sometimes be heard doing this when they leave local parks after a picnic. None of these ploys can work, however, unless the soul-calling ritual has already been properly observed.

Lia's *hu plig* took place in the living room of her family's apartment. There were so many guests, all of them Hmong and most of them members of the Lee and Yang clans, that it was nearly impossible to turn around. Foua and Nao Kao were proud that so many people had come to celebrate their good fortune in being favored with such a healthy and beautiful daughter. That morning Nao Kao had sacrificed a pig in order to invite the soul of one of Lia's ancestors, which was probably hungry and would appreciate an offering of food, to be reborn in her body. After the guests arrived, an elder of the Yang clan stood at the apartment's open front door, facing East 12th Street, with two live chickens in a bag on the floor next to him, and chanted a greeting to Lia's soul. The two chickens were then killed, plucked, eviscerated, partially boiled, retrieved from the cooking pot, and examined to see if their skulls were translucent and their tongues curled upward, both signs that Lia's new soul was pleased to take up residence in her body and that her name was a good one. (If the signs had been inauspicious, the soul-caller would have recommended that another name be chosen.) After the reading of the auguries, the chickens were put back in the cooking pot. The guests would later eat them and the pig for dinner. Before the meal, the soul-caller brushed Lia's hands with a bundle of short white strings and said, 'I am sweeping away the ways of sickness.' Then Lia's parents and all of the elders present in the room each tied a string around one of Lia's wrists in order to bind her soul securely to her body. Foua and Nao Kao promised to love her; the elders blessed her and prayed that she would have a long life and that she would never become sick.

[…]

When Lia was about three months old, her older sister Yer slammed the front door of the Lees' apartment. A few moments later, Lia's eyes rolled up, her arms jerked over her head, and she fainted. The Lees had little doubt what had happened. Despite the careful installation of Lia's soul during the *hu plig* ceremony, the noise of the door had been so profoundly frightening that her soul had fled her body and become lost. They recognized the resulting symptoms as *qaug dab peg*, which means 'the spirit catches you and you fall down'. The spirit referred to in this phrase is a soul-stealing *dab*; *peg* means to catch or hit; and *qaug* means to fall over with one's roots still in the ground, as grain might be beaten down by wind or rain.

In Hmong–English dictionaries, *qaug dab peg* is generally translated as epilepsy. It is an illness well known to the Hmong, who regard it with ambivalence. On the one hand, it is acknowledged to be a serious and potentially dangerous condition. Tony Coelho, who was Merced's congressman from 1979 to 1989, is an epileptic. Coelho is a popular figure among the Hmong, and a few years ago, some local Hmong men were sufficiently concerned when they learned he suffered from *qaug dab peg* that they volunteered the services of a shaman, a *txiv neeb*, to perform a ceremony that would retrieve Coelho's errant soul. The Hmong leader to whom they made this proposition politely discouraged them, suspecting that Coelho, who is a Catholic of Portuguese descent, might not appreciate having chickens, and maybe a pig as well, sacrificed on his behalf.

On the other hand, the Hmong consider *qaug dab peg* to be an illness of some distinction. This fact might have surprised Tony Coelho no less than the dead chickens would have. Before he entered politics, Coelho planned to become a Jesuit priest, but was barred by a canon forbidding the ordination of epileptics. What was considered a disqualifying impairment by Coelho's church might have been seen by the Hmong as a sign that he was particularly fit for divine office. Hmong epileptics often become shamans. Their seizures are thought to be evidence that they have the power to perceive things other people cannot see, as well as facilitating their entry into trances, a pre-requisite for their journeys into the realm of the unseen. The fact that they have been ill themselves gives them an intuitive sympathy for the suffering of other's and lends them emotional credibility as healers. Becoming a *txiv neeb* is not a choice; it is a vocation. The calling is revealed when a person falls sick, either with *qaug dab peg* or with some other illness whose symptoms similarly include shivering and pain. An established *txiv neeb*, summoned to diagnose the problem, may conclude from these symptoms that the person (who is usually but not always male) has been chosen to be the host of a healing spirit, *a neeb*. (*Txiv neeb* means "person with a healing spirit.") It is an offer that the sick person cannot refuse, since if he rejects his vocation, he will die. In any case, few Hmong would choose to decline. Although shamanism is an arduous calling that requires years of training with a master in order to learn the ritual techniques and chants, it confers an enormous amount of social status in the community and publicly marks the *txiv neeb* as a person of high moral character, since a healing spirit would never choose a no-account host. Even if an epileptic turns out not to be elected to host a *neeb*, his illness, with its thrilling aura of the supramundane, singles him out as a person of consequence.

In their attitude toward Lia's seizures, the Lees reflected this mixture of concern and pride. The Hmong are known for the gentleness with which they treat their children. Hugo Adolf Bernatzik, a German ethnographer who lived with the Hmong of Thailand for several years during the 1930s, wrote that the Hmong he had studied regarded a child as 'the most treasured possession a person can have'. In Laos, a baby was never apart from its mother, sleeping in her arms all night and riding on her back all day. Small children were rarely abused; it was believed that a *dab* who witnessed mistreatment might take the child, assuming it was not wanted. The Hmong who live in the United States have continued to be unusually attentive parents. A study conducted at the University of Minnesota found Hmong infants in the first month of life to be less irritable and more securely attached to their mothers than Caucasian infants, a difference the researcher attributed to the fact that the Hmong mothers were, without exception, more sensitive, more accepting, and more responsive, as well as 'exquisitely attuned' to their children's signals. Another study, conducted in Portland, Oregon, found that Hmong mothers held and touched their babies far more frequently than Caucasian mothers. In a third study, conducted at the Hennepin County Medical Center in Minnesota, a group of Hmong mothers of toddlers surpassed a group of Caucasian mothers of similar socioeconomic status in every one of fourteen categories selected from the Egeland Mother–Child Rating Scale, ranging from 'Speed of Responsiveness to Fussing and Crying' to 'Delight'.

Foua and Nao Kao had nurtured Lia in typical Hmong fashion (on the Egeland Scale, they would have scored especially high in Delight), and they were naturally distressed to think that anything might compromise her health and happiness. They therefore hoped, at least most of the time, that the *qaug dab peg* could be healed. Yet they also considered the illness an honor. Jeanine Hilt, a social worker who knew the Lees well, told me, 'They felt Lia was kind of an anointed one, like a member of royalty. She was a very special person in their culture because she had these spirits in her and she might grow up to be a shaman, and so sometimes their thinking was that this was not so much a medical problem as it was a blessing.' (Of the forty or so American doctors, nurses, and Merced County agency employees I spoke with who had dealt with Lia and her family, several had a vague idea that 'spirits' were somehow involved, but Jeanine Hilt was the only one who had actually asked the Lees what they thought was the cause of their daughter's illness.)

Within the Lee family, in one of those unconscious processes of selection that are as mysterious as any other form of falling in love, it was obvious that Lia was her parent's favourite, the child they considered the most beautiful, the one who was most extravagantly hugged and kissed, the one who was dressed in the most exquisite garments (embroidered by Foua, wearing dime-store glasses to work her almost microscopic stitches). Whether Lia occupied this position from the moment of her birth, whether it was a result of her spiritually distinguished illness, or whether it came from the special tenderness any parent feels for a sick child, is not a matter Foua and Nao Kao wish, or are able, to analyze. One thing that is clear is that for many years the cost of that extra love was partially borne by her sister Yer. 'They blamed Yer for slamming the door,' said Jeanine Hilt. 'I tried many times to explain that the door had nothing to do with it, but they didn't believe me. Lia's illness made them so sad that I think for a long time they treated Yer differently from their other children.'

During the next few months of her life, Lia had at least twenty more seizures. On two occasions, Foua and Nao Kao were worried enough to carry her in their arms to the emergency room at Merced Community Medical Center, which was three blocks from their apartment. Like most Hmong refugees, they had their doubts about the efficacy of Western medical techniques. However, when they were living in the Mae Jarim refugee camp in Thailand, their only surviving son, Cheng, and three of their six surviving daughters, Ge, May, and True, had been seriously ill. Ge died. They took Cheng, May, and True to the camp hospital; Cheng and May recovered rapidly, and True was sent to another, larger hospital, where she eventually recovered as well. (The Lees also concurrently addressed the possible spiritual origins of their children's illnesses by moving to a new hut. A dead person had been buried beneath their old one, and his soul might have wished to harm the new residents.) This experience did nothing to shake their faith in traditional Hmong beliefs about the causes and cures of illness, but it did convince them that on some occasions Western doctors could be of additional help, and that it would do no harm to hedge their bets.

Source

FADIMAN, A. (1997) *The Spirit Catches You and You Fall Down: a Hmong child, her American doctors, and the collision of two cultures*, New York, The Noonday Press, pp. 10–23.

READING B

Birth and broken promises

UNICEF

There was high excitement in the village, the kind of joy and optimism that only a new baby can bring. Ayodele was a beautiful baby, full of limitless potential, her whole life before her. For this moment, as should be the case at the birth of any child, everyone set aside their fears and doubts about the future, their anxieties about family health and growing enough food. They congratulated the baby's parents and contemplated the resurgent hope that new life always brings.

At the same time, on the other side of the Atlantic, there was a birth of a different kind, one to which great hope was also attached. An unprecedented number of country presidents and national leaders gathered in New York for the World Summit for Children. It was September 1990, a time of unusual optimism in the world.

The child-health revolution, begun decades earlier, was in full swing during the 1980s as a worldwide immunization drive saved millions of young lives. The cold war was over and there was widespread expectation that money that had been spent on arms could now be devoted to human development in a 'peace dividend'. The World Summit for Children seemed in itself a sign that the world had moved into a new and brighter phase in which its policy makers and politicians could gather to consider how to guarantee children a better life rather than to deal with the implications of superpower rivalry.

The World Summit reflected the world's hopes for children. Leaders promised to ratify the Convention on the Rights of the Child, which had been unanimously approved by the United Nations General Assembly just the year before. They signed on to ambitious goals to reduce child mortality, increase immunization coverage, deliver basic education and a whole raft of other measures by the year 2000. There was hope that the combination of a specific legal framework together with an action plan with time-tied, concrete goals would transform children's lives worldwide over the decade to come. Children's survival, development, protection and education were no longer matters of charitable concern but of legal obligation. The Declaration to which the world's leaders signed their name was bold and unequivocal: 'The well-being of children requires political action at the highest level.' The cause of children, for perhaps the first time in human history, was at the top of the world's agenda.

Eleven years on

Ayodele is now 10 years old, going on 11 – and, though she does not know it, she has been let down. Her life is much the same as it would have been for a girl of her age in 1990. She is hard at work. The grain needs to be pounded for the nightly meal. This job is far from being her first of the day: She has already collected four large bowls full of water, which she has carried back to her family's compound on her head; she has helped in the fields, cleaned the house and has looked after her younger brothers and sisters. Yes, she would like to go to school, but it is very expensive to buy the books and, besides, her family needs her at home.

Ayodele's life provides one small piece in the jigsaw of evidence that shows that the most optimistic assessments both in her own village and in New York at the time of her birth have not been realized. While she survived her first five years of life, two of her siblings born since the World Summit did not, dying from childhood diseases against which they could have been immunized or which were easily treated. Ayodele's learning potential was far from realized. Schools are not the only place in which learning occurs, and she has grasped, by precept and example, many of the important skills she will need to negotiate life in the village and beyond. But she cannot read or deal with any but the most basic ideas of number; she has no knowledge of the world beyond her local town; and she has no idea of her own rights.

Children of the 1990s

One child cannot stand for the whole world, but the picture for the human family in its entirety, while it has some bright spots that were a lot darker back in 1990, reflects a largely unfulfilled promise to children like Ayodele. The group of children born at the start of the last decade of the 20th century was the largest generation of children the world has ever known. If all those born at the time of the World Summit were reduced proportionately to a cohort of 100 children, what would they look like? – and what would their experience in the last 10 years have been?

Of the 100 children, 55 would have been born in Asia, including 19 in India and 18 in China. Eight would have come from Latin America and the Caribbean, seven from the Middle East and North Africa, 16 from sub-Saharan Africa, six from CEE/CIS and Baltic States and eight from industrialized countries.

The births of 33 of these children went unregistered: As a result they have no official existence, no recognition of nationality. Some of them have no access to health facilities or to school without this official proof of their age and identity.

Around 32 of the children suffered from malnutrition before the age of five and 27 were not immunized against any diseases. Nine died before the age of five. Of the remaining 91 children, 18 do not attend school, of whom 11 are girls. Eighteen of the children have no access to safe drinking water and 39 live without sanitation.

The difference between the life experiences and living conditions of these 100 children and a comparable cohort of 11-year-olds in 1990 is not anything as great as the international community would have wished when it began its undertakings a decade ago. Eleven years on from the World Summit, world leaders are again to gather in New York to consider the state of the world's children, looking back over the years since the fine words of the Declaration were expressed and since key, specific goals were set to improve children's lives. The data presented to them will show that the progress has been patchy, the record a mixture of conspicuous achievement and dispiriting failure.

Source

UNICEF (2002) *The State of the World's Children*, New York, United Nations Children's Fund (UNICEF).

READING C

Cases of malnutrition in Mali

Katherine Dettwyler

[Fatoumata and Oumou were a set of identical twin girls.] They were their mother's first and second children. Their mother, Aminata, was approximately 16 years old, and unmarried. The twins' father, who had not been allowed to marry her, did not contribute anything to their support. Aminata lived in a large compound containing one elderly woman, this woman's four adult sons, and their wives and children. Aminata was the foster child of a wife of one of the adult men in the compound.

I first encountered the twins when they were 14 months of age. […] I often gave Aminata advice, and occasionally money to buy fish, and for several months I brought her home-made formula (powdered milk, sugar, oil, water). In addition, when the twins had the measles, I bought the ingredients for oral rehydration solution and showed Aminata how to mix and administer it. […] [T]heir case is described here because it provides a particularly clear illustration of the constraints placed on women and their children by the social structure of a patrilineal society.

The twins were born at home, so birth weights are not available. I did not measure them when I first met them at 14 months of age. At 15 months of age, during the hot season, both twins caught the measles. Fatoumata had an especially serious case, probably because she was already more severely malnourished than her twin. For two weeks neither twin ate any solid food, and both became dehydrated. I provided oral rehydration solution and tried to convince their mother to take them to the hospital, but she refused. They eventually got better, though it took several months for them to recover fully and begin eating normally again. […]

Although I did not measure their heights, photographs reveal that Fatoumata was already several centimeters shorter than her sister. My field notes from this visit describe them as follows: 'reddish hair, no tissue in buttocks or thighs, sunken eyes, sunken fontanelles, sores on their faces, vacant stares, can barely crawl.' At 19 months, they could not walk or talk. They were still nursing and eating only a little food, primarily rice or millet breakfast porridge.

Oumou began to walk when she was 24 months old, and Fatoumata at 26 months … The children were still nursing at this time, and were eating all the adult foods, including rice and millet with various sauces. The mother requested that I stop providing formula, because she 'didn't have time to give it to them.' At the time, I did not understand this statement, but as the study progressed, the truth of her assertion became apparent. The twins were weaned at 28 months of age, and their mother reported that they ate more food than before being weaned.

The twins were 3 years and 4 months old at the end of the study. They could walk, but not run, could say only the words for 'mother' and 'water,' and spent their days standing listlessly in the doorway of their house …

What factors contributed to malnutrition in this case? At first, I was inclined to attribute it to their mother's seemingly callous indifference to their welfare … She had asked me to stop bringing formula because it took too much time to give it to the children. In addition, she said that the children were a burden to her, that she had little chance of marrying with two small children, and that she would be in a better position for getting out of the compound if they died. As I probed into the motivations underlying these statements, the reality of her position in the family and the conditions of her life became clear.

As described earlier, Aminata lived in a compound based around four adult brothers and their elderly mother. When Aminata herself was 3 years old, she had been given to her father's sister as a foster child. A common practice throughout West Africa, child fostering involves sending young children to live with relatives for a variety of reasons (e.g., to provide labor for paternal relatives, to keep an elderly grandmother company in a rural village, or to help a female relative care for a newborn baby). Foster children often have low status in the household, and they may not be accorded the same access to scarce resources as the other children in the family (Bledsoe, Ewbank, and Isiugo-Abanihe 1988; Bledsoe 1991).

After several years, Aminata was passed on again as a foster child, from her aunt to this woman's daughter (her own cousin), who was a young adult at the time. This woman, in turn, had married into the family of four brothers, as the second wife of the third brother. In this strongly patrilineal, age-conscious society, a man's status in the family depends on his birth order, with the oldest surviving brother being the head of the family. Likewise, a woman's status depends both on the status of her husband and on her position as his first, second, third, or fourth wife. Generally speaking, first wives have higher status than later wives. This meant that Aminata was the foster child of the second wife of the third brother in a compound of four adult men. Thus, Aminata was the foster child of a woman who also had low status in the household.

In addition to her low structural position in a large, patrilineal family, Aminata was several years older than any of the children in the family. During 1982 and 1983, she was responsible for the vast majority of the heavy manual labor in the compound, including virtually all of the millet pounding, firewood chopping, water hauling, and clothes washing. She also did the majority of the cooking. Even though there were five other adult women in the household, Aminata was never allowed to rest. Partly to escape the drudgery of her existence, she used to 'go out at night' with a group of boys and girls her own age.

When she was 15 years old, Aminata became pregnant by one of her 'friends.' The adult men of the compound did not approve of this man, and her life became even worse. The birth of twins, usually viewed as a blessing, was an excessive burden for an unmarried, adolescent girl. Her work load did not change while she was pregnant or after the twins were born, and she was routinely beaten by the women of the compound for her indiscretion in becoming pregnant before marriage. Although the twins' father wanted to marry Aminata, her foster fathers would not allow it.

On a relative scale of socioeconomic status, Aminata's compound would be considered 'above average' for the community. It contained four adult male wage earners, all of whom were skilled laborers. The compound itself was large, with cement-block houses, and the other children of the family were only mildly malnourished, which is typical of children in the community. Therefore, money was available in the family; Aminata, however, had no access to it. If she needed money to take her children to the doctor or to buy the food I suggested, she had to ask her cousin, who in turn had to ask her husband. These requests were seldom granted. When she had to spend the day at the river washing clothes, she used to leave the children with a friend, because no one at her own compound would watch them for her.

She felt that there was little she could do to change her situation or to improve her children's health given her lack of resources. She really *didn't* have the time to give them formula or to administer oral rehydration solution every 15 minutes when they were dehydrated from measles or diarrhea. Pryer and Crook (1988:19) have noted, 'especially during illness when appetite fails, small children need to be fed frequently during the day, which is very time-consuming, and can be especially difficult for mothers from poor families who may have other domestic and economic responsibilities.'

Follow-Up

In 1989, I returned to Aminata's compound. She was no longer living there, but I was able to relocate her in a neighboring community. According to Aminata, the smaller of the twins, Fatoumata, died in 1984 of malaria. Shortly thereafter, Oumou was sent to live with Aminata's own parents (whom she had not seen in many years) in Mopti, a large port town on the Niger River northeast of Bamako. Once both the twins were 'out of the way' (her phrase), Aminata's foster family arranged for her to be married to a man of their choosing.

Since her marriage in 1984, Aminata has had three more children, of whom two survive. The first child, a boy, is now 4 years old. The second, a girl, died in 1986 in Mopti while Aminata was visiting Oumou. According to Aminata, this child died from the measles. That was the last time Aminata saw Oumou, and she has no plans to visit her again. The third child, another boy, is now one year old. The two surviving children have weights and heights that place them in the 'mildly malnourished' category.

Aminata reports that she is very happy in her marriage and content with her life. She married into a large extended family with many adult women to share the work. She is the first of two wives of one of the older brothers. The women take turns doing the domestic labor, and she only has to work two days each week. Looking back on her childhood and adolescence, she says that although she had to work very hard, she learned how to do everything well, so that now her life is comparatively easy. She says she tries not to think of Fatoumata and Oumou because it makes her sad. She feels no personal responsibility for Fatoumata's death, or for the death of her younger daughter. When I asked, 'Do you think there is anything you could have done to prevent their deaths,' she replied, 'You can search for medicine, and give your children medicine, but if it is their time, Allah will take them no matter what you do.' Aminata does not admit to any bad feelings toward her foster family, or blame them for contributing to Fatoumata's death or Oumou's separation from her.

Fatoumata and Oumou were two of the most severely malnourished children in the study. Their malnutrition … had many contributing causes. If Aminata had not been a foster child, or if she had gotten pregnant by a man her foster fathers liked (so they could have been married), if she had

had only one child instead of twins, or if the adult women of the compound had helped more with the household labor – if any one of a number of factors had been different, her children would have been healthier.

References

BLEDSOE, C. (1991) The Trickle-Down Model Within Households: Foster Children and the Phenomenon of Scrounging. *In* The Health Transition: Methods and Measures. Health Transition Series No. 3, J. CLELAND and A.G. HILL, eds. Pp. 115–131. Canberra: Australian National University Press.

BLEDSOE, C.H., D.C. EWBANK, and U.C. ISIUGO-ABANIHE. 1988. The Effect of Child Fostering on Feeding Practices and Access to Health Services in Rural Sierra Leone. Soc Sci Med, 27(6):627–636.

PRYER, J., and N. CROOK. 1988. Cities of Hunger: Urban Malnutrition in Developing Countries. Oxford: Oxfam.

Source

DETTWYLER, L. (1998) 'The biocultural approach in nutritional anthropology: case studies of malnutrition in Mali' in BROWN, P. (ed.) *Understanding and Applying Medical Anthropology*, London and Toronto, Mayfield Publishing Company, pp. 395–3.

Chapter 4

Children and violence

Heather Montgomery

CONTENTS

When you have studied this chapter, you should be able to:

1   Discuss the ways in which children are the victims of violence and the multiple effects that violence has on children, encompassing not only physical pain and injury but also psychological harm.

2   Examine the various roles that children play in relation to violence amongst peers as victims, perpetrators, witnesses, colluders and peacemakers.

3   Consider the ways children are affected by, as well as inducted into, civil conflicts.

4   Analyse the role of children in armed conflicts and discuss whether young people should be allowed to fight.

5   Examine the ways in which children and their communities have attempted to end violence in their lives.

1 INTRODUCTION

As the previous chapters have discussed, children are subject to many forms of adversity, for example, poverty or ill health. This chapter examines another form of adversity that many children face, that of violence. This is a huge topic which can be tackled in a number of ways, for example by looking at the effects of war on children in Africa and Asia, physical or sexual abuse of children in the North, structural violence against children in the form of government policies, or symbolic forms of violence, looking at how images and representations of violence in the media affect children. It is difficult to cover all these topics in one chapter and the focus is necessarily limited. The chapter concentrates on three different situations where children experience violence: at home, among peers at school and in the wider society (in the context of armed conflicts). There is obviously an overlap between these situations and they are not meant to be mutually exclusive. It is an unfortunate fact that children may experience violence in their families and among their peers, and may also become involved in armed conflict.

This book focuses on children's experiences locally and globally and this chapter emphasizes that violence against children should not be exoticized; it is not something that occurs only in other countries or in other families. Many children experience violence, whether they live in a Sierra Leonean war zone or experience bullying at school or domestic violence in the UK. Although the forms of violence that children experience may be different, the important point is that many children, throughout the world, have daily experiences of violence which can have negative impacts on their physical or emotional health. This chapter therefore moves from ideas about children and violence in very localized contexts – within families and with peers at school – through to the broader community and on to the international perspective. It also analyses the different roles that children take on in relation to violence, such as victim, perpetrator, witness, colluder and peacemaker.

In Western thought, children and violence exist in an ambivalent, and much debated, relationship with each other which centres around whether children are naturally good, gentle, kind and loving or naturally wicked and cruel (see Montgomery, 2003). While the image of the gentle, meek child is integral to the Christian New Testament, many other Christian teachings, especially those in the Old Testament book of Proverbs and in the practices of some seventeenth-century Puritan sects, point to the inherent badness of children that must be controlled by punishment. Others have seen in children a particular form of violence, typified by cruelty to animals and to smaller children, which is linked to the innate savagery of children and their existence in a pre-civilized state. Nineteenth-century naturalists and archaeologists pointed to children as the closest available 'savages' who, like the 'exotic primitives' of Australia and North America, existed in a wilful, amoral and cruel state. C. Staniland Wake, an anthropologist writing in 1878, drew close parallels between children and 'native peoples', claiming that both were characterized by an innate viciousness towards others that glorified in violence for violence's sake. He wrote of a '*cruelty* so noticeable among children [and Native Americans], so much so indeed, that it may be described as one of the most distinguishing traits of boyhood' (Wake, 1878, p. 5). While the racism inherent in such statements may sound shocking nowadays, especially when written in such an objective, scientific tone, the casual assumption that violence and children are connected continues. The view that children, and especially boys, are cruel to animals, pulling the legs off spiders or tormenting cats, is commonplace.

However, the idea that children are cruel and violent is countered by the view that children are in fact naturally good and that any cruelty is a result of adult corruption. Ideas of children's innocence, gentleness and kindness can be traced back to the Romantic period in European history, characterized by philosophers such as Jean-Jacques Rousseau and poets such as William Wordsworth. For the Romantics, children had a visionary quality and represented humanity in its uncorrupted state. They were born good and lacking in all violence and it was civilization that imposed violence on them.

Allow about 10 minutes

ACTIVITY 1   Representations of children and violence

Study the pictures overleaf. How do you react to them? In which do you see children as innocent and in which do you see them as violent? Why do you feel this?

COMMENT

These four pictures convey very different images of children and violence. It is hard to look at them without assigning innocence to some and violent intentions to others. The first image seems to show two girls play-fighting. They are smiling and apparently playing rather than hitting each other in anger. They are more likely to be seen as playing rough-and-tumble or romping than as committing violence. The second picture shows a child who is the victim of violence rather than a perpetrator. It is significant that both pictures show girls, in that, because of their gender, they are more likely to be seen as non-violent. In Western societies, girls are invariably seen as less aggressive, less violent, more caring and at greater risk of being victims of violence than its perpetrators (and this is largely backed up by crime statistics that suggest that girls are less likely than boys to commit violent crimes). In the final two pictures, however, vulnerability and innocence have gone and been replaced with images of children as threatening and dangerous. The fact that they are male might encourage the conclusion that they are violent. Their age is also significant. Teenagers are more likely to be seen as violent, and to pose a greater threat than younger children.

SUMMARY OF SECTION 1

- Children and violence exist in an ambivalent relationship to each other.
- In Western thought, children can be perceived as inherently violent and naturally cruel. Conversely, they are also seen as inherently gentle and lacking in violence.
- Boys are more likely to be seen as violent and aggressive than girls, and teenagers as more violent than younger children.

2 VIOLENCE IN THE HOME

2.1 Violence towards children

For many children, the place where they experience most violence is in the home. Since the American paediatrician Henry Kempe first publicized the 'battered child syndrome' in 1962, the extent and nature of child abuse in the home has increasingly been recognized, and become the subject of research, legislation and social care practice. Following on from Kempe's claims that some children were routinely beaten and ill treated within their own families, other issues such as sexual abuse and emotional abuse have also come to the fore. The National Society for the Prevention of Cruelty to Children (NSPCC) released a statement in 2002 which said:

> Home Office figures show that the rate of child homicide in England and Wales has not dropped over the last 25 years. In each generation of children, more than a thousand will be killed before reaching adulthood. Most will die at the hands of violent or neglectful parents and carers.

> (NSPCC, 2002)

The home is still the environment where children are most at risk, despite the widespread fears over 'stranger danger'. In the UK, in 2001, 65 children under seven were killed by their parents or carers (NSPCC, 2002). Even if children themselves are not the direct victims of violence at home, they can witness domestic violence carried out by one parent on another.

Allow about 10 minutes

A C T I V I T Y 2   **Different forms of violence**

Read through the list below. Which of these behaviours do you consider to show violence towards children? Why do you consider some of these to be forms of violence, and some not?

1   Being hit with a cane
2   Being shouted at
3   Overhearing parents arguing
4   Being told that you are stupid or ugly
5   Being smacked
6   Witnessing one parent hit another
7   Being tied into a cot or high chair
8   Being told 'I hate you' by a parent
9   Being humiliated in front of friends

C O M M E N T

All the above might be considered different forms of violence against children. Although only hitting with a cane or being smacked involve the imposition of physical violence and pain, it is possible to argue that the others show some form of violence towards children. Humiliating a child or telling them 'I hate you' can be seen as a type of psychological violence that damages the well-being of a child. Whether or not these behaviours are seen as violence towards children depends in part on cultural attitudes. For example, parents in Vietnam expressed shock and outrage to one researcher over 'tying' a child into a pushchair (Burr, 2000), a behaviour seen as so unremarkable in the UK as to be not worthy of comment. Indeed, the issue of restraint is a striking one because it may be seen as protecting children and ensuring their safety in the UK, yet considered inappropriate in Vietnam.

It may also depend on personal interpretation and individual experiences of being either a child or a parent. Furthermore, the intention needs to be taken into account. Many people argue that smacking is an acceptable form of discipline, seeing it as an effective form of training for good behaviour. Those who are opposed to smacking view it as a form of violence and unacceptable.

What constitutes violence towards children must therefore be seen in its cultural context – it must be acknowledged that practices and attitudes will differ markedly even within quite similar cultural contexts. There are some practices that are universally regarded as abusive and constituting violence towards children, such as sustained beating or shaking. However, there are other practices that are more contested. A clear example here is smacking, which remains widely practised in the UK, yet is looked upon with horror in Scandinavia where it is considered violent and abusive. In these countries, it is seen as an abuse of adult power against people who are smaller, weaker and more vulnerable. Similarly, what is considered violence towards children changes over time. In the 1970s in the UK, corporal punishment was widespread in British schools and viewed as a useful disciplinary tool for teachers. Now it is banned and if it occurred would be classified as assault.

While all societies have ideas about what constitutes unacceptable violence towards children, definitions of abuse vary across societies. For example, in certain Inuit societies of Canada, children are 'toughened up' from an early age by being made to plunge their hands repeatedly into icy water. Among

A fourteen-year-old Inuit child helping his father skin a caribou on Island Nunavut, Canada.

some groups in Amazonia, boys are encouraged to show the bravery they will need to hunt later on by putting their hands in a wasp's nest and getting stung hundreds of times. From a Western perspective, these practices might seem cruel, or even violent, but amongst the people who practise them they are regarded as a necessary way of disciplining children and teaching them the skills they need to know later. Jill Korbin writes:

> The parent who 'protects' his or her child from a painful, but culturally required, initiation rite would be denying the child a place as an adult in that culture. That parent, in the eyes of his cultural peers, would be abusive or neglectful for compromising the development of his child.
>
> It is equally sobering to look at Western child-rearing techniques and practices through the eyes of these same non-Western cultures. Non-Western people often conclude that anthropologists, missionaries, or other Euro-Americans with whom they come into contact do not love their children or simply do not know how to care for them properly. Practices such as isolating infants and small children in rooms or beds of their own at night, making them wait for readily available food until a schedule dictates that they can satisfy their hunger, or allowing them to cry without immediately attending to their needs or desires would be at odds with the child-rearing philosophies of most ... cultures.
>
> (Korbin, 1981, p. 4)

In short, particular ways of treating children may be seen as violent in one cultural context, but as necessary restraint or even positive training in others. It is important to take account of these different cultural beliefs about violence, especially when making judgements about what counts as abusive. So far we have concentrated on violence towards children in the home. Next we turn to violent behaviour by children themselves. Of course, in practice the two are often connected, especially where a young child's misbehaviour provokes a violent reaction from a parent, initiating an escalating cycle of aggression (Patterson, de Baryshe and Ramsay, 1989).

2.2 Children's violence

There has been a great deal of work done by psychologists on violence and aggression in children, looking at whether this is part of a normal and natural developmental process or whether it is pathological. Cole and Cole define aggression as 'an act in which someone intentionally hurts another' (1996, p. 406). They then split this definition to look at instrumental aggression which is committed in order to obtain a specific goal, and hostile aggression which is aimed at hurting another person or showing dominance. They emphasize that intention is important and that discussions of children and violence should distinguish aggression from rough play. One of the earliest studies on this issue was carried out by Nicholas Blurton Jones (1972). He looked at the characteristics of aggression and rough-and-tumble play in an attempt to draw a distinction between violent and non-violent behaviour in children. Based on detailed studies of facial and bodily movements, he claimed that aggression is composed of '*frown, fixate, hit, push*, and *take-tug-grab*', whereas rough-and tumble is characterized by *laugh-playface, run, jump, hit-at* and *wrestle*' (quoted in Schaffer, 1996, p. 278).

He also claimed that these behaviours occurred in different contexts. For example, aggression is much more likely to occur when children are competing to play with the same toy, while play-fighting involves cooperating in a shared game. Children taking part in rough-and-tumble tend to play with smiles on their faces and to come back for more, whereas when children perceive aggression they are more likely to stay away from the other child. Blurton Jones also found that children who indulge in rough-and-tumble are no more likely to be violent in other contexts than those who do not.

In situations where children are in conflict, they express aggression in different ways according to their age and gender. Girls are less likely to use physical violence than boys and rely on emotional or psychological violence. Also, children's expressions of aggression become increasingly verbal as they get older. While two year olds will use what physical force they can, by the age of ten children are more likely to tease or humiliate other children. As Durkin suggests, children may have more scope to become aggressive as they get older.

> Older individuals have more mechanisms available for acting aggressively. Not only do they have bigger, stronger, and better coordinated bodies, and in some cases access to more dangerous weapons, but they have also increasing competence in nonphysical means of aggression, such as verbal and nonverbal communications, and more sophisticated social understanding (so that, for example, they have a better sense of what will hurt someone else's feelings).

(Durkin, 1995, pp. 397–8)

While this chapter mainly concentrates on the very different ways children experience and express violence in a range of situations, it is worth briefly noting some of the different hypotheses about why children are violent. Some psychologists and anthropologists have used theories from socio-biology to explain children's violence. These claim that violence is instinctive in humans and part of mankind's adaptive strategies for survival. Furthermore, they claim, boys are more likely to be violent than girls because of the effects of testosterone – their aggression is biologically determined. However, this is problematic, partly because research is inconclusive about the effects of testosterone (Durkin, 1995). Also, not all boys are violent or even aggressive and, in a society where aggression is downplayed, there is little evidence for these ideas. Girls are usually socialized to be less aggressive than boys and physical aggression in girls is viewed differently, and more negatively, than in boys. It is therefore difficult to know if girls are naturally less aggressive than boys or conditioned to be so. Indeed, such ideas do not take cultural conditioning into account and, as this section will go on to show, there are large variations cross-culturally in incidence and type of aggressive behaviour in children.

Other theorists claim that aggression and violence are learned rather than being innate. For example, Albert Bandura put forward a 'social-learning theory' of aggression (1977). This, he claimed, showed that children learned to be violent through observation. He pointed to the social factors in their lives and argued against looking at individual predispositions to violence. Bandura considered that violent behaviour is socially transmitted through parents, community and the media. When children see someone they admire or respect being aggressive and getting the results they want, they copy this and become violent themselves.

Most studies on children's violence have been based on children in North America or Europe. The work of anthropologists offers a broader perspective, demonstrating the power of cultural expectations in shaping children's behaviour, and in determining whether children's actions are considered violent. The following quote is from Napoleon Chagnon's *Yanamamo: the fierce people* (1968), concerning a group of Amerindians in Venezuela whose society is associated with the raiding of neighbouring communities, the killing of rivals, a high level of intra-group violence and physical violence inflicted by men on women.

> Despite the fact that children of both sexes spend much of their time with their mothers, the boys alone are treated with considerable indulgence by their fathers from an early age. Thus, the distinction between male and female status develops early in the socialization process, and the boys are quick to learn their favored position with respect to girls. They are encouraged to be 'fierce' and are rarely punished by their parents for inflicting blows on them or on the hapless girls in the village. Kaobawä [his father], for example, lets Ariwari beat him on the face and head to express his anger and temper, laughing and commenting on his ferocity. Although Ariwari is only about four years old, he has already learned that the appropriate response to a flash of anger is to strike someone with his hand or with an object, and it is not uncommon for him to give his father a healthy smack in the face whenever something displeases him. He is frequently goaded into hitting his father by teasing, being rewarded by gleeful cheers of assent from his mother and from the other adults in the household.
>
> (Chagnon, 1968, p. 84)

Amongst the Yanamamo, violence is classified as fierceness and is prized and appreciated. Children are therefore encouraged to show violent behaviour, in a way that would be unacceptable in other societies. However, this violence is also highly gender specific; fierceness in girls is not acceptable among the Yanamamo, even in self-defence, and is dealt with severely.

In other societies, a child who lashed out and regularly hit their parents or other children may well be seen as being disturbed or as showing inappropriate levels of violence and aggression. Even within a society, the norms of acceptable behaviour are different for boys and girls, and for younger and older children. Furthermore, different sections of the community, as well as individuals, have differing standards as to what they consider to be violent behaviour. These are also setting-specific, with different behaviours considered to be acceptable or non-acceptable, depending on whether they are occurring in the home, the classroom, the playground or on the football pitch.

Yanamamo children practising their hunting skills in Roraima, Brazil.

SUMMARY OF SECTION 2

- Violence against children can take the form of emotional, psychological, sexual or physical abuse.

- Children's violence has to be contextualized by reference to the norms of a particular society, while recognizing that, even within a society, these norms may be contested.

- The levels of aggression deemed acceptable amongst children may vary according to gender, age and the site of the violence.

3 VIOLENCE AMONGST PEERS

3.1 Bullying – children as victims

Isolated child in a playground.

In countries of the North, much of children's daily life is divided between home and school. It is therefore in schools that many children experience violence amongst their peers and they may either be bullied or themselves become bullies.

READING

In Reading A, Dan Olweus, a psychologist specializing in children and bullying, looks at typical bullies and their victims in Sweden, although much of what he writes of Sweden is equally applicable to non-Scandinavian countries in Europe and North America. Read the extract, looking in particular at the links between home life and school behaviour, and noting the particular characteristics of those who are bullied and those who bully.

COMMENT

This extract indicates that there is no clear division between violence between peers at school and violence at home. Olweus makes the point that 'Violence begets violence' – children who are exposed to violence at home are more likely to be violent at school. They are also likely to have had insufficient warmth and love from their parents. Later on in the article, Olweus claims that bullies are more likely than others to commit acts of violence later in life. He therefore sees a continuum between aggression at home, bullying at school and later criminality. However, this 'cycle of abuse' theory can be contested. Not all researchers agree that children who experience violence go on to commit it. Indeed, their experiences of violence may make them more empathetic and less likely to inflict violence on others. It would also be interesting to speculate on how far these findings could apply to the Yanamamo in Venezuela. Clearly, by Olweus's criteria, Yanamamo male children are very likely to grow up to be bullies but, in a society which encourages fierceness, this may well be seen as positive.

Much of Reading A is about what Olweus calls the typical characteristics of victims and bullies. It is important not to exaggerate these characteristics, implying that some children will inevitably either be bullied or become bullies. This runs the risk of overlooking the fluidity of roles that children take – they can be both victim and bully, depending on the circumstances. There is also a danger of overlooking the other roles that children may play in bullying, such as those of witnesses, peacemakers or colluders (those children who do not actively take part in bullying but encourage it to occur).

Allow about 10 minutes

A C T I V I T Y 3   The effects of bullying

After reading Olweus's article, think about the effects of bullying. Make two lists – one of the possible physical effects and one of the psychological effects. In his article, Olweus concentrates largely on boys, but think back to the previous section where the differences between girls' and boys' experiences and ways of showing aggression were mentioned. Do you think that there would be any differences between the effects on boys and girls? To what extent do you regard bullying as a form of violence against children?

C O M M E N T

When children are bullied, they may experience physical violence in the form of being hit or threatened. On the psychological level, they can be ostracized from their group, teased, humiliated, belittled or simply ignored, and can suffer loss of self-esteem and confidence. You may have written down other forms of violence present in school bullying.

In general, both boys and girls are subject to all these forms of bullying. However, there are some gender differences. Boys are more likely to commit physical acts of bullying while girls resort to emotional bullying. Girls are at less risk of direct attack from other children but are more subject to indirect attacks in the form of exclusion or ostracism from the group.

Bullying can have very damaging consequences for children. The quotes below are taken from a problem page of the charity Bullying Online. In them, children express their fears of bullying and clearly do see it as a form of emotional, as well as physical, violence.

Dear Liz

I'm 14 in March and I'm being bullied constantly. In nearly every class I sit by myself because nobody wants to sit next to me. One of my few friends hangs around with other people because I think he is frightened if he is with me he will get bullied. Please help me. I'm sick to death and sometimes I feel like killing myself. I wish I was dead. I have been to the doctor.

Mike

Dear Liz,

I go to a village school where there aren't many other children. Some of them are being very spiteful and not letting me play with them. They call me names and hit me when they think the teacher isn't looking. I'm aged 10 and my mum has been trying to get it stopped.

Lucy

(Bullying Online, 2002)

For some children, going to school can be a violent and alienating experience. One survey carried out anonymously in Sheffield, UK, found that 27 per cent of the 6,758 junior and middle school children surveyed were bullied 'sometimes' or more often and 10 per cent faced bullying once a week or more (Smith *et al.*, 1999, p. 121). It is further claimed that sixteen children commit suicide in the UK each year as a result of bullying (Marr and Field, 2001). Yet it is only fairly recently that bullying has been recognized as a serious problem and seen as a form of violence against children. There has been a tendency among adults to see it as playing or teasing which occasionally gets out of hand or to see it as an inevitable fact of playground life which children will eventually grow out of (Smith *et al.*, 1999).

Bullying in schools is not only a problem for the North. Although there is little research on the subject, studies from Ethiopia suggest that it is also a serious problem in the South. A study of one classroom in Addis Ababa reported:

> Bullying and snatching objects (books, bags, etc.) are the most frequently occurring forms of violence, followed by physical violence (hitting, kicking, etc.). Attempts of rape at school are frequent among students, particularly among high school students (20 per cent of the total violence counted) …

> A study in eight schools around Addis Ababa revealed that … [n]early 90 per cent of students reported that they have either repeated classes or dropped out of school due to violence.

> (Ohsako, 1999, pp. 363–4)

Within schools, violence may also come from teachers, who bully or humiliate children or use physical punishment. This is especially common in countries where teachers' methods of discipline are subject to few regulations. Many children find school a hostile and violent environment with its rigid hierarchies and punitive sanctions for breaking rules.

The following quotations come from a study of children in countries of the South, many of whom try to combine working with going to school.

> [Teachers] pinch us … throw erasers at us … pull our hair … hit us with big sticks … make us kneel, hands raised and put books on our hands. (Philippines)

> They beat us with a cane or a bamboo stick on our palms or back … At times they also push our head under a table and hit us on the buttocks. (Bangladesh)

> When my parents did not buy exercise books, the teacher beat me. (Ethiopia)

> (Woodhead, 1999, p. 42)

3.2 Children as perpetrators

There has been a great deal of research on the personalities of bullies (for an overview, see Smith *et al.*, 1999) and explanations given for their behaviour in terms of family background or attachment to parents. Some of the findings of this research are summarized in Reading A. In another article, Olweus (1993) suggests that bullies are more likely to hold favourable views of violence, have a marked tendency towards aggression towards both adults and other children, have a strong need to dominate and feel more powerful than other children and feel little empathy for those they are bullying. But, as stated earlier, it is important to bear in mind that children can be both bullies and bullied in different contexts. There is also some evidence that children who are bullied may resort to violence themselves as a form of self-defence. Here, a boy in Australia recounts becoming a bully:

> HARRY: I used to fight all the time in year seven.
>
> MARTIN: Why was that?
>
> HARRY: People didn't like me and they'd try to hit me and I'd react.
>
> MARTIN: And when did things start to change?
>
> HARRY: When I fought back.
>
> MARTIN: Do you think if you hadn't fought back that would have been a big problem?
>
> HARRY: Yeah it would have been.
>
> (Mills, 2001, p. 69)

In other contexts also, children may turn to violence as a form of defence, aiming to be more violent than those of whom they are afraid. For example, street children in Brazil face an often brutal life where they are threatened and susceptible to violence from the police and the wider community, including older street children. Some children therefore turn to violence as a way of protecting themselves, using violence as both self-defence and a means to survival. Here, a child from Recife, Brazil, discusses his use of violence.

Once when I earned money, I bought a Beretta. I spent ten days snatching watches, 'Pah, pah' [his onomatopoeic rendition of children stealing watches]. First I bought a Mauser and then I held it against a lady's neck. I swiped her money and a bunch of videocassettes. I spent more than a month with the gun, stealing. Then I sold it and with the money I'd stolen and the money from the gun I bought a thirty-eight. Then I stole some more, sold that gun, and bought the Beretta.

I went to the street and a kid saw that my pockets were bulging, he tried to take my money. I pulled out the gun and pointed it at him. He took my money [anyway]. I said, 'Give it back you asshole or I'll shoot you. You think I steal so you can come and take my money?' He gave me the money and I yelled, 'Run!' He ran and I went 'Bam!' but I missed. 'Take another!' I missed again. When I shot again he fell. I said, 'Shit, I killed a boy.' I took off. The next day the kid had a Band-Aid on his toe. I only shot him in the toe.

(Hecht, 1998, p. 34)

Street children, Brazil.

3.3 Children as peacemakers – peer mediation

One response to witnessing bullying is to stand by and watch it happen. Alternatively, and more positively, children themselves can often act as mediators or peacemakers. Some of the most successful anti-bullying schemes have been those set up or run by children and have involved confronting the bully about the impact of his or her behaviour on others. Other schemes have involved setting up school bullying courts where children are 'tried' by a jury of their peers, while in others children counsel victims of bullying. In the following example, pupils at a school in Scotland talk about the anti-bullying programme that they have taken part in, emphasizing their role as peer mediators and counsellors.

The children in this project have tackled the issue of bullying head on and feel that they have made a significant difference to their school and community.

Children comforting a friend.

You help them [children who are bullied] with a procedure of acknowledging the fact that they're being bullied and the fact that there is somebody who is there to listen to them and who can help them do something about it, and give them different options on different routes that they can take. And they have to choose which is basically what we do here. We don't force them to do things, we simply tell them what can be done and then they decide on the best way of handling their business.

In most cases I did, I found that … there's never a bully who does anything by themselves, there's always a friend who is, the friends are more threatening than actually the bully. And if you actually collar them by themselves, the bully, they eventually become very, very vulnerable and it's, that's when, that's how we basically approach them. You do not approach them with their friends, you approach them by themselves …

There is an advantage of us, the students dealing with the bullying rather than the teachers because students are more likely to open and feel comfortable with other students … Because if there was a scheme where it was just teachers doing it, I assure you, no student would be up there, because why would you want to go up to a teacher and start talking to them unless you are comfortable with them. Because teachers know they have authority over you but other students are on the same level as you and you are more likely to open up to them than you are to a teacher.

(Glenn, quoted on BBC Online, 2002)

SUMMARY OF SECTION 3

- Children take on different but sometimes overlapping roles in bullying, those of victim, perpetrator, colluder, witness and peacemaker.
- Bullying can affect children's well-being and is a form of physical and psychological violence.
- Children who bully often hold favourable views of violence, show aggression towards both adults and children, have a strong need to dominate and feel more powerful than other children and feel little empathy for those they are bullying.
- Bullying is not confined to countries of the North.
- Children can act as peer mediators, tackling bullying and holding the perpetrators to account.

4 VIOLENCE WITHIN ARMED CONFLICTS

The final area of violence examined in this chapter involves children caught up in armed conflict, as victims, perpetrators or witnesses in violence affecting whole communities. It is important to emphasize that the three sites of conflict discussed in this chapter – family, schools and the community – are in no way exclusive. It is also important to stress that, in some parts of the world, criminal violence and repressive law enforcement measures (including harsh prison regimes) affect children's daily experiences of violence. Furthermore, gun violence against children is not limited to armed conflict. In some cities in the USA, children are as likely to be affected by violent death from guns as children living in a war zone. Psychologist James Garbarino refers to these as 'war-zone neighbourhoods', where

> almost every fourteen-year-old has been to the funeral of a playmate who was killed, where two-thirds of the kids have witnessed a shooting, and where young children play a game they call 'funeral' with the toy blocks in their preschool classroom.
>
> (Garbarino, 1999, pp. 17–18)

This section, however, will concentrate on the effects of armed conflict on children. These go far beyond injury and death to children and cause suffering to many children who are not directly involved. For example, during the Iraqi invasion of Kuwait in 1990, researchers found that children living in Kuwait suffered from anxiety and sleeplessness, loss of appetite, unexplained crying, bed wetting and unexplained physical symptoms such as headaches and stomach problems, even when they had not directly

Two Iraqi Kurdish children in a refugee camp outside Diyarbakir, southeast Turkey.

witnessed acts of violence. There were also rises in social problems such as truancy, poor academic performance and verbal and physical conflicts with teachers and other adults (King, 1999). At the end of the Gulf War, concern shifted away from Kuwaiti and on to Iraqi children, both those in the Kurdish and Shia communities of Iraq, who opposed Saddam Hussein and suffered persecution from state sources, and those who suffered as a result of the lack of food and medical care in the country, caused by the embargo on Iraq. These children too may be seen as casualties of war.

4.1 Violence within communities

READING

The long-standing conflict in Northern Ireland has had many repercussions for children. The effects of the terrorist and counter-terrorist activities have been extensively studied by Ed Cairns, who, in Reading B, looks at how violence affected children during the 1970s and 1980s. This reading was published in 1987, and consequently provides an account of Northern Ireland at a particular time in history. Although the situation is different today (2003), the reading gives a good sense of how children experience the everyday effects of living in a civil conflict. It also emphasizes that, even in a modern, wealthy society such as the UK, war affects children's lives. As you read through it, note the various forms of violence that children suffer, both physical and emotional.

COMMENT

In this extract, Cairns looks at the physical and the psychological effects of war on children. The majority of children in Northern Ireland may not have been subjected to actual physical assault or have witnessed it directly, but Cairns points to the stress and difficulties many children faced under these circumstances. Many families were forced to move when they experienced violence because of their religion or their organizational affiliation. War, even a 'low level' conflict such as Northern Ireland, disrupts the daily patterns of people's lives, making children's families and homes part of the conflict.

The Good Friday Agreement of 1999 was supposed to bring a formal end to much of the terrorist violence in Northern Ireland. However, people have been killed since and sectarianism remains entrenched. Other social problems have also become more visible in Northern Ireland since 1999. Crime has risen, drugs have become more widely available and young people have continued to be caught up in violence. Older youths are subject to arbitrary justice from paramilitary squads who threaten and carry out beatings or knee-cappings as punishment for a range of antisocial offences such as joyriding and taking or supplying drugs. Many of the victims of these are young men under eighteen. In 1999–2000, 47 youths under eighteen were punished by Republican and Loyalist paramilitary groups, compared with 25 in 1997–98 (BBC Online, 2001). These groups claim to keep law and order in their respective communities, believing that these young people deserve their punishment and that, through such acts, order is kept. In other

Catholic youths throwing stones at British army vehicles as they patrol the Ardoyne area of Belfast, 2001.

instances, being from the wrong part of the community in the wrong place is enough to be beaten up. Neville, aged seventeen, expresses this feeling of insecurity well.

> They just want to know if you're a Protestant or a Catholic. And if you're in the wrong area, like, that's you hammered. You might as well book your hospital place now.
>
> (Thomson, 2002, p. 16)

Once again, in a situation such as Northern Ireland, children cannot be labelled simply as the victims of violence. Some children have also been perpetrators, throwing stones at soldiers or calling abuse. Some were simply passive witnesses to violence, while others were more active colluders. Some have been very politicized, seeing the conflict as a struggle of ideologies, others were socialized into violence by their families or their communities at a very young age. As Ciaran, aged seventeen, told researchers about his own induction into violence:

> Time I was sent out, by the father, out to the police, wi' bottles – to throw at them. I was only five or six. I knew, well I knew it was wrong but I thought it was right because that's what I was taught to do.
>
> (Thomson, 2002, p. 16)

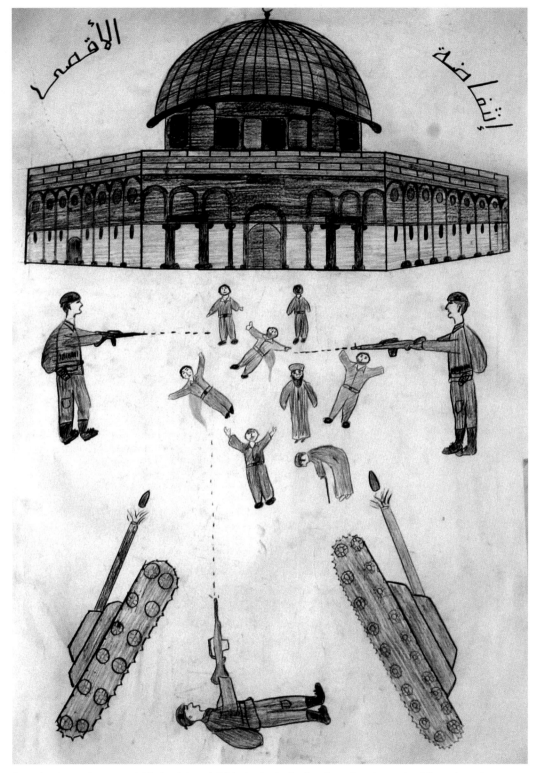

Drawing by a six-year-old Palestinian child in Jenin. It depicts Israeli tanks and soldiers shooting civilians outside the Dome of the Rock, Jerusalem.

Another drawing by a six-year-old Palestinian child. It shows a child with stones in front of a barricade of burning tyres. An Israeli tank is in the foreground while a Palestinian flag flies overhead.

Allow about 20 minutes

ACTIVITY 4   Children's induction into violence

Read the quotation below and make notes on the questions that follow it.

> In Palestine rioting and stone throwing brought the local children to the attention of the world's media. However, far from being a childish behaviour … stone throwing amongst children in Palestine has been elevated to a military art with specific roles assigned to children of different ages. Those aged 7–10 years are given the job of rolling tyres into the middle of the road. These tyres are then set alight in order to disrupt traffic and attract Israeli soldiers. The next youngest age group (11–14 years) use slingshots to attack passing cars. These two groups are used to prepare the ground for … the 'veteran stone throwers'. These young people use large rocks and inflict the worst damage on passing traffic and hence 'they are the most sought after by the Israelis'. This command structure is coordinated by older youths who from the vantage points they occupy determine which cars to attack for example, or when to retreat when the soldiers advance.

(Cairns, 1996, pp. 112–13)

1   Do you see throwing stones at soldiers as 'childish' behaviour or is it an example of political violence among children?

2   Are these Palestinian children victims of violence or perpetrators of it? Should this affect the ways the Israelis treat them?

COMMENT

These children have been raised in an atmosphere of violence and, to them, the Israelis are the enemy. They have suffered both direct violence in the form of family members killed or arrested and indirect violence in the form of prolonged curfews. Given this, it seems naive to dismiss their stone throwing as childish behaviour. The Israeli government, like the UK government, has found it very difficult to know how to react to young boys throwing stones at its soldiers. It is hard to know how politically aware and astute these children are, and therefore how knowingly violent, or whether they have been persuaded to take part by peer pressure or the chance to join in a group activity. It depends largely on your perception of children. If you believe that children are innocent, both of bad intent and of ideological motivation, then stone throwing is simply game playing even when they inflict actual harm. If, however, you believe that it is possible for children to be politically motivated and committed to a cause, then young people throwing stones are taking part in political violence.

There may also be another explanation for throwing stones at soldiers. In the absence of anything else to do, it may occur due to boredom. The children in Gaza and the West Bank have to cope with long curfews, while children in Northern Ireland also express a sense of frustration about their situation and their inability to change it.

> Like something when we throw [things] cos you've nothing to do – the streets are boring … most of the tax money goes on helicopters and paying police. The money could be going on parks and theatres and football grounds and all that there. [I prefer] police out, parks, and all that stuff in.
>
> (Luke, fourteen, quoted in Thomson, 2002, p. 16)

Children who are pictured throwing stones or rioting raise further questions about manipulation, not only by adults within their communities but also by the national and international media. Children may be encouraged to act up for the cameras or their political ideals may not be discussed, leaving their actions uncontexualized. The political beliefs of those who view the images will also alter how these children are seen – whether as nascent terrorists, freedom fighters or vulnerable children playing at war.

4.2 Children and the armed forces

The dual role of children as both perpetrators and victims of violence becomes very clear when looking at child soldiers. Despite international treaties, thousands of children worldwide fight in armies and paramilitary forces. Article 38 of the United Nations Convention on the Rights of the Child (UNCRC) states that no child under the age of fifteen should fight. Supplementary international treaties, such as the 1999 Maputo Declaration on Child Soldiers and the 2000 Optional Protocol to the UNCRC on children in armed conflict, state that children under eighteen should not be involved as combatants in armed conflict. However, in 1999 Amnesty International claimed that there were at least 300,000 children under eighteen actively involved in armed conflict in countries as diverse as Sierra Leone, Liberia, Congo, Sudan, Uganda, Sri Lanka and Burma (Amnesty International, 1999). The increase in availability of smaller, lighter weapons has made it easier for children to go into combat and fight alongside adults. Many others are not actual combatants but are used to plant or clear mines, as reconnaissance, as bearers and suppliers to the front line or as general ancillary workers, cooking, cleaning, keeping guard or delivering food.

Child soldiers in Sierra Leone, Burma and Uganda

Child soldier with a gun in Sierra Leone.

Concern about child soldiers grew in the 1990s, with the conflict in Sierra Leone in particular providing many iconic images of child soldiers. The image of a child soldier is a difficult one. To see a young child with a machine gun or a rocket launcher is to look at a deeply incongruous and ambiguous image of childhood. Is this child a victim or a perpetrator of violence or both? Usually the story told of these children is that they were taken unwillingly by an army or quasi-military group and subjected to indoctrination and intimidation, sometimes given drink and drugs and sent out to kill. Two children from Burma and Uganda recount how they became soldiers.

Zaw Tun, aged fifteen, was forcibly conscripted into the Burmese army

I was recruited by force, against my will. One evening while we were watching a video show in my village three army sergeants came. They checked whether we had identification cards and asked if we wanted to join the army. We explained that we were under age and hadn't got identification cards. But one of my friends said he wanted to join. I said no and came back home that evening but an army recruitment unit arrived next morning at my village and demanded two new recruits.

Those who could not pay 3,000 kyats had to join the army, they said. I could not pay, so altogether 19 of us were recruited in that way and sent to Mingladon [an army training centre].

(BBC World Service Online, 2002)

Susan, aged sixteen, abducted by the Lord's Resistance Army in Uganda

One boy tried to escape [from the rebels], but he was caught ... His hands were tied, and then they made us, the other new captives, kill him with a stick. I felt sick. I knew this boy from before. We were from the same village. I refused to kill him and they told me they would shoot me. They pointed a gun at me, so I had to do it. The boy was asking me, 'Why are you doing this?' I said I had no choice. After we killed him, they made us smear his blood on our arms ... They said we had to do this so we would not fear death and so we would not try to escape ... I still dream about the boy from my village who I killed. I see him in my dreams, and he is talking to me and saying I killed him for nothing, and I am crying.

(Human Rights Watch, 2001)

Not surprisingly, these children tend to downplay their actual involvement in violence. Their recruitment, they claim, was involuntary and when they took part in atrocities they did so out of fear and coercion. In many cases, no doubt, this is true. However, it is also important to note that some children have been willing volunteers, finding in these armies a sense of purpose and comradeship and learning skills of loyalty, teamwork and independence.

The wars in Sierra Leone and Uganda in the 1990s were particularly brutal and it is not surprising that children have been caught up in atrocities. Even so, child soldiers have often provoked particular fear as being exceptionally brutal and without pity or mercy. Children who are recruited into paramilitary or state armies are often brutalized by having seen family members killed. Sometimes they have known nothing other than war and violence. They are seen as easy to manipulate and many have learned to distrust adult authority.

There is therefore ambivalence about child soldiers. While they, and their supporters, claim that they are among war's victims, others have claimed that they are the perpetrators of violence and must be called to account for their actions. Kofi Annan, the Secretary-General of the United Nations, asked the United Nations Security Council in 2002 to approve the prosecution of those child soldiers in Sierra Leone over the age of fifteen who were involved in murder, mutilation and rape (McGreal, 2000).

Children in Cambodia under the Khmer Rouge

In 1975, Pol Pot's army, the Khmer Rouge, took over Cambodia and attempted to enforce an extreme Maoist communist regime, replacing all that went before. They restarted the calendar, renaming 1975 Year Zero. Their regime was murderous and, during the next four years, over 1 million Cambodians were killed and up to another 2 million died from starvation or

The people line up to be put to the sword.

Drawing by a Cambodian child depicting events under Pol Pot's Khmer Rouge, a period that lasted from 1975 to 1979.

exhaustion. The Khmer Rouge emptied the cities of people, forcing everyone to live off the land. Professionals, those who knew a foreign language and, at one time, even those who wore glasses were murdered. Much of this was accomplished by indoctrinating children and forcing them to denounce and kill suspect adults. Family life was discouraged and repressed. Everyone was forced to live in communal work camps, but at the age of eight most children were sent away to live with other children under two or three senior Khmer Rouge officials. Traditional norms of respect for elders were suppressed and the 'Comrade Child' was praised as being 'pure and unsullied by the corrupt past of the adults' (Ponchaud, 1977, p. 143). Special spy units, *Kang Chhlop*, were composed mainly of children and were used to spy on adults. One Cambodian woman recalled the power given to children under the Khmer Rouge:

> In the Pol Pot times children could catch an adult if they thought they had done wrong. They could beat the adult. For example, if an adult was caught stealing fruit a child could tell the soldiers: 'look they are our enemies'. Then the soldiers would set a chair for the child to stand on so that they could beat the adult's head.

(Boyden and Gibbs, 1997, p. 44)

Children rose quickly up the ranks of the Khmer Rouge and it was not unusual for children to be in charge of workcamps at the age of twelve. Camps run by these children became notorious for the extreme and arbitrary violence inflicted on the inmates. Children, even more than adults, appeared particularly cruel. Even after Cambodia was liberated in 1979 by the Vietnamese, there remained a 'residual fear of children' in the country (Boyden and Gibbs, 1997, p. 98).

Children in contemporary rural Cambodia. Despite the tranquillity of this scene, researchers in contemporary Cambodia talk of a 'residual fear' of children caused by the atrocities committed by children under the Khmer Rouge.

4.3 Why shouldn't children fight?

The UNCRC (1989) set the age limit for armed combat at fifteen years old. Many argued that fifteen was too young and inconsistent with the UN definition of a 'child'. An Optional Protocol to the UNCRC was proposed, which aimed to exclude young people under eighteen from involvement in any hostilities and set strict standards for their recruitment into military service. The next reading is an extract from a debate on this issue which appeared in the *New York Review of Books* around the time the optional protocol was being proposed, in 1999.

READING

There are many reasons why, ideally, children should not be allowed to join armies, but there are also reasons why children might want to fight and to protect themselves and their families. In Reading C, John Ryle puts forward a controversial argument about letting children fight and the reasons why, in some instances, they should. His argument is countered by Amnesty International's Martin Macpherson. Which viewpoint do you most agree with? Why?

COMMENT

John Ryle argues that if children are in peril, then they have a right to self-defence and to protect their families. To keep them out of the army may compromise other rights, such as the right to have an opinion, to bodily integrity, to protection of life and property. He is particularly concerned to draw a distinction between voluntary and forced recruitment, claiming that this is more of a problem than age. In contrast, Martin Macpherson argues that children should never fight and sees the distinction between voluntary enrolment and force as untenable. He defines a child as any person under eighteen and feels that this line can, and must, be drawn to protect children from armed conflict. (Note that the UNCRC Optional Protocol on Child Soldiers was formally adopted by the UN General Assembly in May 2000. It has since been signed by a number of countries, but by no means all.)

Part of the idea of childhood innocence is the notion that children should be free from ideological motivation or political involvement. Yet, as John Ryle argues, there may be circumstances in which children should fight for a cause in which they believe. An important case here is that of the role of youth movements against the apartheid regime in South Africa. Children took an active part in the struggle, raising questions about whether, in the face of an illegal and brutal regime, it is morally right for children to fight. Often children were specifically targeted by the police and subjected to arbitrary whippings, detentions, tear-gassing or shootings. Between 1984 and 1986, 300 children were killed by the police, 1,000 wounded, 11,000 detained without trial, 18,000 arrested on charges related to protesting and 173,000 held in police cells (Cairns, 1996, p. 113). Given these statistics, it can be argued that South African children had no choice but to fight back. They were being directly targeted and their actions were in self-defence. Since the end of apartheid, the Truth and Reconciliation Committee has been set up to examine the injustices of the apartheid era. However, rather than celebrating children's resistance and their important role in the struggle, it has reduced many children to the role of victim, looking at crimes against them but not always recognizing their organization, their political commitment or their bravery.

Although the majority of child soldiers are in countries of the South, historically child soldiers and sailors have played an important part in European military history. One of the first acts of the Duke of Wellington when leading troops during the Napoleonic Wars was to put a stop to boys under eighteen (often in fact aged between ten and twelve) buying commissions in the army and leading troops into battle. More recently, in Europe during the First World War, children of fifteen signed up to fight and, even when they were obviously under age, the authorities turned a blind eye to their recruitment. Similarly, towards the end of the Second World War, Nazi Germany conscripted fifteen-year-olds into the army to make up for the numbers lost on the Russian front. There is also a long tradition in the UK of sending children to sea as a form of education and apprenticeship, from all classes – even royal children, such as Edward VII, who was sent to sea at fourteen in 1855.

Allow about 10 minutes

A C T I V I T Y 5   Child soldiers in Britain

In the UK, in 2001, there were 6,000 soldiers under the age of eighteen serving in the armed forces. In March 2002, under pressure from the European Union, the government stated that these soldiers would no longer be sent into combat positions. However, Article 38 of the UNCRC states that fifteen is the minimum age for recruitment and there is no law which forbids children under eighteen to fight. What do you think are the arguments for and against keeping soldiers under eighteen out of armed combat?

C O M M E N T

Until March 2002, the British government argued that, as there was no conscription, serving in the military was voluntary and therefore it was allowing young people the choice to serve their country if they so wished. Critics of this policy pointed to the discrepancy between children being allowed to fight in the UK army at sixteen, while still being considered children under international law. Furthermore, during the Gulf War in 1991, five British child soldiers were killed in action, which many saw as unacceptable. Barry Donnan, a young man who signed up to join the British Army at sixteen and saw combat in the Gulf War at seventeen, clearly sees this policy as potentially damaging to young people.

> Perhaps if I'd been a bit older then, you know I'd probably have had a better chance of getting back to a bit of normality afterwards. And I think, being so young, with so many multiple incidents, effectively, you know you're at a point where … your nature's changing, your character's changing, and I think probably that will just stay with me for the rest of my life … I would say being young … made its differences.

(The Open University, 2003)

These accounts of child soldiers in Asia, Africa and Europe all draw attention to the ambiguous status of young people who take up arms. These ambiguities also surface when deciding how they should be treated. This is the topic of the next section, which looks at strategies for re-integrating child soldiers, especially in Africa.

4.4 Strategies for reintegrating child soldiers

Allow about 10 minutes

A C T I V I T Y 6   **Rehabilitating child soldiers**

Child soldiers in several African countries have been guilty of committing atrocities against civilians. To what extent do you feel that child soldiers ought to be held accountable for their crimes?

C O M M E N T

For many, the rehabilitation of child soldiers is very problematic. The term 'rehabilitation' is itself contested, as it implies that responsibility is removed from the society that generated the violence in the first place and that it is the individual children who are at fault and need to be resocialized. Others have argued that, whatever they have done, they are still children and cannot be held responsible for actions that they did not necessarily understand. However, many of those who have suffered because of the violence of child soldiers believe that they should be tried and punished. There is a great reluctance to see them as anything other than the perpetrators of particularly gruesome acts. As one child soldier from Sierra Leone told a researcher:

> Five years of my life was characterized by cutting limbs, killing, raping and drug abuse. Here I am. I cannot trace my relatives. I beg for food in the streets of Freetown. Even if I find my relatives, who will want to take a child like me? ... My innocence was exploited, my development was violently suppressed, my identity contaminated almost irreparably; my parents and anything that gave me a sense of safety was annihilated.

(International Bureau for Children's Rights, 2000)

The issue of rehabilitating child soldiers is a very fraught one. Successful rehabilitation depends strongly on the circumstances of the war and the actions of the children.

> Communities that have been caught up in war view children's involvement in violence in ways that are contingent on the nature, length and ferocity of the conflict; the choice or lack of choice the young had in participating; the actions they carried out; and the consequences for members of the family. Clearly attitudes to the young who fight against oppression and for liberation differ profoundly from attitudes to the young who kill and maim as members of warring groups.

(Reynolds, 2001)

This second group represents the greatest challenge to those who try to break the cycle of violence and return children to their communities. For example, encouraged by local mosques and churches, some adults in Sierra Leone have become foster parents to former child soldiers, attempting to teach them about family life and to trust adults again. But adults in other communities have not felt able to have child soldiers back among them until they have been disarmed and debriefed by an outside agency. In this instance, healing cannot take place only in the community and a third party is involved. To this end, some agencies have set up camps where children are counselled and reintegration is attempted. This may involve children confronting their victims and being forced to account for themselves and ask for forgiveness. But many of these children also need to come to terms with what happened to them and to forgive those who forced them into becoming child soldiers. In one such centre in Uganda, thirteen-year-old Charles Oranga describes meeting the man who kidnapped him and forced him into becoming a soldier:

> I felt like killing my kidnapper when I first met him … But then I was told that he had only done it because he was forced to – and I later did the same thing as well.

> That made me see the other side: it is not hard to forgive someone when they tell you that. We ended up playing football together. He's not a friend, but I have no hatred anymore.

(Wazir, 1999, p. 1)

At the time of writing, in Uganda and Sierra Leone, such projects are having some success, but the number of children involved is still small. The scale of the problem is also overwhelming. Not only do these children have emotional scars but they often have physical ones too. One project in Sierra Leone removes the tattoos and scars that children were marked with (or in some instances inflicted on themselves) which branded them as members of a particular militia. By getting rid of these markers, it is hoped that children will not be permanently reminded by their bodies of the atrocities that they witnessed and committed.

No single model or method has been found most effective for rehabilitating child soldiers or indeed any children so dramatically affected by violence, especially those caught up in brutal conflicts in Africa and Asia. While Western experts tend to look to therapy and counselling, some commentators have begun to question whether this is an appropriate response. Indeed, many now prefer to emphasize models based on healing and forgiveness rather than counselling or psychological help (see Reynolds, 2001). Community mediation has had some successes and some non-governmental organizations support it as a way of ending the violence that dominates those countries. The role of children themselves in this is also crucial. They must be seen not as passive victims who need to be 'rehabilitated' but as active agents who can rebuild their communities and act as peacemakers in the reintegration process.

However, this is far from straightforward. When resources are scarce, as they usually are in war-torn countries, rehabilitation of child soldiers is often a low priority. When communities have been destroyed, it is impossible to reintegrate a child into a community that no longer exists. Furthermore, many wars in which children are involved do not have a clear ending, so that anxiety remains entrenched. Community mediations and child peacemakers are therefore no panacea. They must be seen as one more strategy alongside rebuilding communities and countries destroyed by war, supporting people's attempts to work and to gain education for their children. Helping child soldiers should be seen in the context of the resources that a country has and the way it chooses to spend them.

SUMMARY OF SECTION 4

- War affects many aspects of society and therefore all children in societies at war are affected by violence, even if they do not experience violence directly.
- Children are involved in armed conflict in many countries, not only in the South. In Northern Ireland, children have suffered as a consequence of the military and paramilitary presence.
- Children can be targeted directly by military and paramilitary groups and be either forced to become involved or punished for not doing so.
- Some child soldiers join for ideological reasons or to protect their homes and families.
- It is very difficult to reintegrate children into their community if they are perceived to have been responsible for violence against it. Western-style counselling has proved inappropriate in many instances. Community reintegration programmes, where the emphasis has been placed on healing and forgiveness, have had greater success in some African countries.

5 CONCLUSION

This chapter has concentrated on three main situations where violence affects children and on the variety of the roles that children play: victim, perpetrator, witness, colluder and peacemaker. It has looked at individual and social experiences of violence, examining what is normal and abnormal child behaviour and whether violence is innate or learned. It has also broadened out these discussions to look at the ways child violence is differently understood in a range of cultural contexts. What is clear from this examination is that children at both a local and a global level experience multiple and complex forms of violence which shape their experiences of childhood, and which constitute, for many, an extreme form of adversity.

This chapter and the previous two have looked at three different forms of adversity as they affect children. Clearly there is an overlap between them: children suffer health consequences as a result of war and they may become impoverished if they are forced to flee their homes as a result of armed conflict. Similarly, poverty can lead to civil unrest and uprising which in turn place children at risk from armed conflict. In the final two chapters of this book, we shall be looking at the ways in which adults and children have attempted to alleviate these afflictions in their lives and the measures they have taken to survive these adversities.

REFERENCES

AMNESTY INTERNATIONAL (1999) *Child Soldiers: one of the worst abuses of child labour*, London, Amnesty International (AI Index IOR 42/01/99).

BANDURA, A. (1977) *Social Learning Theory*, Englewood Cliffs, NJ, Prentice-Hall.

BBC ONLINE (2001) *Paramilitary-style attacks double*, http://www.news.bbc.co.uk/hi/english/uk/northern_ireland/newsid_1503000/1503496.stm (accessed 9 July 2002).

BBC ONLINE (2002) *We made a difference!* http://www.bbc.co.uk/education/schools/getinvolved/casestudies/malory.shtml (accessed 17 January 2002).

BBC WORLD SERVICE ONLINE (2002) *Children of Conflict: child soldiers*, http://www.bbc.co.uk/worldservice/people/features/childrensrights/childrenofconflict (accessed 15 January 2002).

BLURTON JONES, N. (1972) *Ethological Studies of Child Behaviour*, Cambridge, Cambridge University Press.

BOYDEN, J. and GIBBS, S. (1997) *Children of War*, Geneva, United Nations Research Institute for Social Development.

BULLYING ONLINE (2002) *Children's Problem Page*, http://www.bullying.co.uk/children/pupil_problems.htm (accessed 15 January 2002).

BURR, R. (2000) *Understanding Children's Rights,* Unpublished PhD thesis, Brunel University.

CAIRNS, E. (1996) *Children and Political Violence*, Oxford, Blackwell.

CHAGNON, N. (1968) *Yanamamo: the fierce people,* New York, Holt, Rinehart and Winston.

COLE, M. and COLE, S. (1996) *The Development of Children*. New York, W. H. Freeman and Company.

DURKIN, K. (1995) *Developmental Social Psychology*, Oxford, Blackwell.

GARBARINO, J. (1999) *Lost Boys*, New York, The Free Press.

HECHT, T. (1998) *At Home in the Street: street children of Northeast Brazil*, Cambridge, Cambridge University Press.

HUMAN RIGHTS WATCH (2001) *The Voices of Child Soldiers*, http://www.hrw.org/campaigns/crp/voices.htm (accessed 15 January 2002).

INTERNATIONAL BUREAU FOR CHILDREN'S RIGHTS (2000) *Exploring International Standards Relating to Children Affected By Conflict*, (Draft) Judgement of the International Tribunal For Children's Rights, 3–6 April, Colchester, England.

KING, E. (1999) *Looking into the Lives of Children: a world-wide view*, Albert Park, Australia, James Nicholas Publishers.

KORBIN, J. (1981) *Child Abuse and Neglect: cross-cultural perspectives*, Berkeley, University of California Press.

MARR, N. and FIELD, T. (2001) *Bullycide. Death at Playtime: an exposé of child suicide caused by bullying*, London, Success Unlimited.

McGREAL, C. (2000) 'Annan wants UN to try teenagers for war crimes', *Guardian*, 7 October.

MILLS, M. (2001) *Challenging Violence in Schools*, Buckingham, Open University Press.

MONTGOMERY, H. (2003) 'Children in time and place' in WOODHEAD, M. and MONTGOMERY, H. (eds) *Understanding Childhood: an interdisciplinary approach*, Chichester, John Wiley and Sons Ltd/The Open University (Book 1 of the Open University course U212 *Childhood*).

NATIONAL SOCIETY FOR THE PREVENTION OF CRUELTY TO CHILDREN (2002) *Call for National Strategy on Child Deaths*, http://www.nspcc.org.uk/html/information/callfornationalstrategyonchilddeaths.htm (accessed 1 May 2002).

OHSAKO, T. (1999) 'The developing world' in SMITH, P. K., MORITA, Y., JUNGER-TAS, J., OLWEUS, D., CATALANO, R. and SLEE, P. (eds) *The Nature of School Bullying: a cross-national perspective*, London, Routledge.

OLWEUS, D. (1993) *Bullying at School: what we know and what we can do*, Oxford, Blackwell.

THE OPEN UNIVERSITY (2003) U212 *Childhood*, Audio 8, Band 4, 'Child soldiers', Milton Keynes, The Open University.

PATTERSON, G. R., DE BARYSHE, D. and RAMSAY, E. (1989) 'A developmental perspective on anti-social behaviour', *American Psychologist*, **44**, pp. 329–35.

PONCHAUD, F. (1977) *Cambodia Year Zero*, London, Penguin.

REYNOLDS, P. (2001) 'Cultural Norms and Morals Regarding the Protection of Children from Warfare', paper presented at the conference 'Filling knowledge gaps: a research agenda on the impact of armed conflict on children', Florence, 2–4 July.

SCHAFFER, H. R. (1996) *Social Development*, Oxford, Blackwell.

SMITH, P., BOWERS, L., BINNEY, V. and COWIE, H. (1999) 'Relationships of children involved in bully/victim problems at school' in WOODHEAD, M., FAULKNER, D. and LITTLETON, K. (eds) *Making Sense of Social Development*, London, Routledge/The Open University.

THOMSON, R. (2002) 'Presentation to seminar on children, violence and violence prevention', co-hosted: Forum Children and Violence/ESRC Violence Research Programme, April.

WAKE, C. S. (1878) *The Evolution of Morality*, London, Trübner and Co.

WAZIR, B. (1999) 'Africa's child soldiers face their victims', London, *Observer*, 5 December.

WOODHEAD, M. (1999) 'Combatting child labour: listen to what the children say', *Childhood*, **6**(1), pp. 27–49.

Sweden

Dan Olweus

Definition of bullying

A student is being bullied or victimized when he or she is exposed, repeatedly and over time, to negative actions on the part of one or more other students. It is a negative action when someone intentionally inflicts, or attempts to inflict, injury or discomfort upon another – basically what is implied in the definition of aggressive behavior (Olweus, 1973b; Berkowitz, 1993). Negative actions can be carried out by physical contact, by words, or in other ways, such as making faces or mean gestures, and intentional exclusion from a group. Although children or youths who engage in bullying very likely vary in their degree of awareness of how the bullying is perceived by the victim, most or all of them probably realize that their behavior is at least somewhat painful or unpleasant for the victim …

   In this context, it is also natural to consider briefly the relationship between bullying and teasing. In the everyday social interactions among peers in school, there occurs a good deal of (also recurrent) teasing of a playful and relatively friendly nature – which in most cases cannot be considered bullying. On the other hand, when the repeated teasing is of a degrading and offensive character, and, in particular, is continued in spite of clear signs of distress or opposition on the part of the target, it certainly qualifies as bullying. Here it is thus important to try and distinguish between malignant and more friendly, playful teasing, although the line between them is sometimes blurred and the perception of the situation may to some extent depend on the perspective taken, that of the target or of the perpetrator(s) …

Characteristics of typical victims

The typical victims are more anxious and insecure than students in general. Further, they are often cautious, sensitive, and quiet. When attacked by other students, they commonly react by crying (at least in the lower grades) and withdrawal. In addition, victims suffer from low self-esteem, and they have a negative view of themselves and their situation. They often look upon themselves as failures and feel stupid, ashamed, and unattractive.

   The victims are lonely and abandoned at school. As a rule, they do not have a single good friend in their class. They are not aggressive or teasing in their behavior, however, and accordingly, one cannot explain the bullying as a consequence of the victims themselves being provocative to their peers (see below). These children often have a negative attitude toward violence and use of violent means. If they are boys, they are likely to be physically weaker than boys in general (Olweus, 1978) …

   In-depth interviews with parents of victimized boys indicate that these boys were characterized by a certain cautiousness and sensitivity from an early age (Olweus, 1993). Boys displaying such characteristics (perhaps combined with physical weakness) are likely to have had difficulty in asserting themselves in the peer group and may have been somewhat disliked by their age mates … At the same time, it is obvious that the repeated harassment by peers must have considerably increased their anxiety, insecurity, and generally negative evaluation of themselves. In sum, the typical reaction patterns or personality traits characterizing children who have been identified as victims (and who, by definition, have been exposed to bullying for some time) are likely to be both a cause, and a consequence, of the bullying.

… There is also another, clearly smaller group of victims, the *provocative victims*, who are characterized by a combination of both anxious and aggressive reaction patterns. These students often have problems with concentration, and behave in ways that may cause irritation and tension for those around them. Some of these students may be characterized as hyperactive. It is not uncommon that their behavior provokes many students in the class, thus resulting in negative reactions from a large part of, or even the entire class. The dynamics of bully/victim problems in a class with provocative victims differ in part from problems in a class with passive victims (Olweus, 1978).

A follow-up study of two groups of boys (Olweus, 1993) who had or had not been victimized by their peers in school (from grades 6 through 9) shows that the former victims had 'normalized' in many ways as young adults at age 23 … In two respects, however, the former victims had fared much worse than their non-victimized peers: they were more likely to be depressed and had poorer self-esteem. The pattern of findings clearly suggested that this was a consequence of the earlier, persistent victimization which had left its mental scars on their minds.

Characteristics of typical bullies

A distinctive characteristic of typical bullies is their aggression toward peers – this is implied in the definition of a bully. But bullies are often aggressive toward adults as well, both teachers and parents. Generally, bullies have a more positive attitude toward violence than students in general. Further, they are often characterized by impulsivity and a strong need to dominate others. They have little empathy with victims of bullying. If they are boys, they are likely to be physically stronger than boys in general, and the victims in particular (Olweus, 1978).

A commonly held view among psychologists and psychiatrists is that individuals with an aggressive and tough behavior pattern are actually anxious and insecure 'under the surface.' The assumption that the bullies have an underlying insecurity has been tested in several of my own studies, also using 'indirect' methods such as stress hormones (adrenaline and noradrenaline) and projective techniques. There was nothing in the results to support the common view, but rather pointed in the opposite direction: the bullies had unusually little anxiety and insecurity, or were roughly average on such dimensions (Olweus, 1981, 1984, 1986; see also Pulkkinen and Tremblay, 1992). They did not suffer from poor self-esteem.

These conclusions apply to the bullies as a group (as compared with groups of control boys and victims). The results do not imply that there cannot be individual bullies who are both aggressive and anxious.

It should also be emphasized that there are students who participate in bullying but who do not usually take the initiative – these may be labeled *passive bullies*, *followers*, or *henchmen*. A group of passive bullies is likely to be fairly mixed and may also contain insecure and anxious students (Olweus, 1973a, 1978) …

Bullies are often surrounded by a small group of two or three peers who support them and seem to like them (Cairns, Cairns, Neckerman, Gest and Gariépy, 1988). The popularity of the bullies decreases, however, in the higher grades and is considerably less than average in grade 9 (around age 16). Nevertheless, the bullies do not seem to reach the low level of popularity that characterizes the victims …

As regards the possible psychological sources underlying bullying behavior, the pattern of empirical findings suggests at least three, partly interrelated motives (in particular for male bullies who have so far been studied more extensively). First, the bullies have a strong need for power and dominance; they seem to enjoy being 'in control' and to subdue others. Second, considering the family conditions under which many of them have been reared (see below), it is natural to assume that they have developed a certain degree of hostility toward the environment; such feelings and impulses may make them derive satisfaction from inflicting injury and suffering upon other individuals. Finally, there is an 'instrumental component' to their behavior. The bullies often coerce their victims to provide them with money, cigarettes, beer, and other things of value (see also Patterson, Littman and Bricker, 1967). In addition, it is obvious that aggressive behavior is in many situations rewarded with prestige (e.g. Bandura, 1973) …

Development of an aggressive reaction pattern

In light of the characterization of the bullies as having an aggressive reaction pattern – that is, they display aggressive behavior in many situations – it becomes important to examine the question: What kind of rearing and other conditions during childhood are conducive to the development of an aggressive reaction pattern? Very briefly, the following four factors have been found to be particularly important (based chiefly on research with boys; for details, see Olweus, 1980; see also Loeber and Stouthamer-Loeber, 1986):

- The basic emotional attitude of the primary caretaker(s) toward the child during early years (usually the mother). A negative emotional attitude, characterized by lack of warmth and involvement, increases the risk that the child will later become aggressive and hostile toward others.

- Permissiveness for aggressive behavior by the child. If the primary caretaker is generally permissive and 'tolerant' without setting clear limits on aggressive behavior toward peers, siblings, and adults, the child's aggression level is likely to increase.

- Use of power-assertive child-rearing methods such as physical punishment and violent emotional outbursts. Children of parents who make frequent use of these methods are likely to become more aggressive than the average child. 'Violence begets violence.' We can summarize these results by stating that too little love and care and too much 'freedom' in childhood are conditions that contribute strongly to the development of an aggressive reaction pattern.

• Finally, the temperament of the child. A child with an active and hotheaded temperament is more likely to develop into an aggressive youngster than a child with a quieter temperament. The effect of this factor is less powerful than those of the two first-mentioned conditions.

These are main trends. In individual cases, other factors such as the presence of an alcoholic and brutal father may have been of crucial importance, and the causal pattern may appear partly different …

It should also be pointed out that the aggression levels of the boys participating in the analyses above (Olweus, 1980) were not related to the socioeconomic conditions of their families such as parental income level, length of education, and social class. Similarly, there were no (or only very weak) relations between the four childhood factors discussed and the socioeconomic conditions of the family (Olweus, 1981).

References

BANDURA, A. (1973) *Aggression: a social learning analysis*, Englewood Cliffs, NJ, Prentice-Hall.

BERKOWITZ, L. (1993) *Aggression: its causes, consequences, and control*, New York, McGraw-Hill.

CAIRNS, R. B., CAIRNS, B. D., NECKERMAN, H. J., GEST, S. D. and GARIÉPY, J. L. (1988) 'Social networks and aggressive behavior: peer support or peer rejection?', *Developmental Psychology*, **24**, pp. 815–23.

LOEBER, R. and STOUTHAMER-LOEBER, M. (1986) 'Family factors as correlates and predictors of conduct problems and juvenile delinquency' in TONRY, M. and MORRIS, N. (eds) *Crime and Justice*, Vol. 7, Chicago, IL, University of Chicago Press.

OLWEUS, D. (1973a) *Hackkycklingar och översittare. Forskning om skolmobbning*, Stockholm, Almqvist and Wicksell.

OLWEUS, D. (1973b) 'Personality and aggression' in COLE, J. K. and JENSEN, D. D. (eds), *Nebraska Symposium on Motivation 1972*, Lincoln, University of Nebraska Press.

OLWEUS, D. (1978) *Aggression in the schools: bullies and whipping boys*, Washington DC, Hemisphere Press (Wiley).

OLWEUS, D. (1980) 'Familial and temperamental determinants of aggressive behavior in adolescent boys: a causal analysis', *Developmental Psychology*, **16**, pp. 644–60.

OLWEUS, D. (1981) 'Bullying among school-boys' in CANTWELL, N. (ed.), *Children and Violence*, Stockholm, Akademilitteratur.

OLWEUS, D. (1984) 'Aggressors and their victims: bullying at school' in FRUDE, N. and GAULT, H. (eds) *Disruptive Behavior in Schools*, New York, Wiley.

OLWEUS, D. (1986) 'Aggression and hormones: behavioral relationship with testosterone and adrenaline' in OLWEUS, D., BLOCK, J. and RADKE-YARROW, M. (eds) *Development of Antisocial and Prosocial Behavior*, New York, Academic Press.

OLWEUS, D. (1993) 'Victimization by peers: antecedents and long-term outcomes' in RUBIN, K. H. and ASENDORF, J. B. (eds) *Social Withdrawal, Inhibition, and Shyness in Childhood*, Hillsdale, NJ, Erlbaum.

PATTERSON, G. R., LITTMAN, R. A. and BRICKER, W. (1967) 'Assertive behavior in children: a step toward a theory of aggression', *Monographs of the Society for Research in Child Development*, **32**, pp. 1–43.

PULKKINEN, L. and TREMBLAY, R. E. (1992) 'Patterns of boys' social adjustment in two cultures and at different ages: a longitudinal perspective', *International Journal of Behavioral Development*, **15**, pp. 527–53.

Source

OLWEUS, D. (1999) 'Sweden' in P. K. SMITH, Y. MORITA, J. JUNGER-TAS, D. OLWEUS, R. CATALANO and P. SLEE (eds) *The Nature of School Bullying: a cross-national perspective*, London, Routledge.

READING B

Children and the Northern Ireland conflict

Ed Cairns

Bombs kill children too

Mention the impact of violence upon children in Northern Ireland and what immediately springs to mind is the psychological impact of violence on children. However, before going on to examine this popular and relatively well researched topic it is necessary to remember what people appear to have forgotten, that the violence in Northern Ireland kills children too. Perhaps this is something that people want to forget. It has been said that the greatest taboo subject of our modern technological age is death, particularly the death of a child. Maybe this accounts for the apparent lack of interest in the physical impact violence has had on children in Northern Ireland.

Another possible explanation for the lack of interest in this topic is the difficulty in obtaining information about the child victims of violence. Indeed, despite the fact that the Northern Irish conflict is perhaps one of the most intensely reported, most closely studied conflicts ever, no one knows exactly how many children have died, how many have been maimed, and how many injured. Murray (1982) has estimated that between 1969 and 1977 some 103 people under the age of seventeen years have been killed (or 8 per cent of the total) while the present author estimates that between 1969 and 1983 some 150 children under fourteen years have been killed or injured. These latter figures are at best however 'guestimates'. The reason for this lack of hard data is, first, that official statistics do not give a breakdown of victims in terms of age (or indeed in terms of sex or religion). The only other possible source is press reports. But here, as indeed with official statistics, there are particular problems. Often, for example, a victim may be identified as a schoolboy or a schoolgirl without an exact age being given. A headline therefore that states 'Schoolboy shot in murder bid' could mean that a five-year-old has been shot or an eighteen-year-old. Yet another difficulty in compiling statistics in this area is deciding whether a child has really been a victim of the troubles or not. And finally there is perhaps the most sensitive issue of all, at least as far as local reporting is concerned, that is the question of attributing blame.

All these problems are well illustrated when one attempts to examine what information is available on children who have been killed and injured over the course of the last fifteen years. For example, even deciding who exactly the first child victim was is not a simple task. Was it, as some would claim, the five-year-old girl killed in February 1971 when she was knocked down by an army vehicle? Or was she simply the victim of a simple everyday traffic accident? Such accidents were of course by no means rare, particularly when at one time thousands of British troops, plus their vehicles (many of them gigantic armoured personnel carriers with restricted vision for the driver) were crowded into the narrow streets of Belfast and Derry. If this child was not the first victim then that dubious honour must fall to the seventeenth-month-old girl who, in that phrase which so well describes the position of children in Northern Ireland was, in September 1971, 'caught in crossfire' during an attack on an army patrol in Belfast. This incident illustrates the problem involved in deciding who to blame for such deaths.

Was this the fault of the army for opening fire when children were nearby, or was it the fault of the IRA for attacking the army in the first place? A sterile argument it could be suggested, yet one which on many occasions has generated much heat in Northern Ireland, particularly where the deaths of children have been concerned.

Typical of this search for blame perhaps is the case of Brian Stewart. Brian was thirteen years old when he was shot in the head by a rubber bullet. He died six days later. At the time the army claimed he was part of a rioting mob which attached a foot patrol of soldiers. Local residents however claim that when Brian was shot no rioting was going on. Since then his mother, aided by the National Council for Civil Liberties, has been urging the European Human Rights Commission to find that the British Government was in breach of the human rights convention by using rubber bullets (now replaced by plastic bullets) as riot control weapons. Once again this is not an isolated incident, several children have been killed or injured by rubber or plastic bullets often in contentious circumstances. Sadly, this case also illustrates another fact of life in Northern Ireland. And that is that in most cases, victims of the violence, be they adults or children, are soon forgotten by all except their immediate family. Only those children whose deaths in some way became a *cause célèbre*, such as Brian Stewart, are still remembered today …

Sources of stress

For every child who has been killed or injured in the troubles there have been many more who at some time must have felt their life was threatened and more still who have had to witness the horror of death or injury inflicted upon others. Often the other has been a close friend or relative. This is because, as the pattern of violence has changed slowly but surely over the years, deaths and injuries have resulted less from street rioting or even bomb explosions and more from single acts of assassination. Many of these assassinations have taken place at the victim's place of work or, more often, in his (most victims have been men) own home. As a result hundreds of children in Northern Ireland have had to witness their father's murder. For example, according to press reports, the most recent assassination victim at the time of writing [mid-1980s] had just seconds before his death been holding his three-year-old daughter in his arms. On another occasion a whole classroom of elementary school children watched as their school teacher was gunned down and on more than one occasion school bus drivers – easy targets in the rural areas where they are employed – have been similarly dealt with in front of their young charges.

Not a lot of information is available about children who have been indirectly victimised in this way either by being forced to witness terror at first hand or by themselves being terrorised. Researchers are obviously sensitive to the fact that such children may, for some time, be in a delicate psychological state which probing or questioning could easily exacerbate. However, some information is available though often obtained by indirect means. For example, McKeown (1973) in the course of a survey of all post-primary schools in Northern Ireland asked the question, 'Has there been any harassment of pupils on their way to and from school?' Over 70 per cent of the 255 schools polled responded and of these 51 per cent reported that indeed such harassment had occurred. In fact forty-eight schools reported assaults on pupils including fifty seriously injured and one child killed.

Nor has harassment simply been confined to children coming and going to school. The most serious form of harassment during the early 1970s was centered around the place where children have the most right to feel safe – their home. With the outbreak of street violence at the beginning of the troubles many families found themselves living in the 'wrong' area – that is in an area where, in religious terms, they were in a minority. In this situation these families often became scapegoats for the intensely felt anger of the time. Thus 'intimidation' as it became known was for a time one of Belfast's most serious problems. This phenomenon has been graphically described by Darby and Morris (1973), who explain that in many cases intimidation took the form of actual physical violence. Children or sometimes pets might be attacked, mothers or fathers beaten or jostled, eggs, stones, petrol bombs or bullets directed through windows or doors, homes ransacked, furniture piled up in the streets and burned and in some cases the actual houses themselves were burnt down. In other cases threats were simply used, perhaps in the form of anonymous letters or phone calls or slogans were painted on walls. More subtle intimidation might take the form of neighbours becoming less friendly, for example refusing to talk to housewives at the shops, not allowing children to play with their friends and so on.

The result of all of this was what Darby and Morris (1973) have described as 'the largest enforced population movement in Europe since the Second World War.' During the period August 1969 to February 1973 they estimate that somewhere between 8,000 and 15,000 families moved home as the result of intimidation. In other words, somewhere between 30,000 to 60,000 people were forced to leave their homes in the Greater Belfast area alone. Many of these refugees were children and Murray and Boal (1980) in their research attempted to focus specifically on families with children who moved home because of intimidation. To do this, they compared those households with children who moved home between 1969 and 1972 either because of intimidation, or for other more normal reasons. Of the 353 households in their study, about one third had moved because of intimidation, broadly defined. Of these intimidated families the majority (66 per cent) had moved because of direct attack or threat either to their home or members of their family. The remaining households in the group indicated that they had moved simply because of the general level of violence in their area. And if the results of this survey are representative then they suggest that children may have accounted for well over half of those forced to flee their homes at this time. This is because, while only 10 per cent of the 'ordinary' households had four or more children, 35 per cent of the intimidated families fell into this category. Further, the intimidated households, particularly those directly threatened, were more likely to be single-parent families and also more likely to be working-class families with younger children. Additionally while 'ordinary' movers tended to remain within the same local area within Greater Belfast, and therefore presumably closer to schools, family and friends, the intimidated more often than not were forced to move to another district often Murray and Boal (1980) noted, not even adjacent to their original district. Thus for the intimidated, due to a combination of having younger children and the great distance moved, a change of school was more often involved. Finally, and perhaps not surprisingly, the mothers of the families that were forced to move were more likely to express dissatisfaction with their new environment than did the mothers from other families.

References

Darby, J. and Morris, G. (1973) 'Intimidation in housing', *Community Forum*, **2**, pp. 7–11.

McKeown, M. (1973) 'Civil unrest: secondary schools survey', *The Northern Teacher*, Winter, pp. 39–42.

Murray, R. (1982) 'Political violence in Northern Ireland 1969–1977', in Boal, F. W. and Douglas, J. N. H. (eds) *Integration and Division: geographical perspectives on the Northern Ireland problem*, London, Academic Press.

Murray, R. C. and Boal, F. W. (1980) 'Forced residential mobility in Belfast 1969–72' in Harbison, J. and Harbison, J. (eds) *A Society Under Stress: children and young people in Northern Ireland*, Somerset, Open Books.

Source

CAIRNS, E. (1987) *Caught in the Crossfire: children and the Northern Ireland conflict*, Syracuse, Appletree Press.

Children at arms

John Ryle

In the 1980s the standard image to emerge from the world's disaster zones was a skeletal child with despairing eyes, clutching the hand of an aid worker. Soon this was displaced by another stereotype, a bearded guerrilla fighter brandishing an AK-47, its forward-curving magazine silhouetted above his head. Today these two images have morphed into the figure of the child soldier, a gun-toting sub-teen with wrap-around shades and a threatening demeanour, a child who is clearly not on his way to school.

The kid-with-a-Kalashnikov is already a cliché, and picture editors are now likely to demand more arresting images from the battlefield (a seven year old with a rocket-propelled grenade launcher, say, preferably a girl). But the child-at-arms is still the defining image of the troubled lands of the South, of the realm of war and hunger. He or she has come to represent a whole array of things that have gone wrong with the world: the loss of innocence, the destruction of youth, the collapse of order, the continuing spread of war.

Because we sentimentalise children and disprize soldiers, the very term 'child soldier' sets up a disturbing resonance. Formerly we felt sorry and angry about the fate of children in disaster zones. Now we feel sorry and fearful. According to a report from Amnesty International, *In the Firing Line*, there are at least 300,000 under-18s actively engaged in combat, in 36 armed conflicts round the world, a dozen of them in Africa. Such young people are the focus of a campaign by Amnesty and other human rights organizations to outlaw their participation in armed conflict. The proposal is to expand the UN Convention on the Rights of the Child to include a new protocol banning military recruitment below the age of eighteen (the current limit is fifteen). This move is opposed by a number of countries, including the United States and Britain, where sixteen year olds are still recruited into the armed forces.

Like others of my generation growing up in England in the 1960s and 1970s I was a child soldier myself, from the age of fourteen to sixteen, a less than willing recruit to a ramshackle organization known as the Combined Cadet Force. We were, in theory, potential conscripts in the event of the reintroduction of national service. I was also a member of Amnesty International. On Thursdays I learned to shoot; on Saturdays I rattled a collection box outside the school chapel. Since then I have worked as an anthropologist and aid worker in various African countries. A day a week playing war games as a schoolboy does not, of course, qualify you to understand what it is like to be a bush fighter, but talking to trigger-happy teenage sentries in Uganda, Somalia, Sudan and elsewhere has made me come to doubt that these *kidogos* – little ones – to use the Swahili term widespread in East and Central Africa, see their situation in the terms that human rights researchers do, any more than I did when I was a military cadet. I doubt that they even accept that they are children. And, in the case of seventeen year olds, I am not sure they are wrong.

Despite the near universal adoption by governments of the existing Child Rights Convention (the United States and Somalia share the distinction of being the only countries in the world that have not ratified it) the definition of childhood is by no means as universal as the Convention implies. At the start of the war in Sudan most of the senior class in the secondary school in the town where I had worked went to the bush to join the Southern rebel army. These sixteen and seventeen year olds were from a pastoralist culture where young men were traditionally expected to be warriors. Their uneducated younger brothers in the village had most likely already been initiated into adulthood, a rite of passage that can occur in Nilotic societies at any age after puberty. Although Southern Sudanese are quite as shocked as we are by ten or eleven year olds in the line of battle (such things have come to pass as the war has become more widespread and brutal), they do not necessarily consider it inappropriate for a sixteen year old to bear arms.

Faced with the horrors of the current wars in Africa and elsewhere it seems churlish to question the Amnesty Campaign. It is certainly imperative to reduce the dreadful abuse of children in conflict, both as victims and as perpetrators. But it is also necessary to consider the wisdom of trying to control these evils by expanding the definition of childhood. Africa is a young continent, demographically speaking. Most of its inhabitants are under eighteen. That is to say, the majority of Africans are children, in terms of the UN convention. But there are many places where a seventeen year old would no longer be considered a child, and might well be expected to take on the role of an adult, quite possibly the head of a household. For many such, as the Amnesty report acknowledges, the choice is likely to be soldiering or starvation. In Africa, when there is no state to protect you, a gun may be the only way to ensure that you and your family have food – and that someone else doesn't take it away from you.

It's a shame – it's more than a shame – but if I were a seventeen year old in Southern Sudan, say, or Somalia today, I would get myself a gun as soon as I could. I'd join a guerrilla force or a militia – whatever it took. And if I were the responsible adult in my family it would be not just my right, but my obligation to acquire the means to defend myself and my weaker relatives. If a foreigner – or anyone else – told me that I was a child, and therefore had to be protected from military service, I would laugh at them as people who understood nothing.

The proposed extension of the UN Convention risks jeopardizing, in the name of children's rights, this right to self-defence, a right which may include bearing arms. Western countries with representative governments have, in many cases, quite properly legislated this right away; but the situation is different where there is no state, where there is no other source of security …

Youths with guns may well become monsters; they are liable to terrorize, rather than defend, local people. It would be a far better thing if they could learn the arts of peace. But none of this is an argument for forcing seventeen year olds into the Procrustean bed of the Child Rights Convention. Human rights campaigners need more realistic and culturally convergent ways of tackling the problem. Transparency in the arms trade is the first desideratum – and stricter controls on it the second. With respect to rights, the key issue when considering the involvement in military activity of sixteen year olds and over is not their age; it is whether they are volunteers or not. Many child soldiers are forcibly recruited and this, of course, is a manifest abuse. But it is the fact of conscription that is the issue, not chronological age. Whether the victims are sixteen or eighteen – or twenty-one – is of lesser importance. Most armies in the world, not just in Africa, would be in breach of the new age limit on recruitment that is proposed in the additional protocol to the Convention on the Rights of the Child.

Although there is undoubtedly a case for establishing principles of good practice in military recruitment, principles that well-ordered countries can aspire to, the danger of enacting them into international law, a body of law that is already more honoured in the breach than the observance, is that they will distract from the more fundamental and unambiguous issue of forced recruitment. Forced recruitment is an issue that everyone, combatant and human rights worker, should be able to agree on. The right that must be asserted is the right not to be forced to fight. To do this is enough of a struggle in itself.

Post Script

Letter to the Editors of the New York Review from Martin Macpherson of Amnesty

John Ryle is mistaken when he says Amnesty International is seeking to expand the definition of childhood in its campaign on children in armed conflict. The United Nations Convention on the Rights of the Child, an international human rights treaty ratified by 191 countries (only the US and the collapsed state of Somalia have not ratified), defines childhood in Article 1 as '*every human being below the age of eighteen years unless, under the law applicable to the child, majority is attained earlier*' and increasingly international law uses the benchmark of eighteen years as the age below which special protection should be afforded.

The Convention on the Rights of the Child in Article 19 enshrines the right of those under eighteen to protection '*from all forms of physical or mental violence, injury or abuse ...*' although Article 38, which deals specifically with children in situations of armed conflict, establishes fifteen, not eighteen, years as the minimum age for recruitment into armed forces of states or parties and participation in hostilities. Many governments, UN agencies, the Red Cross and Red Crescent Movement, and non-governmental organizations, such as those supporting the Coalition to Stop the Use of Child Soldiers, which are seeking to raise the age of recruitment into armed forces and participation in hostilities, are simply trying to correct an anomaly in the convention and not redefine childhood.

John Ryle's review also attempts to justify recruitment of children into armed forces providing recruitment is voluntary. Such a position is simplistic as the distinction between forced and voluntary recruitment is often imprecise and ambiguous. Children may join armed forces for a range of reasons, including family connections, lack of alternative employment opportunities, a parental belief that the child will benefit from a period of military discipline, peer pressure, adventure, a desire for revenge, or ideological beliefs. But regardless of how children are recruited, the treatment of child soldiers is often abusive, and mentally and physically hazardous in itself. Even with regular government armed forces children are often subject to 'toughening-up regimes' which may be detrimental to their mental and physical well-being, as well as to punishments which can lead to death or permanent physical or mental injuries …

Ryle's argument that any attempt to protect children's rights is to force them into 'the Procrustean bed of the child rights convention' is disturbing. Human rights standards – whether for adults, children, women, refugees, or any other group – are based on the concepts of universality and nondiscrimination. To argue against this demonstrates a fundamental lack of understanding of the role of all human rights standards which seek to provide equal protection for all.

In his review John Ryle gives examples of child soldiers on the continent of Africa to support his argument that the definition of childhood is not universally accepted and argues for more realistic and culturally convergent ways of resolving the child soldier problem. And yet, it was the Organization of African Unity (OAU) in 1990 which adopted the African Charter on the Rights and Welfare of the Child, which defines a child as 'every human being below the age of 18 years' and prohibits the recruitment of children …

The involvement of children in armed forces is not inevitable. There is no excuse or acceptable argument for abusing and exploiting children as combatants. The recruitment and participation of children in armed conflicts is a decision made by governments or by leaders of armed opposition groups. It is unforgivable that children and young persons are encouraged to commit barbaric acts as well as being the victims of grave human rights abuses. It is time to exclude children from participating in war, and the optional protocol to the Convention on the Rights of the Child on the Involvement of Children in Armed Conflict which raises to eighteen years the minimum age for participation in hostilities into armed forces is a significant contribution to this goal.

Martin Macpherson
Adviser, International Organization
Amnesty International
London

Source

RYLE, J. (1999) 'Children at arms', *New York Review of Books*, New York, **46**(4), 4 March.

Chapter 5

Intervening in children's lives

Heather Montgomery

CONTENTS

When you have studied this chapter, you should be able to:

1   Give reasons why children's well-being concerns all of society rather than just individual families.

2   Comment on the issues surrounding interventions in children's lives based on ideas of charitable rescue.

3   Discuss the rationale behind fulfilling children's potential by investment in early childhood development programmes.

4   Discuss the shift in policies and practices away from fulfilling children's needs towards understanding their role as social actors.

5   Examine the role of children's rights commissioners and ombudsmen in ensuring children's rights are implemented.

1 INTRODUCTION: WHY INTERVENE IN CHILDREN'S LIVES?

Earlier chapters in this book looked at different types of adversity faced by children. Despite changes in thinking as to what constitutes poverty, ill health or violence, a consistent feature is that individuals, organizations and the state have regularly intervened in children's lives in an attempt to alleviate these adversities. The final chapters of this book look at these interventions. This chapter focuses on adult-led interventions. The last chapter examines ways in which children themselves have attempted to improve their lives.

Most parents have always wanted the best for their children, and within families there are many discussions about the best way to raise children. This chapter does not deal with individual parents' attempts to improve their children's lives or to be better parents. Instead, we look at attempts by adults and society in general to intervene in the lives of children, ranging from the work of local charities to national governments and international agencies.

While we concentrate on interventions in children's lives which have their roots in European history, often based on Christian belief, it is important to note that the special status of children is recognized by almost all of the world's major religions, and believers are encouraged to show kindness towards children and to protect them. For example, the idea of social service and helping the needy is central to Islamic teachings. One of the five pillars, or central beliefs, of Islam is the obligatory tax, the *zakat*, which helps the vulnerable. Islam recognizes that poor children, and those without fathers, are particularly disadvantaged, and need education and health care. In Theravada Buddhism (as practised in South East Asia and Sri Lanka), poor and vulnerable boys are brought by monks to their local temple where they are fed, clothed and educated to a high standard.

One of the Buddhist monks in the Chiang Rai province of Thailand who look after a child orphaned by AIDS.

Allow about 10 minutes

A C T I V I T Y I   Why children?

Both adults and children are vulnerable to a range of adversities. Why do you think that children should have special claims to protection and intervention to protect them from harm?

C O M M E N T

As previous chapters of this book have shown, children's growth, development and well-being are often particularly affected by adversities such as ill health, poverty and violence. So one reason why children have special claims to protection is that they are a particularly vulnerable group and society should target its resources towards them. Although certain categories of adults, such as the elderly or people with disabilities, have particular needs, adults as a whole are less vulnerable. There are also other reasons why children are given special protection. Children are relatively powerless to act for themselves, therefore adults should act to defend their best interests.

A second argument for intervening to alleviate adversity concerns children's future potential. Children are targeted because they are seen as an investment. Investment implies a return, and, using this reasoning, children are singled out for special measures because they are the productive adults of the future. Because they have longer lives ahead of them than older people, investing in children, especially in the early years, will have greater benefits in the future for the whole of society. More generally, children are the way that society will replicate itself.

A third way of approaching this issue is based on children's rights. Within this approach children are seen as social actors in their own right, as fellow human beings who have a call on society's time and resources, not out of charity, but because they are equal members of society who contribute to society in the present.

In the rest of this chapter we look in turn at each of these three different approaches to intervening in children's lives.

Children are seen as a special priority because:

- They are especially vulnerable to adversity, relatively powerless to act for themselves, and need protection.
- They are human potential and represent an investment in the future of society.
- They are social actors in their own right.

2 RESCUING CHILDREN

One way of intervening in children's lives has relied on viewing them as victims – as dependent, passive, weak and powerless. When children have faced adversity, therefore, adults have attempted to protect them, stepping in, if need be, to rescue them from their circumstances. Ideas about rescuing children have a long history, and, although this approach is now controversial, it has not entirely vanished. This section looks at different ways in which adults have attempted to rescue children throughout history, focusing on three examples: the establishment of foundling hospitals in Europe from the thirteenth century onwards; the growth of philanthropic efforts to rescue children from poverty, exploitation and moral corruption in Victorian England; and the earliest international work of the Save the Children Fund in the twentieth century. At the end of the section we pose the question of which children should be 'saved' and in which circumstances.

2.1 Foundling hospitals

The word 'hospital' was used during this period for any institution which dealt with the ill or destitute, so the terms 'foundling hospital' and 'foundling home' can be used interchangeably.

Some of the famous examples of rescuing vulnerable children are foundling hospitals, set up in Europe from the thirteenth century onwards. Until the foundation of these institutions, orphans, illegitimate children and children of the poor were often abandoned. Foundling hospitals were set up to save children from the threat of abandonment, or even infanticide. The most famous foundling hospitals were in Italy, in particular the Spedale degli Innocenti in Florence, founded in 1419. Foundling homes later spread to France, Portugal and Spain. Typically, children entered the homes through a wheel. A turning mechanism allowed a parent to place the child in a cradle on the outside wall, turn the wheel to take the infant inside and ring a bell to alert an attendant. Abandonment could thus be done anonymously, although many parents left a token, such as a button or a piece of ribbon, in the baby's hand in order that they might be able to identify and reclaim the child later on, possibly when their circumstances improved. Children were cared for in these homes through a system of wet-nurses who fed them.

Foundling hospitals came to England much later, the first and best known being founded in London by Thomas Coram in 1741. Shocked by the numbers of abandoned and dead babies he saw in the streets of London, Thomas Coram set up a home for children whose parents could not afford to

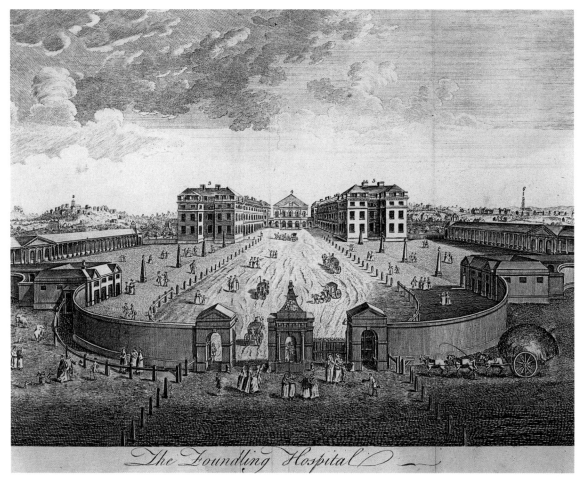

The London Foundling Hospital founded by Thomas Coram in 1741.

look after them. It aimed to rescue children whose lives would otherwise be lost or wasted, and turn them into productive citizens. Unlike the punitive workhouses, set up in the seventeenth century for the absolutely destitute, the London Foundling Hospital aimed to care for and educate children rather than just feed and house them. Children were placed with wet-nurses and fostered outside the hospital until they were old enough to come to the school. Later they became apprentices, joined the army, or went into domestic service. The Foundling Hospital did not discriminate against children who were illegitimate, but was based on a philosophy of protecting and helping children because they were particularly vulnerable.

Despite the good intentions, the mortality rates at the Foundling Hospital were, however, extremely high, running at over 75 per cent. Although in the parish workhouses the rate of death for children was 90 per cent (Harris, 2001), the overcrowded conditions of the Foundling Hospital and the general lack of hygiene meant that Thomas Coram had little impact on the rate of child death in London. In general, 75 per cent of children in London died before their fifth birthday, so that while children who survived the Foundling Hospital may have been better educated than other poor children, their chances of survival were just as precarious.

THOMAS CORAM, ESQ.^R

Thomas Coram
(1668–1751).

The setting up of homes such as the London Foundling Hospital and the Spedale degli Innocenti in Florence exemplifies particular efforts to rescue children. Foundling hospitals in general viewed all children at risk of abandonment as vulnerable and therefore in need of rescue, whatever the circumstances of their birth. Unlike parish charity, which often refused help to illegitimate children, foundling hospitals did not punish children for the sins of their parents. Rather they designated children as the helpless victims of their parents' inability to look after them. The establishment of the foundling hospitals in both Italy and England was based on ideas of Christian charity, in particular on the ideal of generosity towards the poor and more vulnerable. Thomas Coram was a devout Protestant who saw the establishment of the London Foundling Hospital as a Christian duty: not only was he saving lives, but he was also saving souls and turning children into useful members of society. He encouraged others to donate or leave legacies to his home.

In contrast to the Christian-inspired generosity of private individuals, there was little state help available to children at this time, whether in the form of education, health care or protective legislation. Indeed, state policy towards children could be punitive. While infants might be seen as innocent victims of abandonment, older children were often dealt with much more harshly. Children as young as ten could be punished as adults in England, and there are accounts from the early eighteenth century of a boy of ten being hanged for stealing a penknife and of a girl of fourteen hanged for stealing a handkerchief (Fyson, 1977).

2.2 Rescuing children in Victorian England

Nineteenth-century England saw an expansion of philanthropy as well as an increasing state interest in children's well-being. It was also the era when ideas about childhood, and particularly about children's innate innocence, became most clearly articulated. Within this ideology, children were special and free from corruption. Consequently, it was argued, they should be sheltered from the realities of the adult world in order to protect their specialness and vulnerability. Adults therefore set about rescuing children in a number of ways, both through their own efforts for individual children and through wider legislation. The nineteenth century saw the first laws designed specifically to improve children's lives by regulating their employment and promoting schooling (Cunningham, 2003).

Campaigns were also initiated to rescue children from the worst forms of child labour, such as mill work and chimney sweeping, and from the exploitation of child prostitution: from both physical exploitation and from moral corruption. Journalist W. T. Stead's campaigns against child prostitution in the 1880s, for example, were characterized by moralistic, and highly sensationalist, stories of young girls 'swept irresistibly on and on to be destroyed in due season, to give their place to others who will also share their doom' (Stead, 1885, p. 2). His attempts at rescue were equally sensational – he proved how easy it was to buy children for sexual purposes by purchasing a fourteen-year-old girl from her mother and publicizing how he had both bought and then rescued her. Stead's fellow campaigner, Josephine Butler, used very similar rhetoric about child prostitutes in Brussels.

> In certain of the infamous houses in Brussels there are immured little children, English girls of from ten to fourteen years of age, who have been stolen, kidnapped, betrayed, carried off from English country villages by every artifice and sold to these human shambles.

(Butler, 1910, p. 221)

Cartoon which appeared in the French magazine *L'Assiette au beurre* on 23 March 1907. The caption reads: 'There's no need to be frightened my dear, I'm not one of those who kill – I pay!'

Butler, too, made every effort to save girls such as these and bring them back to England, thereby reinforcing the ideology of rescue which lay at the heart of concerns about children in this era. However, it is clear that looking only at passive, helpless victims who need rescuing, whether from abandonment, factory work or prostitution, overlooks important issues such as the social, economic and political contexts of children's lives. Children worked through necessity, and their wages often ensured the survival of their families. There is evidence that child prostitution in the Victorian era, although common, had more to do with financial necessity and the lack of economic options for poor women and girls, and less to do with the more dramatic sounding kidnapping and betrayal that captured the imagination of Josephine Butler and W. T. Stead (Walkowitz, 1980).

Similar images of the child as a victim in need of rescue exist in the work of one of Victorian England's most famous social reformers and champions of poor children – Dr Thomas Barnardo. In 1866, Barnardo was on the verge of becoming a missionary in China, but a visit to the East End of London showed him a hitherto unimagined level of squalor and misery that existed among children.

Street urchins taken in by Dr Barnardo circa 1875.

Allow about 10 minutes

A C T I V I T Y 2   **Children as victims**

Read through the description below of Dr Barnardo's first trip to the East End of London, recalled in his autobiography. How does he portray these boys? To what extent does he contextualize their lives?

> There on the open roof, lay a confused group of boys, all asleep. I counted eleven … The rags that most of them wore were mere apologies for clothes … I realised the terrible fact that they were absolutely homeless and destitute, and were almost certainly but samples of many others; it seemed as though the hand of God Himself had suddenly pulled aside the curtain which concealed from my view the untold miseries of forlorn child-life upon the streets of London.
>
> (Barnardo quoted in Walvin, 1982, p. 154)

C O M M E N T

Barnardo portrays these children as poor victims of circumstances. He does not comment on why they might be living like this, or on the social conditions surrounding them. He does not mention their families or the role of the state in their lives. His response to them is one of pity, for their poverty and the lack of basic necessities such as clothes and somewhere to live. His concern led him to found a series of homes for boys and girls, where they could be fed, housed and educated. He was much less interested in changing the wider political and social conditions in which they lived. His was a humanitarian response to individual children with individual needs. The wider implications of why so many children should have been destitute in a city as wealthy as London were not explored.

By viewing children as victims of their parents' neglect or of their circumstances, it was possible to make direct, targeted interventions in their lives. Hungry children could be fed, homeless children housed, prostitutes rescued, young chimney sweeps prevented by law from remaining in this occupation. Intervention, therefore, had a very specific focus on alleviating suffering. Much less was done to bring about greater social equality or to tackle the root causes of poverty and social inequality. The concentration on children meant that such issues tended to be avoided. If children were suffering, it was due to the neglect of their parents, not the social and economic system which was founded on the need for a constant supply of cheap labour.

However, there was also an increasing recognition that children might need rescuing not only from factories or brothels but also from their own families. Although foundling hospitals implicitly acknowledged that children may be at risk from their parents, this was made explicit at the end of the nineteenth century by the formation of societies such as the National Society for the Prevention of Cruelty to Children (NSPCC). In 1881, Lord Shaftesbury, a British philanthropist, was asked by a Liverpool clergyman to introduce a bill into Parliament to prevent parental cruelty to children. At first he refused, arguing that the matter was 'of so private, internal and domestic a character as to be beyond the reach of legislation' (quoted in Hendrick, 1997, p. 45), but he later supported the Bill. In 1889 the Prevention of Cruelty to, and Protection of, Children Act came into force. It made the ill treatment and neglect of children illegal and created a new offence of causing suffering to children. It also enabled police and magistrates to remove children from their parents if cruelty was suspected. Within five years, 5,400 parents had been convicted of cruelty to children in England (Walvin, 1982). This Act was the forerunner of twentieth-century child protection legislation and the basis on which specialist social work to protect children was founded.

2.3 International charity

Eglantyne Jebb (1876–1928), founder of the Save the Children Fund.

Until the twentieth century, most attempts to save children were confined to children within national boundaries, so that, for example, Dr Barnardo's organization was set up specifically to help poor children in the UK. In the twentieth century, however, the narrowness of the focus became more problematic and the idea that rescuing children had to transcend national boundaries became more prominent. In this vision, protecting children became an international concern, beyond political or national factions.

European missionaries had been working with children and adults overseas for many years, offering medical help, food and education in the hope of their conversion to Christianity. However, specific large-scale organizations, set up to rescue children because they were helpless victims rather than potential converts, did not begin in the UK until after the First World War. With Germany and her allies defeated and with the victorious nations of France and the UK imposing punitive sanctions on their enemies, one consequence was a blockade which meant that food supplies became very limited and many children in Austria and Serbia faced starvation. Their plight attracted the attention of Eglantyne Jebb, who in 1919 started the first overseas relief agency for children – the Save the Children Fund (SCF).

Jebb estimated that up to five million children were starving in Eastern and Central Europe and resolved to set up a special fund to help them. She was greeted with a great deal of hostility at first because she was raising money for what were perceived as 'enemy children', of whom it was said, 'These children had much better die,' and, 'They will only grow up to fight us' (Jebb, 1929, p. 5). Furthermore, others questioned her motives for doing this at a time when British children were also suffering from serious social problems. However, the basis of her work was that *all* children should be saved regardless of their ethnicity or where they lived. Jebb claimed in 1919 'The SCF pays no regard to politics, race or religion. A child is a child whether red or white, brown or black' (Jebb quoted in Wilson, 1967, p. 183).

By the 1920s, therefore, SCF was helping children both overseas and in the UK. Because her intention was to put children first, regardless of race or background, the links between the local and the global in the work of SCF are evident.

> It was during the winter of 1920–21 that the economic distress of our own country became such that the SCF felt itself called upon to issue appeals for British children. It is true that, unhappily, the distress in

many countries abroad remained of a character far more desperate and terrible than that which prevailed at home. But the system of world organization in the interests of the children which had been adopted was not based on the principle of dividing up the countries into those which gave and those which received. Rather it required the recognition of a dual duty from all countries – a duty towards the poorest children of the world, the victims of war, epidemics, massacre, famine, and bankruptcy, and a duty towards their own children who in normal times should never be allowed to sink into such extreme destitution.

(Jebb, 1929, p. 13)

The SCF took as its basis the premise that rescuing children from suffering should be seen as a humanitarian rather than a political issue. However, Jebb was astute enough to recognize the political causes of children's suffering. A committed pacifist, she was acutely aware that children were suffering as a direct result of the political intransigence of the nations that were victorious in the First World War. Nevertheless, her argument was that children were the innocent victims of adult wars who should not be tainted by the guilt of their governments. In 1922, the SCF was active in the Russian famine, again an unpopular cause because the communist 'Red' government of Lenin had defeated the 'White' army (a coalition of anti-communist forces supported by the UK). In 1922, Jebb made a silent promotional film about the work of SCF in Russia, using stark and disturbing images of starving and dying children. Once again, her message was 'All wars, just or unjust, disastrous or victorious, are waged against the child' (Jebb, 1929, p. 9).

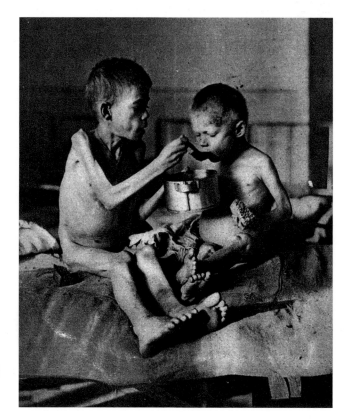

Promotional postcard from 1922 showing a Save the Children Fund feeding project in Russia.

Box 1   The Declaration of Geneva

Although the SFC was one of the earliest charities which worked for children overseas, Eglantyne Jebb herself was interested in more than charity. Throughout her work she emphasized that children should be fed and sheltered as a *right*. After much lobbying by Jebb, this principle was enshrined in international law. In 1924, the League of Nations (the precursor to the United Nations) agreed The Declaration of Geneva. The full text reads as follows:

> By the present Declaration of the Rights of the Child, commonly known as the 'Declaration of Geneva', men and women of all nations, recognizing that mankind owes to the child the best that it has to give, declare and accept it as their duty that, beyond and above all considerations of race, nationality or creed:
>
> 1. The Child must be given the means requisite for its normal development, both materially and spiritually.
>
> 2. The Child that is hungry must be fed, the Child that is sick must be nursed, the child that is backward must be helped, the delinquent child must be reclaimed, and the orphan and the waif must be sheltered and succoured.
>
> 3. The Child must be the first to receive relief in times of distress.
>
> 4. The Child must be put in a position to earn a livelihood and must be protected against every form of exploitation.
>
> 5. The Child must be brought up in the consciousness that its talents must be devoted to the service of its fellow men.
>
> (Jebb, 1929, pp. 39–40)

Allow about 15 minutes

ACTIVITY 3   **Children's entitlements and rights**

In her fundraising work, Eglantyne Jebb used very strong images of suffering children to raise money. It is clear from the Declaration of Geneva that she also envisaged a time when children would not have to rely on charitable rescue. The Declaration looks forward to a time of universal rights for children. Make brief notes on how you see the child conceptualized in the Declaration. What assumptions are made about the child?

COMMENT

The Declaration of Geneva is an attempt to get away from ideas about assistance for children based on individual charitable contributions. It also assumes that 'normal development' is a universal given, reflecting the evidence from scientific studies of children's growth and development which were well known by the 1920s. It emphasizes that adults have a duty to look after children and that this is the responsibility of everyone, at every level. Although there are some aspects of the Declaration that can be seen as protectionist (meaning that governments and parents are expected to make decisions on behalf of the child), it assumes that children are worthy of saving in their own right and as a future generation. There is no such thing as an enemy child or a child that does not deserve these rights. The responsibility for ensuring that the rights enshrined in the Declaration are enforced lies at national and international level and it places the good of children above consideration of national politics. It also positions the child as having responsibilities towards society and looks forward to the day when children are active contributors to society.

Since 1919, the SCF has undergone radical changes and now campaigns for children's rights rather than their rescue. Save the Children organizations have been set up throughout the world, and they are now co-ordinated through the International Save the Children Alliance.

In its early incarnation, SCF was inspired by the priority of rescuing children from starvation and associated miseries. Other organizations which have been subsequently established around the world have adopted similar aims, some focusing on a specific aspect of adversity that children face, such as child prostitution or child labour, others having a wider remit. Some of these organizations seek to shift the focus towards enabling children to participate more in discussions about their own lives (see Chapter 6).

Ideas about children needing rescue are now specifically rejected by Save the Children Alliance, who are trying to work in partnership with children, rather than imposing charity. They have now replaced images of passive, dependent children in their fundraising campaigns. Their images now show positive pictures of children as resourceful and resilient and being cared for within their communities rather than being rescued by outsiders. Yet there is a tension for agencies who try to raise funds to help children. They are aware that children are more likely to attract donations if they look appealing, passive and vulnerable. If children are perceived as social actors, or even as a threat, adults are less likely to wish to rescue them, or help them in other ways. In 2002, Angela Penrose, of Save the Children UK, discussed the dilemma faced by her organization between fundraising and the promotion of positive images of children.

> When we fund raise, we also sometimes face difficulties in promoting certain groups of children. Over the years, we have found obviously that young children create greater sympathy than adolescents who may also be having problems.

> Perhaps girl children create greater sympathy than boys, and obviously, although we would be working with child soldiers, sometimes they present an image that is violent, and doesn't raise sympathies.

> I think things did change after the Ethiopian famine in the mid 1980s. I think after that, many agencies looked to themselves and said, what are we promoting, if we continually promote children as helpless victims?

> (The Open University, 2003a)

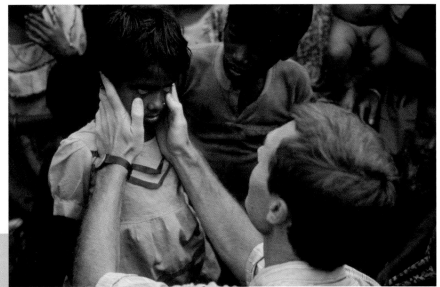

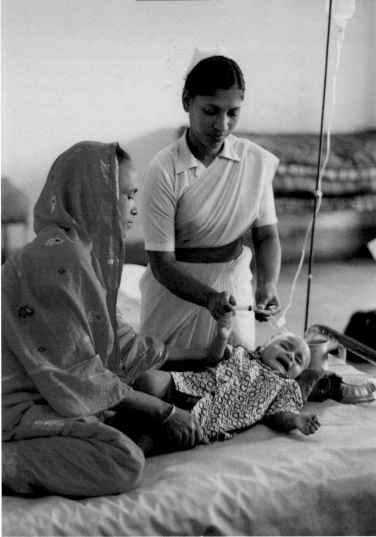

A Danish doctor examining a child suffering from tuberculosis in Bangladesh. Agencies such as Save the Children Alliance are now reluctant to use such images, preferring to show local people helping themselves rather than relying on outsiders, as in the photograph of the Bangladeshi nurse.

A Bangladeshi nurse at the Chittagong Mother and Baby Hospital cares for a sick baby.

In *Children: noble causes or worthy citizens?* (1997), Karl Eric Knutsson looks at how perceptions of children have changed and how this has affected interventions in their lives. The basis of Knutsson's argument is that charity, while it has its place in certain circumstances, condemns children to be passive objects of concern. He goes on to argue that children are not 'noble causes' but 'worthy citizens' who should be enabled to play a positive role in society because they are equal to adults and bear the same rights.

READING A

Now read Reading A, which is an extract from Knutsson's book. In this extract Knutsson sums up many of the themes of this section. He looks at the theoretical basis of ideas about charity, the motivations behind it, the types of charitable interventions undertaken on children's behalf and why children continue to be seen as vulnerable and in need of rescue. Knutsson then goes on to identify other ways of conceptualizing children and intervening on their behalf (approaches which will be followed up in Sections 3 and 4).

As you read, think about how far you identify with the distinction Knutsson draws between children as noble causes and as worthy citizens.

COMMENT

Knutsson argues that children are noble causes because the image of a suffering child, whose suffering can be alleviated by adult intervention, and who is reliant on adult responsibility, is an appealing one. However, he goes on to claim that there is another side to this: that many people are in fact reluctant to spend money or pay taxes in support of children that they deem unworthy of such support and that only certain children are seen as 'noble causes'. Knutsson also draws attention to the structural inferiority of children, which keeps them weak and vulnerable and therefore inevitably 'causes' for adults.

Children are rarely seen as worthy citizens as this implies an equality and partnership which is usually denied to them. While he acknowledges the compassionate impulse behind charity, Knutsson is critical of the short-term, emergency focus of much charitable intervention. He argues that charity is not enough because it presupposes that certain groups of people, usually in positions of power, can turn the lives of children into causes which can be improved. He argues that charity does not question power differentials between people and does not look at the underlying causes of suffering.

2.4 Which children should be rescued?

As this book has emphasized, children are not a homogeneous group, but are differentiated by, among other factors, age, gender, ethnicity and religion. All these factors affect how children experience, and react to, adversity. But they also affect the way interventions are planned and experienced by children. What might be beneficial for certain groups of children may have different, and unthought of, implications for others. In situations of extreme adversity, adults sometimes have to make difficult decisions to save only younger children, or girls, or healthy children. Within families, choices also may have to be made between devoting time and resources to one particular child who is ill, disabled or in trouble and looking after other children. Some of these issues have already been discussed in earlier chapters (notably Chapter 3). This section takes the analysis further by looking at situations where children alone are singled out for interventions, and at situations where some children are rescued, but not others.

Four young members of the Kindertransport. These children arrived in March 1939 aboard the US liner Manhattan, as part of a group of 88 German-Jewish children who were resettled in the UK. What happened to their parents is not known.

In some situations, children generally have been targeted for special protection but at the expense of their families and wider community. An example here is that of the Kindertransport, the granting of asylum and visas to German-Jewish children before the Second World War, which enabled them to escape to the safety of the UK. Very few countries were willing to admit Jewish people and the British Jewish Refugee Committee petitioned Parliament to allow large numbers of Jewish children between the ages of five and seventeen into Britain. Because they were children, they were singled out as weak and vulnerable and therefore in need of special protection (although their parents were also arguably as vulnerable). Over 10,000 children came to Britain in 1938 and 1939 without their parents and, in many instances, their parents did not survive the Holocaust. While this was undoubtedly a measure to assist, and even save, these children, the idea of helping children, and only children, is highly problematic. The next activity provides an illustration of this issue drawn from more recent history.

Allow about 15 minutes

A C T I V I T Y 4 **Children or families?**

Between 1992 and 1994, the Bosnian city of Sarajevo was at the centre of a civil war in the former Yugoslavia. Its inhabitants were being besieged by Serb forces and death was a daily reality for many in the city. A blockade was also in force, making food scarce. Under the circumstances a charity called the Children's Embassy organized an evacuation of children from Sarajevo. Throughout this period, a young woman called Elma Softic kept a diary. In the following extract she records her thoughts about the evacuation of the children from the city. Read the extract and make notes on the issues raised. Do you think that children should be saved in all circumstances, even when the rescue comes at the expense of the community?

18 May 1992

Today, under the auspices of the Children's Embassy, a convoy of children left Sarajevo for Split. The Children's Embassy called on everyone who has any sort of means of transport (except for bicycles, motorcycles, and horse-drawn vehicles) to participate in the transport of the children. The column was about ten kilometres long. Television cameras filmed the sorrow and grief of the scene. It was dreadful to see the trucks under whose tarpaulins were crammed the children and their tearful mothers. The life of Sarajevo is leaving. The children and their mothers are leaving. Sarajevo is not merely bleeding to death – it is dying of old age. The young men are being killed, the young women are leaving along with their children. The strength, creativity and intelligence of this city are leaving.

I don't know what to think about this. Keeping the children in Sarajevo means condemning them to possible death or to certain suffering – starvation is doubtless knocking on the doors of the families of Sarajevo. But by escorting them out, we are condemning to death the future of this city, the city that exists now and that its citizens love. What is more important: the life of the individual or the group? I have always believed that a thriving and promising society is impossible without healthy, courageous, strong, and self-confident individuals. However, is the life of each of these young people more important than the survival of the community? There was a time when I would have said yes without hesitation, but now I am no longer sure.

(Softic, 1995, p. 31)

C O M M E N T

There are no right or wrong answers here. Clearly, it is a deeply emotive issue. For some children, removal from the city would be in their best interests, and maybe individual families would be more concerned with the life of their child than with abstract issues of the survival of the city. Others might argue that evacuating a few thousand vulnerable children does nothing to address the situation of the rest of the people, or tackle the geopolitical problems that caused the conflict. However, this small extract shows how problematic the idea of rescuing children is in reality and how difficult the decisions are that have to be made by parents and communities in the face of a crisis.

In other instances, too, certain children have been rescued while others were not, for example from the Romanian orphanages in the 1980s. After the regime of President Ceausescu was toppled in 1989, the grim conditions in these orphanages were widely publicized. Ceausescu had banned contraception and abortion, with the consequence that large numbers of children were born to parents in Romania who could not afford to meet the basic needs of their children, and so had little choice but to place them in the care of state orphanages. Furthermore, a high proportion of these children were from Roma families, who had been forbidden by the government from carrying out street trading, their traditional occupation, on the grounds that individual trading was against the policies of the centralized economic state. When children were born, therefore, they became an economic burden where once they had been an asset, and they were often placed in institutions as a way of ensuring the survival of the rest of the family. Conditions in the institutions were extremely poor. Although the children were given food, shelter and clothing, they had little else. Medical care was minimal and the use of dirty needles meant that a high proportion of these children became infected with HIV/AIDS. The orphanages were very understaffed and the people who worked there were seldom able to give the children any human contact. Indeed, the children were often tied to their beds to prevent them from falling and hurting themselves.

When these conditions became known, there were many attempts to save children from these institutions. Drawing explicitly on ideas of rescuing helpless children, schemes were set up to help people from North America and Europe adopt them, remove them entirely from these institutions and raise them outside of Romania. Many children were rescued in this way, and

A Romanian orphanage, 1989.

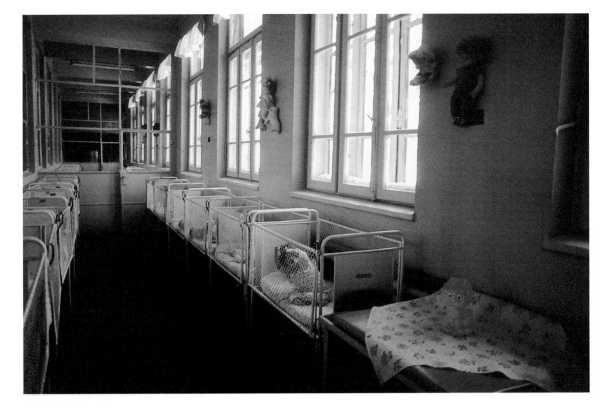

the quality of care given to them by their new families was substantially better than the care they would have received had they stayed in Romania.

On the surface, the case of Romanian orphanages seemed straightforward. Here were children in desperate circumstances who needed saving. Kind-hearted people could take pity on them and either adopt them or send money so that the orphanages could be improved. Yet the reality was more complicated, and shows the dangers of rescuing children without taking into account wider political and economic issues. While many children were taken out of the orphanages, thousands of others were left behind. The children who were adopted tended to be younger and healthier, leaving behind older, more disturbed and disabled children who needed more resources to ensure their long-term well-being. Furthermore, the emphasis on rescuing relatively few children obscured other issues. Many of these children were not orphans but had been put in institutions by parents unable to cope with them. It can be argued that money would have been better spent supporting families, returning children to their care and investing in the whole country rather than in rescuing a few hundred children.

The situation in Romania is still extremely complex. Since 1989, the Romanian government has made strenuous efforts to improve the lives of children in these orphanages. But the country is still very poor and families are still struggling. Improving the state institutions for children has also had the unintended effect of increasing the numbers of children placed in orphanages, as their parents perceive them to be better off when raised by the state than in conditions of poverty at home.

SUMMARY OF SECTION 2

- There is a long-standing tradition in Europe of rescuing abandoned or suffering children.

- The idea of rescuing children relies on the belief that children are particularly vulnerable and powerless and have no power to change their situation.

- Conceptualizing the child as a victim in need of rescue can decontextualize the social, economic and political circumstances of child suffering. Understanding the child as a victim does nothing to bring about greater social equality or to tackle the root causes of poverty and suffering.

- International help for children has been undertaken since the end of the First World War. It has been based on the premise that aiding children is non-political.

- Eglantyne Jebb's work with the Save the Children Fund (SCF) led to the first Declaration of the Rights of the Child in 1924, which enshrined in law the principle that children had the right to special protection *because* they were children.

- Sometimes decisions are made as to whether children should be saved rather than adults. Also, the rescue of a particular child, or group of children, may come at the expense of other children or of their families or wider community.

3 FULFILLING CHILDREN'S POTENTIAL

In this section we turn to the second approach to intervening in children's lives, introduced in Activity 1. This is based on the idea of children fulfilling their potential to be active and useful participants in society when they are older. This need not preclude ideas about rescuing children; indeed, one of Thomas Coram's aims was to rescue children so that they could be useful to society later on (see Section 2.1). Fulfilling children's potential takes Thomas Coram's vision a step further. It means understanding children as 'human capital'. Instead of seeing them as a burden on society, they are viewed as an investment which will bring rewards in the future. According to this view, adults must take responsibility for children's well-being, not just out of charity or for sentimental reasons, but because they are the next generation of society and an investment in the future. The demographics of Western Europe bear this out. As the population ages, there will be more and more old people being supported by a declining workforce (the children of today). Many people face a poorer old age because there is an insufficiently large working population paying taxes to provide the services they need. Far from being a burden on society, therefore, children are necessary for its continued existence.

Some ways of intervening in children's lives, therefore, recognize that children have needs and potential, which, if fulfilled, will reap benefits for all. A good example here is education. It is beneficial to the whole of a society to have a literate, well-educated population. In countries of the South, there is, for example, a strong positive correlation between educating girls and the survival rate of their children once they become mothers: that is, the higher the girls' level of education, the higher the survival rate of their children (see Stainton Rogers, 2003). From the perspective of human capital, a dead child represents a wasted opportunity and investment.

Throughout the 1960s and 1970s, many national and international organizations targeted their resources at keeping children growing up in the poorest countries of the world alive by vaccination programmes, ensuring access to clean water, health care and education. Initiatives such as mass vaccination programmes led to the near elimination of diseases such as smallpox and there was a determined effort to deliver practical, tangible services to children and, where appropriate, to their mothers. All these initiatives were aimed at producing the next generation of children who were healthy and educated and could contribute positively to their own societies. It was a move away from the idea of children as passive victims who could do little about their fate except wait helplessly for rescue through charity handouts. It assumed that given the right resources, especially in their earliest years, children could and would grow up to be productive citizens.

Much of this intervention work has focused on the early years of childhood. As Chapter 3 showed, children between the ages of nought and five are the most vulnerable to ill health, and most at risk from killer infectious diseases. For this reason, under-five mortality rates are very sensitive indicators of the overall health and wealth of a nation. Countries where these rates are low are invariably those which are richer and where children have better acess to health care, education and social service provision. Agencies such as the United Nations Children's Fund (UNICEF) have, therefore, focused a great deal of attention on early childhood development programmes, arguing strongly that these should be seen as a an investment for the future.

Allow abut 10 minutes

UNICEF was founded in 1946. Originally called the United Nations Children's Emergency Fund, and set up to help children at the end of the Second World War, it is now known simply as the United Nations Children's Fund. This represents a change in its focus and a move away from the notion of charitable rescue in its ideology.

A C T I V I T Y 5   **Investing in children**

Read through the following passage from UNICEF's 2001 report, the *State of the World's Children,* which focuses on early childhood development programmes. List at least four reasons why UNICEF claims that investing in early childhood brings positive benefits to the whole society.

> The rights of children and the cause of human development are unassailable reasons for investing in early childhood. The neurosciences provide another rationale that's hard to refute as they demonstrate the influences of the first three years on the rest of a child's life.
>
> In addition, there are also compelling economic arguments: increased productivity over a lifetime and a better standard of living when the child becomes an adult, later cost-savings in remedial education and health care and rehabilitation services and higher earnings for parents and caregivers who are freer to enter the labour force.
>
> And there are social reasons as well: Intervening in the very earliest years helps reduce the social and economic disparities and gender inequalities that divide a society and contributes to including those traditionally excluded.
>
> And political reasons: A country's position in the global economy depends on the competencies of its people and those competencies are set early in life – before the child is three years old.
>
> (UNICEF, 2001, pp. 12–13)

C O M M E N T

This passage begins with a general claim about children's rights and development. Then UNICEF identifies the following five reasons why investing in children in their early years is important.

1   Evidence from neuroscience shows that the first three years of life is a critically important period in terms of a child's neurological development; their mental capacities can be affected by, for example, poor nutrition and an unstimulating environment.

2   There are economic arguments that suggest that money invested early in childhood is more cost effective than remedial help later.

3   Providing care for children frees the time of children's care-givers so that they can work and provide more income for the family.

4   Early childhood programmes can reduce social inequalities, particularly concerning gender.

5   A healthy, well-educated workforce will bring political benefits to the country.

For all these reasons, UNICEF suggests that spending money on children early on is not charity but an investment that will reap future rewards for the whole society.

The idea, taken up by UNICEF, of the importance of early child development programmes involves an important shift in priorities for intervention, beyond merely ensuring child survival. One of the pioneers of this approach was Robert Myers. His book, *The Twelve Who Survive*, was published in 1992 at a time when large-scale programmes of immunization, oral rehydration and food distribution had had a significant impact on child survival. The title of the book referred to the fact that by the early 1990s twelve out of every thirteen children born in the world survived their infancy. Given this, Myers argued that it is critical to look beyond child survival at issues such as the quality of children's lives and the fulfilment of their potential after the age of five. In Reading B, Myers argues why spending money on very young children is not just a question of saving them, or prolonging their survival, but a necessary investment in the future of society that will bring benefits to everyone.

READING

Now read Reading B, 'Why invest in early childhood development?', which is an extract from Robert Myers' *The Twelve Who Survive*. Which of Myers' arguments do you find most compelling? Why?

COMMENT

Robert Myers' book marked a shift away from prioritizing physical health and focused instead on issues such as education and quality of life. Myers is interested in children's long-term futures, which he believes are best supported by early childhood intervention programmes. He goes on to develop eight arguments as to why children's best interests should be promoted through early childhood development programmes. All except the first one – the human rights argument – suggest that children have needs and potential that should be fulfilled, both for the individual child's good and for the good of the community and society in general. Myers claims that investing in young children can have a significant impact on their later lives, which will in turn enrich their society. The emphasis of Myers' book is on improving the prospects for young children growing up in the poorest countries of the world. But much of the research evidence for this approach comes from interventions targeting poverty within affluent countries of the North, especially the USA and countries in Europe.

3.1 Early childhood programmes in the USA and UK

Ideas about fulfilling children's potential by concentrating on their early years have been behind some of the early childhood development projects in countries of the North, in particular the long-standing Head Start programme in the USA and the more recent Sure Start and Starting Well initiatives in the UK.

Head Start was set up in the 1960s in the USA as part of President Lyndon Johnson's 'War on Poverty'. The differences between the rich and the poor had become increasingly obvious in 1960s America. A study in 1964 found that half of the nation's 30 million poor were children and that these children

The 'War on Poverty' was an attempt made in the early 1960s in the USA to alleviate poverty and social inequalities by expanding welfare aid to families, providing limited free medical services, public housing and better educational opportunities. President Johnson stated 'No American child shall be condemned to failure by the accident of his birth' (quoted in Woodhead, 1988, p. 445).

lived in homes where their parents had a very low level of education (Zigler *et al.*, 1993). Furthermore, many of these children were black and the civil rights movement, which fought for equal rights for the black community, pushed the government to intervene to ensure greater social equality between white and black as well as between rich and poor. In addition, the government was worried about rising crime and about the poor physical health of many men which was leading to their rejection as unfit for military service, both of which it saw as a partial consequence of poverty. The key to reducing both poverty and social inequality was believed to be education; poorer children were achieving less in school than their middle-class counterparts; they were more likely to be placed in special education streams for children and were less likely to graduate from high school and, therefore, less likely to raise themselves out of poverty.

The Head Start programme was designed to give poorer children an educational boost in their early years so that they could compete with middle-class children when they arrived at school. The premise of the Head Start programme was that the early years of a child's life were particularly critical for growth, development and learning and that money should be invested early in children's services to protect children later in life. Some early advocates for Head Start claimed that money spent on children before the age of five could act as an 'inoculation against failure' in the same way as a targeted medical intervention such as vaccination could prevent disease.

The first Head Start projects, set up in 1965, were originally intended as six-week summer programmes for 100,000 three to five year olds. The rules stated that 90 per cent of the children enrolled had to be from families below the poverty line and that 10 per cent of the places were to go to children with disabilities (Zigler *et al.*, 1993). The programme was, however, extremely popular and in the first summer half a million children took part in a Head Start project. In the following year, 1966, Head Start was expanded so that it became a half day, nine-month programme. Although largely funded by the central government, Head Start was designed to be flexible and sensitive to local needs. There were, therefore, no national standards set, nor an overall curriculum. Nevertheless, Head Start was based on the idea of the 'whole child' and, while education was important, it was understood that in order for children to realize their full potential, education had to take place in conjunction with health projects and familial participation. Therefore, despite differences at a local level, all Head Start programmes covered education, physical and mental health screening and referral, parent education and social services.

Since 1965, over fifteen million children have attended a Head Start programme. In 2002, the US government spent 6.5 billion US dollars on the programme and 915,000 children were enrolled (The White House, 2002). Yet there have been criticisms that Head Start has been overly ambitious and has not fulfilled its promises. As Chapter 2 showed, there are still many poor children in the USA, and Head Start programmes have not reduced the gaps between the rich and the poor. It has not been, as hoped, an 'inoculation against failure'. However, the problems of poverty and social inequality are extremely complex and it was always unlikely that one programme alone could lift children out of poverty. Despite the increased spending on Head Start, it still reaches only one in six of children who might benefit from it.

Head Start project,
New York, 1984.

The idea of a critical period in children's lives has also been questioned by those who believe that there are many critical periods of development when children have different, but equally important, needs. Finally, the lack of universal standards for the Head Start programme means that while some projects are extremely good and of great benefit to children, others are less successful.

Despite all of this, there is evidence of the long-term benefits of Head Start that does suggest the importance of early intervention in fulfilling children's potential. Children who have been to high quality programmes have higher rates of school achievement than their peers who have not. They have lower rates of delinquency, teenage pregnancy, dropping out of school, unemployment and use of welfare services. Some researchers have taken the argument a stage further by carrying out a cost–benefit analysis. Their aim has been to show that a relatively small investment in good pre-school educational services will greatly reduce the need for future spending on special needs education, juvenile delinquency prevention and crime. This is, therefore, an investment not only in children, but in the whole of society. One long-term experimental study carried out in Michigan on 123 children, approximately half of whom had been through a high-quality early childhood programme, found a dramatic difference in outcomes in children's lives. The researchers were able to claim:

> For every $1,000 that was invested in the pre-school program, at least $4,130 (after inflation) has been or will be returned to society – better than the average rate of return to private investors. Returns include reduced costs for education and legal processing for delinquent behavior, and increased lifetime earnings for participants.
>
> (Breedlove and Schweinhart, quoted in Woodhead, 1985, pp. 63–4)

A more recent, more comprehensive economic analysis drew the more modest but still positive conclusion that the benefits of a large-scale public programme like Head Start could offset 40 to 60 per cent of the costs (Currie, 2001).

Head Start provides an example of a programme based on the view that fulfilling children's potential means investing in services for them at a very young age. It is explicitly related to the idea that children are society's future and that investing in children now will benefit the whole of society later on. The same rationale lies behind similar projects set up in the UK. In 1998 the government introduced two programmes, Sure Start in England and Wales and Starting Well in Scotland, which aimed to target poor children in their earliest years, in the belief that early intervention would prevent longer-term problems. Sure Start aims:

> To work with parents-to-be, parents and children to promote the physical, intellectual and social development of babies and young children – particularly those who are disadvantaged – so that they can flourish at home and when they get to school, and thereby break the cycle of disadvantage for the current generation of young children.

> (Sure Start, 2002)

Sure Start concentrates on nought to three year olds, offering family support, advice on nurturing, health services and early learning. Once again, the emphasis in this programme is on investment; money spent on children in the early years of their lives has the greatest impact later on.

3.2 Priorities for early childhood investment

Early childhood development programmes have attracted a great deal of interest and funding from governments and international agencies. However, there have been concerns about the narrow focus of such programmes.

Allow about 10 minutes

A C T I V I T Y 6   **Child care practices in Malawi**

Read through the following extract from the 2001 *State of the World's Children* report published by UNICEF. What do you think the benefits of investing in early child development programmes in Malawi would be? What do you think the limitations of such an approach might be?

> In Malawi, where about 15 per cent of children are orphaned by HIV/AIDS, disease and unrelenting poverty continue to erode the capacity of families and communities to care for their youngest members. More than 90 per cent of the children in rural areas, where 85 per cent of the country's population lives, have no access to any form of organized early childhood care – care that can enhance their right to survival, growth and development.

> In 1999, the Government of Malawi and UNICEF stepped up their efforts on behalf of children from 0–3 years old, developing policies, guidelines and training modules at the central level. Extension workers were trained and local plans of action were developed at the district level. As a result, there is an increased demand for early child care services – a first sign of success. While the number of community-based child care centres is still quite small, demand is rapidly increasing and the benefits of focusing on the needs and rights of young children and their families are becoming more visible.

Local projects use a home visitor model and depend on volunteer community members to serve as caregivers and committee members. The projects focus on six child care practices: care for women, breastfeeding and complementary feeding, food preparation, psychosocial care, hygiene practices and home health practices. Despite abject poverty throughout much of the country, many community members contribute food supplies and work in communal gardens or other income-generating activities to raise money for the centres.

(UNICEF, 2001, p. 34)

COMMENT

Malawi is a very poor country and its children face serious risks to their development, in terms of both their health and their future chances. Investing in early childhood development programmes such as these encourages better nutrition and sanitation standards and educates parents about the steps that they can themselves take to ensure their children's health to the best of their abilities. These relatively simple measures can help boost good health and ensure children's survival.

However, these projects are quite narrowly focused when looked at from the broader perspective of Robert Myers in Reading B. For example, HIV/ AIDS is widespread in Malawi and inevitably affects a child's ability to fulfil his or her potential. This is not simply a health issue but affects family structure, child care, productivity and a range of other issues. Also, these programmes stop when children are three years old and what happens to children after this age is not clear. Part of their rationale is that they prepare children to achieve well in school. But this assumes that quality schools are available for all children to attend, which is not the experience of millions of the world's children. The case for investing in early childhood is powerful, but needs to be set in the context of other competing priorities. This is especially the case in the poorest countries which lack the resources and infrastructure necessary to provide even basic services for children and families (Woodhead, 1996).

SUMMARY OF SECTION 3

- Children can be seen as representing an investment in the future. Promoting their well-being is therefore good for all of society.

- Many policies to improve children's lives have been based on the idea that the best way to realize children's potential is to intervene in the early years, ensuring that basic needs for health, food, shelter and education are fulfilled.

- In the USA, the Head Start programme aimed to provide early education programmes as a way of improving children's life chances, as well as meeting their health and nutritional needs. It has had some significant successes over its history.

- Policies which aim to fulfil children's potential often concentrate on children aged nought to five. Less attention is paid to children in middle and later childhood.

4 ENSURING CHILDREN'S RIGHTS

Finally, we turn to the third approach to improving children's lives introduced in Activity 1, the approach based on a recognition of their rights.

The 1924 Geneva Declaration was the first specific children's rights document in the world. Since then, various international conventions, such as the 1948 Universal Declaration of Human Rights, have had clauses that invoked special protection rights for children. This was followed in 1959 by the United Nations Declaration of the Rights of the Child. However, none of these international instruments adequately protected children in reality.

In 1989, following ten years' preparatory work, the United Nations Convention on the Rights of the Child (UNCRC) was opened for signature. It aimed to be comprehensive and universal and to ensure that children's rights were a matter of law rather than rhetoric. Although based on the 1924 Declaration of Geneva, it differs from it in important ways. The 1924 Declaration conceptualized children as weak and dependent. It emphasized adults' duties towards children and demanded that children should be looked after because of their vulnerability. It also encouraged children to be useful members of society in the future. In contrast, the UNCRC is expressed in terms of children's rights. It is based on the understanding of children as full social beings with rights due to them now, as human beings, covered by the same laws as adults, but with extra rights in recognition of their vulnerability and social status. These rights cover issues such as provision for basic needs such as food and housing and protection from abuse or from degrading punishment or arrest without a proper judicial process, but they also allow for children's participation. (The idea of children's participation is explored more thoroughly in Chapter 6, along with the ways that children themselves have improved their own lives.)

Since the UNCRC was opened for signature, aid agencies such as Save the Children Alliance have tried to bring its recommendations into their work. They have moved away from treating children as the subjects of charitable handouts and instead emphasized the need to fulfil children's rights by providing non-discriminatory access to services to meet their civil, social, political, economic and cultural needs. They have emphasized the importance of children as valuable contributors to society now, rather than as an investment which will reap dividends in the future. This involves envisaging children as human beings rather than as human becomings or, as Knutsson argues in Reading A, seeing children as worthy citizens rather than as noble causes.

Allow about 10 minutes

ACTIVITY 7   Needs and rights

The UK government ratified the UNCRC in 1991, which means that it incorporated the convention's provisions into UK law. It reaffirmed that a child is anyone under 18. It also pledged that it would implement Article 27:

> States Parties recognize the right of every child to a standard of living adequate for the child's physical, mental, spiritual, moral and social development.

> (UNICEF, 2002)

It also ratified Article 28, which concerns the right to free primary education and support and easy access for secondary education, including financial support if a child needs it.

Given this information, read through the following short case study. The account is fictional but based on the situation of many young refugees in the UK. To what extent have Mohammed's rights been met?

> Mohammed is a seventeen-year-old boy who has fled Afghanistan and claimed political asylum in Britain. He left his country because of religious persecution, poverty and because he was afraid of being conscripted into the army. He is living in a single room in bed and breakfast accommodation in London. He shares bathing facilities with five others and has a small gas cooker in his room. He is trying to gain admission into a local school to continue his education and learn English. However, no local college will accept him part way through the year and he does not know if his education authority will pay for it.

COMMENT

Under the UNCRC, because Mohammed is under eighteen he is technically a child. Therefore, when he arrived in the UK the government had a duty to ensure his basic survival through providing him with somewhere to live and enough food and shelter. However, they also had a duty to ensure an adequate standard of living and it is debatable whether or not this has been provided.

Although Mohammed's basic needs are being met, his rights under the UNCRC are not. Initially he can petition his local authority, which has housed him and is providing him with basic needs, for his rights under Articles 27 and 28 to be enforced. However, there are currently many refugee children in the UK who live in temporary accommodation and have still not been given school placements, and, as a seventeen year old, Mohammed may not be seen as a priority. He may also not know how to approach his local authority.

This brief case study shows that ensuring children's rights is not straightforward. Governments may have signed and ratified the UNCRC, but there are practical constraints and issues such as what constitutes an acceptable standard of living are contested. The issue of access to services and children's knowledge of their rights also remains problematic.

4.1 Children's rights commissioners

An ombudsman is a person assigned to investigate complaints against the government or other institution. The word comes into English directly from Swedish, where the language has no feminine equivalent, and this chapter uses 'ombudsman' rather than 'ombudsperson' throughout. Some countries have preferred the term 'children's rights commissioner'.

Guaranteeing children's rights involves looking at their well-being in a broad sense. It includes taking into account their access to services and their quality of life, acknowledging their role as social agents who can change their own lives and who have a right to be consulted and respected for the choices they make. One way of ensuring that children's rights are met, and investigating any complaints about infringements of rights, has been the setting up of children's rights commissioners (known in some countries as children's ombudsmen). These commissioners take on a special responsibility to ensure that children's rights are being supported by the government of the country they are in, and to represent children's interests.

In 1981, Norway appointed the world's first ever ombudsman for children. Since then others countries such as Sweden, Ireland, Peru and Costa Rica have all appointed ombudsmen for children, or children's rights commissioners, who have the responsibility for ensuring that children's rights and interests are protected and that children have a voice in their own futures. According to UNICEF's International Child Development Centre (ICDC), the children's rights commissioner or ombudsman:

> must seek greater justice for children both by improving access to existing rights and by promoting the recognition of human rights not yet embodied in legislation, culture or day-to-day practice in children's lives.

(UNICEF ICDC, 1997, p. 3)

The role and duties of ombudsmen, or children's rights commissioners, differs from country to country, but the idea behind setting up a specific office to deal with children's rights is that it is not enough to say that children have rights; the rights must be actively implemented. Ombudsmen, therefore, influence law, policy and practice, challenge individual breaches of rights, and undertake research into and promote awareness of children's rights. For example, in Israel the role of Ombudsman for Children and Youth exists mainly as a way of tackling violations of individual children's rights. He or she investigates and attempts to resolve complaints through mediation or, where necessary, the law. The ombudsman also acts as an educational service, promoting awareness of children's rights. In contrast, the Swedish Ombudsman for Children and Young Persons cannot intervene in individual cases. His or her remit is to act as a general advocate for children, as well as a source of public information. Other countries, such as Costa Rica, adopt a mixture of these two positions, allowing the ombudsman to intervene in individual cases as well as to lobby for changes in legislation and for investment that will improve the services available to children.

Creating the role of the ombudsman has had some notable successes. In Norway, the ombudsman contributed to legislation banning the physical punishment of children. In Costa Rica, changes to the police, juvenile court and child welfare agency were made after the intervention of the ombudsman, while in New Zealand, the Children's Rights Commissioner has promoted improvements to policies and practices concerning custody disputes and the care of children abused or neglected by their parents. In other instances the role has allowed children themselves to come forward with complaints about individual violations of rights, ranging from sexual abuse, to problems at school, to lack of play facilities (UNICEF ICDC, 1997).

The office of the ombudsman is based on the premise that children are social actors. This means that children are viewed as competent and able to take informed decisions about their own lives. However, there is also a tension in the role, between encouraging children to participate and taking their views seriously and protecting them from the consequences of their actions. For example, in Norway the ombudsman has pushed for a legal ban on cosmetic surgery for under-eighteens, despite protests from girls of sixteen who felt fully competent to make decisions about their bodies. The ombudsman who made this decision, Tronde Waage, said of the dilemma he faced:

[T]here was some resistance among girls from sixteen to eighteen when we proposed to higher the age of cosmetic surgery from sixteen to eighteen, and the resistance was about you do not trust us, you don't trust our competence to make a decision about our own lives. And I had to tell them back, no, I did not because this industry has an enormous power, and it is defining ... how your body should look.

(The Open University, 2003b)

The ombudsman's dilemma – between respecting young people's competence and protecting what he felt were their best interests – is central to current debates about implementing children's rights in practice.

4.2 Implementing children's rights in practice

The final reading for this chapter was written for the Swedish government by academics Jo Boyden and Deborah Levison. Successive governments in Sweden have shown a great commitment to children's rights, setting up the office of the ombudsman and consistently encouraging children's involvement in public life.

READING

Now read Reading C, 'A child-centred vision: new directions' by Jo Boyden and Deborah Levison. This extract argues that implementing children's rights means being committed to supporting their role as social agents. The authors comment on the difficulties inherent in taking this approach, but also point to ways in which children's agency can be acknowledged. As you read, draw up a list of the benefits that doing this might offer.

COMMENT

Boyden and Levison admit that taking children's rights seriously may be difficult because children are traditionally under-represented in social theory and policy. They acknowledge that it will take a major shift in thinking on the part of adults to conceptualize children as competent social actors. However, the benefits of recognizing children as actors and ensuring their full participation in society is that it is the best way of enforcing and implementing children's rights. It enables a more equitable sharing of power between adults and children, and working in partnership with children and consulting them about policies which affect them improves their lives.

The proposal to give children participatory rights is radical. As children's rights advocate Rakesh Rajani argued in an interview conducted in the preparation of this book, making sure that children participate fully in society necessitates a fundamental shift in power from adults to children:

... it is a question of dealing with power. That doesn't mean it's power over adults, or power against adults, but it is a question of sharing power. So that you don't have adults who have all the power, and young people who have none, but rather you have a sharing of the responsibilities, and a sharing of the power. The crucial issue here is –

are adults willing to give up power, are they willing to share the power? That's usually the biggest constraint.

Taking children's rights seriously means recognizing that children are stakeholders in political, social and economic life, and encouraging their full participation in decision making. There may be difficulties in this, as Tronde Waage the Norwegian ombudsman suggested, but, even so, children's opinions are increasingly being sought and taken seriously. On international, national and local levels, groups that work with children are increasingly trying to promote partnerships between themselves and the children with whom they work. They envisage a new relationship, no longer as service provider and recipient, but as equals in an ongoing and evolving partnership.

SUMMARY OF SECTION 4

- The United Nations Convention on the Rights of the Child (UNCRC) is based on an understanding of children as full social beings with rights due to them, not as a special favour from adults, but because they are human beings.
- Ensuring children's rights means reconceptualizing children as active participants in their own lives. It means looking at children as social actors and as competent informants who are partners in improving their own lives rather than recipients of charity.
- The children's rights approach understands needs in the widest possible sense, encompassing the need for basic services as well as access to services.
- Ensuring children's rights is radical, and sometimes controversial, because it necessitates a fundamental shift in power away from adults towards children.

5 CONCLUSION

Adult-led interventions in children's lives have a long history. This chapter has looked at three different ways of intervening in children's lives: rescuing children; fulfilling children's potential; and ensuring children's rights. It is important to note that these are not mutually exclusive; different agencies have a mixture of priorities and agendas in their work with children. Nor are these three categories exhaustive – there are other ways of conceptualizing children and intervening on their behalf. However, by foregrounding these three approaches, we can observe certain continuities, most noticeably the continuing power of ideas about intervening in children's lives based on images of rescuing needy children and of harnessing their potential. It is only very recently that adults have begun to see children as capable agents of change and that policies aimed to help them have viewed them as active participants. Chapter 6 discusses this development in much greater detail.

REFERENCES

BUTLER, J. (1910) *Personal Reminiscences of a Great Crusade*, London, Horace Marshall.

CUNNINGHAM, H. (2003) 'Children's changing lives: 1800–2000' in MAYBIN, J. and WOODHEAD, M. (EDS) *Childhoods in Context*, Chichester, John Wiley and Sons Ltd/The Open University (Book 2 of The Open University course U212 *Childhood*).

CURRIE, J. (2001) 'Early childhood education programmes', *Journal of Economic Perspectives*, **15**(2), pp. 213–318.

FYSON, N. (1977) *Growing Up in the Eighteenth Century*, London, Batsford.

HARRIS, R. (2001) *The Foundling Hospital* [online], http://www.bbc.co.uk/history/society_culture/society/foundling_05.shtml (accessed 12 December 2002).

HENDRICK, H. (1997) *Children, Childhood and English Society 1880–1990*, Cambridge, Cambridge University Press.

JEBB, E. (1929) *Save the Child! a posthumous essay*, London, The Weardale Press Limited.

THE OPEN UNIVERSITY (2003a) U212 *Childhood*, Video 4, Band 5, 'Save the Children', Milton Keynes, The Open University.

THE OPEN UNIVERSITY (2003b) U212 *Childhood*, Audio 8, Band 2, 'Children's Rights Commissioners', Milton Keynes, The Open University.

SOFTIC, E. (1995) *Sarajevo Days, Sarajevo Nights*, Toronto, Key Porter Books.

STAINTON ROGERS, W. (2003) 'Gendered childhoods' in Woodhead, M. and Montgomery, H. K. (eds) *Understanding Childhood: an interdisciplinary approach*, Chichester, John Wiley and Sons Ltd/The Open University (Book 1 of The Open University Course U212 *Childhood*).

STEAD, W. T. (1885) *Maiden Tribute of Modern Babylon*, London, Pall Mall Gazette, Secret Commission.

SURE START (2002) *What is Sure Start?* [online] http://www.surestart.gov.uk/text/aboutWhatIs.cfm (accessed 13 December 2002).

UNICEF ICDC (INTERNATIONAL CHILD DEVELOPMENT CENTRE) (1997) *Innocenti Digest, No. 1*, UNICEF ICDC, Florence.

UNICEF (2001) *State of the World's Children*, UNICEF, New York.

UNICEF (2002) *Full Text of the Convention* [online], http://www.unicef.org/crc/crc.htm (accessed 12 October 2002).

WALKOWITZ, J. (1980) *Prostitution and Victorian Society: women, class and the state*, Cambridge, Cambridge University Press.

WALVIN, J. (1982) *A Child's World*, London, Pelican Press.

THE WHITE HOUSE (2002) *Good Start, Grow Smart: the Bush administration's early childhood initiative* [online], http://www.whitehouse.gov/infocus/earlychildhood/sect5.html (accessed 13 December 2002).

WILSON, F. (1967) *Rebel Daughter of a Country House: the life of Eglantyne Jebb, founder of the Save the Children Fund*, London, Allen & Unwin.

WOODHEAD, M. (1985) *Early Intervention*, Unit 27 of course E206 *Personality and Learning,* Milton Keynes, The Open University.

WOODHEAD, M. (1988) 'When psychology informs public policy: the case of early childhood intervention', *American Psychologist,* **43**(6), pp. 443–54.

WOODHEAD, M. (1996) *In Search of the Rainbow: Pathways to quality in large-scale programmes for young disadvantaged children,* The Hague, Bernard van Leer Foundation.

ZIGLER, E., STYFCO, S. and GILMAN, E. (1993) 'The national Head Start program for disadvantaged pre-schoolers' in ZIGLER, E. and STYFCO, S. (eds) *Head Start and Beyond,* New Haven, Yale University Press.

Different times, different children

Karl Eric Knutsson

Major clusters of perceptions

Perceptions are reality and create reality. When they are firmly held, they express or give rise to deep, powerful, comprehensive and lasting beliefs, attitudes and behaviour. They describe and maintain identities. They map and separate out the various components of our 'reality room', and they define our roles and our lifestyles and influence our views on human rights and obligations.

As far back as historical testimony can take us, perceptions about children, especially suffering children, have been based on views which can be described as 'charitable'. During the nineteenth century, missionaries preceding or accompanying the colonial expansion of the Western powers fostered an ambition to do 'good' by bringing back vivid stories about the hardship and suffering of peoples around the world. This helped strengthen the social and cultural basis for later charitable movements.

'Charity' denotes a wide range of activities which can be viewed as 'good' and worthy of support. Charitable initiatives are mainly recognizable by the intention of their supporters. They also draw strength from feelings of responsibility, kindness and compassion in the face of human suffering and from the identification of good causes with just causes. Further bolstered through the spread of the perception of the innocent and sacred child during the [nineteenth] century, a sense of charity became one of the key elements in the concern for children. Although there can be little doubt that charity is characterized by honourable ambitions, it is also clear that, if we take a closer look at the concept of 'charity', we discover that it is a very complex one. From the perspective of moral philosophy, Immanuel Kant even declared that charity ought to be regarded as obscene.

Charitable actions appeal to a sense of responsibility and help alleviate a sense of guilt. They are easily fuelled by images of suffering children, yet often they do not address the underlying causes of the problems of children. Thus, photos of children with sunken eyes in aged faces are frequently used to generate immediate child-centred actions, but they do not always lead to sustainable and long-lasting efforts to improve the essential support systems for the protection and betterment of children in all their many aspects. Because of these attributes, charitable initiatives in many ways represent the opposite of both the development approach and the child rights' perspective.

Charity as a benevolent concern for others is and will always be an intrinsic element in any well-intentioned effort to better the lot of those suffering from destitution and other ills. However, there is a risk that, once such well-intentioned action is carried out, it may leave the actors with the false impression that dealing with the immediate and obvious problems is the total solution. Moreover, because 'charitable' actions usually respond to urgent cries of distress, the rewards for the providers of charity – in terms of instant gratification – are seen as proof that the problems have indeed been solved, which is usually not the case. A basket of food might represent only a temporary relief in an existence on the margins of starvation and a carefully measured dose of antibiotics may only provide a short-lived respite in a continuing struggle for survival in an unhygienic and life-threatening environment. However, despite these shortcomings, it is equally important that charitable initiatives should not be ignored; nor should they be ridiculed or avoided. Charity has always been and will always remain a driving force of compassionate action. But it is a reasonable demand that the proponents of charity should explore the factors underlying the immediate suffering which triggers the charitable activities, together with the longer-term consequences of these activities. Without such precautions, some of the motivations for charitable initiatives are much less acceptable. Initiatives based mainly on the 'provider's' definition of the needs of the potential recipients can be – and frequently are – counterproductive. Such mistakes may seem clear cut and therefore avoidable, but they are still all too common.

Another cluster of perceptions revolves around the 'emergency–humanitarian' approach to child suffering. Today, the principal goal of this approach is to save children's lives and protect them from hunger, disease and other afflictions caused by natural or man-made disasters. This approach differs from 'charitable' initiatives because of the sense of urgency, the focus of attention, the scale of the problems and the understandable inclination to concentrate on the immediate symptoms of suffering rather than on the causative factors. However, even in emergency situations complementary strategies can be applied. For example, the provision of food, shelter and medical assistance can be combined with efforts to make local schools more effective, and associations can be formed to identify and implement alternative survival and coping strategies and thus mobilize energies, confidence and resources which can help deter migration and the passive abandonment of one's life to the whims of unknown and unknowing outsiders.

A third cluster of perceptions about children has emerged more recently, which is represented by the development approach. The most fundamental and prominent argument for this approach is based on the idea that children ought to be allowed to grow to their full physical and intellectual potential. In a certain way then, the approach is similar to the human rights approach. Another significant rationale is the assumption that, through proper growth, children become more mature, useful and productive citizens as adults.

A fourth cluster of perceptions has been widely embraced in the last few decades. The term used by UNICEF to identify this cluster is 'child survival and development'. This consists of a combination of the elements of the emergency–humanitarian approach and of the development approach. Available technology is applied to combat the 'silent' emergencies caused by poverty, disease and a hazardous and abusive environment. The emphasis is on the need to use a 'cost-effectiveness' calculus to identify feasible goals and strategies which can be promoted despite financial constraints and other obstacles.

All the above clusters of perceptions exhibit an inclination to work as much as possible directly with children in dealing with their needs and problems. Paradoxically, they also frequently share the disadvantage of viewing the suffering child as somehow isolated from the social and cultural space which he or she inhabits. They seem to thrive on an 'isolationist' view of the child in order to satisfy the need for immediate emotional gratification and sometimes also the desire to produce favourable statistics. This view seems to encourage goals and strategies which are very different from those which correctly emphasize the embeddedness of children and childhood in society and the constant interaction of children with society

[…]

Another dominant feature in the recent debate has been identified by Zelizer in *Pricing the Priceless Child*. She points to the 'sharp contradiction … between the public and the private value of children' [1985, p. 216].

Reviewing the situation in North America, Grubb and Lazerson, in an earlier book, reach a similar conclusion.

> Americans fail their children … The saccharine myth of America as a child-centred society, whose children are its most precious natural resource, has in practice been falsified by our hostility to other people's children and our unwillingness to support them.

[1982, p. 5]

Parents may spend lavishly and irrationally on their own children, but their altruism is transformed into miserliness when it comes to public programmes. The 'sacred' child is a luxury commodity restricted to the private sphere. Children in need of public support must show in economic terms that they are worthy of economic investment. This is a widespread attitude in the public debate on children and childhood. Children are worthy causes, but not worthy citizens. Likewise, there is a universal tendency to identify and evaluate children and childhood not on their own terms, but relative to the adult members of society. Such one-sided comparisons understandably and predictably lead to the characterization of children as biologically and socially immature and thus inferior to adults who, by definition, are the yardstick of maturity.

Elise Boulding has pointed to another factor which contributes to perceptions that children are helpless and, consequently, inferior. In *Children's Rights and the Wheel of Life,* she argues that the doctrine of the helplessness of the young and the aged has been developed in those particular circles most concerned with the rights of individuals.

> The convenience of age-segregated social patterns, initially evolved in the West to further the education of the young, ensured that contradicting information from human development research about substantial unused human capacity and ability in the earliest and latest years of life did not penetrate to policymaking circles. What began as a humanitarian concern for the weak has resulted in a depersonalizing and devaluing of individual capacity in the young and the old through a doctrine of protection that has converted persons in these categories from subjects to objects of social concern.

[1979, p. 2]

Boulding's engaged voice brings home with rare strength and vibrancy the fact that the history of childhood to a great extent is a history of exclusion. No matter what changes in analysis, theories and practice we may consider for the betterment of the conditions of children, this process must be reversed.

References

BOULDING, E. (1979) *Children's Rights and the Wheel of Life*, New Brunswick, NJ, Transaction Books.

GRUBB, N. W. and M. LAZERSON (1982) *Broken Promises*, New York, Basic Books.

ZELIZER, V. (1985) *Pricing the Priceless Child*, Princeton, Princeton University Press.

Source

KNUTSSON, K. E. (1997) 'Different times, different children' in KNUTSSON, K. E., *Children: noble causes or worthy citizens?*, Florence, UNICEF, pp. 29–31 and 36–7.

READING B

Why invest in early childhood development?

Robert Myers

The rationale that follows draws upon eight complementary lines of argument for increased support to programmes of early child care and development. These are:

1 *A human rights argument.* Children have a right to live and to develop to their full potential.

2 *A moral and social values argument.* Through children humanity transmits its values. That transmission begins with infants. To preserve desirable moral and social values in the future, one must begin with children.

3 *An economic argument.* Society benefits economically from investing in child development, through increased production and cost savings.

4 *A programme efficacy argument.* The efficacy of other programmes (e.g., health, nutrition, education, women's programmes) can be improved through their combination with programmes of child development.

5 *A social equity argument.* By providing a 'fair start', it is possible to modify distressing socioeconomic and gender-related inequities.

6 *A social mobilization argument.* Children provide a rallying point for social and political actions that build consensus and solidarity.

7   *A scientific argument.* Research evidence demonstrates forcefully that the early years are critical in the development of intelligence, personality, and social behaviour, and that there are long-term effects associated with a variety of early intervention programmes.

8   *Changing social and demographic circumstances.* The increasing survival of vulnerable children, changing family structures, urban–rural migration, women in the labour force, and other changes require increased attention to early care and development …

We turn now to a brief elaboration of each argument.

Children have a human right to develop to their full potential

For many people, the obligation to protect a child's human rights is the most fundamental and convincing reason to invest in programmes to enhance early childhood development.

[…]

Allowing disability and arrested development to occur each year in millions of young children, when it could be prevented, is, then, a violation of a basic human right. The fact that children are dependent on others for satisfaction of their rights creates an even greater obligation to help and protect them, and in this process families may require help.

[…]

Humanity transmits its values through children

We are continually reminded that 'children are our future'. The transmission of social and moral values that will guide that future begins in the earliest months and years of life.

In societies where there is a concern that crucial values are being eroded, there is a strong incentive to find ways in which those values can be strengthened. Early childhood programmes can assist in that effort, both by strengthening the resolve of parents and by providing environments for children to play and learn that include specific attention to desired values.

[…]

Society benefits through increased productivity and cost savings associated with enhanced early childhood development

Without referring to a scientific literature, common sense suggests that a person who is well developed physically, mentally, socially, and emotionally will be in a better position to contribute economically to family, community, and country than a person who is not. And in most countries of the world, that economic contribution begins at a very early age.

Increased productivity   Early childhood programmes have the potential to improve both physical and mental capacity. They can also affect enrolment, progress and performance of children in schooling which is associated with important changes in skills and outlooks affecting adult behaviour …

Income generation   Economic benefits from early childhood programmes may also occur through effects on the employment and earnings of caregivers. Child-care and development programmes offer the possibility of increased labour force participation by women and they can free older siblings to learn and earn as well. They can provide employment for individuals as paid caregivers and can bring new sources of income to local suppliers of materials and services needed to make the programme function.

Cost savings   Another way in which investments in health, nutrition, and psychosocial development during the early years can bring an economic return is through cost savings – by reducing work losses, by cutting the later need for social welfare programmes, by improving the efficiency of educational systems through reductions in dropout, repetition, and remedial programmes, and by reducing health costs.

[...]

The efficacy of other programmes can be improved through joint investment in early childhood development

Early childhood development programmes can affect cost savings in programmes of health, nutrition, and education, as suggested above. But at least as important, integrated attention to child development can increase the effectiveness of health and nutrition programmes ... In addition, child-care and development programmes are potentially useful as vehicles for extending primary health care.

[...]

In a different vein, income-generating programmes for women that respond to child-care and development needs are likely to be more successful than programmes that do not. If proper care for their children is assured, women will lose less work time as a result of child-related concerns (Galinsky, 1986). They will also be able to seek steadier and better-paying employment.

[...]

Programmes can help to modify distressing inequalities

Investments in early childhood development can help to modify inequalities rooted in poverty and discrimination (social, religious, gender) by giving children from so-called 'disadvantaged' backgrounds a 'fair start'. Poverty and/or discrimination produce stressful conditions and unequal treatment that can inhibit healthy and comprehensive development in the early years. For instance, children from poor families often fall quickly and progressively behind their more advantaged peers in their readiness for school, and that gap is never closed.

Boys, traditionally, have been better prepared for schooling than girls and have had more opportunities to enter and continue in school. The differences begin with gender-linked disparities in the patterns and practices of early development that need to be changed if the discrimination is to be overcome. These are often deeply rooted in culture, but there is evidence that integrated attention to early development can produce changes in the way families perceive the abilities and the future of a girl child.

[...]

Children provide a rallying point for social and political actions that build consensus and solidarity

Mozambique, Lebanon, Peru, Sri Lanka, El Salvador, Ethiopia, Iraq and a significant number of other countries are victims of violent actions that place the problem of living together in peace high on the list of social goals. In many locations, lesser political and social tensions make it extremely difficult to mobilise people for actions that will be to their own benefit. In such circumstances, it has been shown that placing 'Children First' can be an effective political strategy.

Perhaps the most dramatic, but short-lived, examples of mobilization around programmes to benefit young children are those in which ceasefires have been obtained between warring groups, as in El Salvador, in order to carry out national immunization campaigns ...

Scientific evidence demonstrates lasting effects of early attention to child development

Evidence from the fields of physiology, nutrition and psychology continues to accumulate to indicate that the early years are critical in the formation of intelligence, personality, and social behaviour. This evidence begins with the not-so-new discovery that brain cells are formed during the first two years of life. But recent research has strengthened the argument for early attention by showing that sensory stimulation from the environment affects the structure and organization of the neural pathways in the brain during the formative period. Thus, opportunities for complex perceptual and motor experiences at an early age favourably affect various learning abilities in later life and are able to compensate, at least partly, for the deficit associated with early malnutrition.

[...]

Changing social and economic conditions require new responses

[...]

Increasing labour force participation by women The increased pressure for women to work for wages and the need to take over men's farming chores as they have migrated to cities or sought work in mines has brought additional burdens affecting child care and creating a need for alternative forms of care. The trend towards increasing labour force participation pre-dates, but has been strengthened by, the world recession of the 1980s. These trends are likely to continue, and even to increase in the coming years.

The mother in these or other settings who works so that she and her family can survive may love her child and believe that she should devote time and energy to her baby, but she may not be able to do so; she needs help.

Modification of traditional family patterns Extended families are no longer as common as they once were. As migration and progressive urbanization occurs, members of an extended family are not as available for child care as in the past. Grandmothers are no longer as easily available, either because they remain in rural areas or because they too are working outside the home in wage-earning jobs. The number of women-headed households has increased. In some developing countries the percentage is high (over 40 per cent in rural Kenya, Botswana, Ghana, Sierra Leone, and Lesotho, according to Youssef and Hertler 1984). In these households, women must work, creating a major need for complementary child care. If care is available, the earnings of these women are more likely than would be the earnings of men to go towards improving the welfare of the children in the household.

[...]

Increased primary school attendance has decreased the availability of older siblings to act as supplementary caretakers. Or, siblings have been forced to drop out of school to provide such care, in which case there is a strong argument for child-care initiatives that will help siblings continue their education, at least to the point of literacy.

Changes in mortality and survival rates Over the last 30 years, the infant mortality rate has been more than cut in half. More children are surviving who in the past would have died an early death. As survival to age one has increased from 5 of 6 in 1960 to 12 of 13 in 1988, the pressure increases to mount programmes for those who survive.

In summary

The rationale developed here brings together several lines of argument supporting the value of investing in early childhood development. Each argument stands on its own, but when combined they are particularly compelling. Whatever the differences in individual predilections and local circumstances, it is clear that the set of arguments provides a strong base from which to argue for investment in programmes of early childhood care and development – by individuals and families, by communities, by governments, by non-governmental organizations, and by international funders.

When early childhood is made a priority, the financial support is forthcoming, even in situations of relative poverty. Financing for early childhood programmes is not the basic problem. The problem is to recognize the value of such programmes and build the personal and political resolve necessary to carry them out.

[...]

References

GALINSKY, E. (1986) *Investing in Quality Child Care: a report for AT & T*, New York, Bank Street College of Education.

YOUSSEF, N. and HERTLER, C. B. (1984) *Rural Households Headed by Women: a priority concern for development*, Rural Employment Programme Research Working Paper, Geneva, International Labour Organisation.

Source

MYERS, R. (1992) *The Twelve Who Survive*, London and New York, Routledge.

A child-centred vision: new directions

Jo Boyden and Deborah Levison

Building public and institutional support for children's rights

A commitment to lasting improvements for children requires more than progress toward the realisation of international standards agreed by social élites. *There is a need in all parts of the world to foster a culture of childhood throughout society that is based on the principles of the CRC [Convention on the Rights of the Child], and to guarantee children a higher priority in social and economic planning and family and community life* (Salazar & Alarcon Glasniovich, 1991). This involves redefining childhood, which is at present a time of exclusion. To an extent, it also implies a reduction in the power of adults. Such changes could lead to some resistance, especially in hierarchical cultures and organisations that prescribe a fixed status for all their members on the basis of gender and generation. Certainly it is important to take into account what adults might be losing by giving children a voice. It is essential also to consider the implications of possible adverse adult reactions in terms of children's wellbeing and integration into society. It needs to be borne in mind too that in many societies a significant proportion of adults are themselves excluded from social, economic and political processes because of their gender, class, ethnic or religious status.

[...]

Achieving widespread recognition and successful implementation of child-centred policy ultimately depends on extended social discourse and action that incorporates all major interested parties. Fundamental issues such as ending traditional forms of discrimination against girls and children with disabilities, changing children's family roles to avoid detrimental child work, and providing for children to participate in social decisions require extensive public discussion in order to arrive at socially supportable solutions. In some countries, such as Brazil, public discussion has led to powerful new laws, even constitutional changes, as well as the mechanisms for applying them in practice. In others, like Vietnam, public consultation has centred on the analysis of children's situation and monitoring of the implementation of the CRC. One of the implications of such examples is that policy measures enhancing the rights and abilities of all people (regardless of age, social status or sex) to participate in free and open discussions, whether in private or public fora, spoken or written, can benefit children substantially. Another is the need in such cases for great *sensitivity to local social and cultural conditions, flexibility, good co-ordination and preparedness to promote decentralized planning, management and administration.*

Collaboration across the full spectrum of civil society is likely to involve *non-traditional partners* such as the private sector. In the Philippines, for example, corporate citizenship has played a major role in improving social

Civil society refers to a network of non-governmental organizations, social and political movements, community-based groups and other agencies which are independent of the government.

provision for children and other groups. Furthermore, close *inter-country and regional co-operation* is often needed to bring about legislative and policy uniformity, especially given that many problems children face, such as trafficking, are trans-national in character. Solitary action in one country to ban children's work in hazardous or exploitative conditions, for example, will not be sustainable without similar and concurrent action in neighbouring countries. In fact, it will merely give other countries a competitive edge in the international market (Levison *et al.*, 1998). There is even a risk that neighbouring countries will introduce opposing policies. Regional co-operation may involve inter-governmental collaboration and close association with national, regional and international NGO [non-governmental organizations] networks and supra-national bodies.

In many post-conflict or transitional societies and in some of the poorest parts of Africa, *creating institutional mechanisms for the support and protection of children may mean starting from scratch*. In some places a concept of social responsibility beyond individual and family charity does not exist. In some, governance at both the national and local levels, and in both the public and non-governmental sectors, is very weak, such that even good child-centred policies are ineffectual. A World Bank (1998) study finds that in weak policy environments, capacity- and institution-building assistance has greater impact than international monetary aid. However, capacity-building projects are also found to have limited effectiveness unless the motivation for reform comes from within the local context. That is, those involved in the projects, whether public sector employees or communities working with non-governmental bodies, must take 'ownership' of institutional change.

In many places, World Bank and IMF programmes have required states to reduce the size of their bureaucracies in the name of fiscal responsibility, further undermining the capacity of already weak social provision. This emphasises the importance of involving powerful international institutions in policy dialogue, to ensure that their goals are consistent with children's best interests. Stabilisation and structural adjustment programmes need to be accompanied by social safety nets to protect the poorest families and children from bearing the brunt of economic adjustment. Children cannot 'adjust' to reduced opportunities in education, malnutrition, and poorer health. The World Bank and the IMF have the power to insist on social safety net programmes, and their member states and governing boards need to mandate that they use this power effectively.

Acknowledging children as change agents

Children everywhere are in a subordinate structural position in relation to adults. In many ways this can be regarded as a logical, inevitable and desirable outcome of the gradual nature of maturation in human beings. Further, as social and technological processes become more complex and demanding, it seems reasonable to expect children in the modern world to take longer to grow into adulthood. This emphasises the virtue of making a distinction between children and adults, which serves to protect the vulnerable and ensure the healthy development of all. Young children in particular should not be expected to take responsibility for situations over which they have no control or do not fully understand. Great care needs to be taken to make sure that the responsibilities born by children are suited to their maturity and capacities and do not expose them to exploitation or hazard.

Nevertheless, new research findings, reported above, suggest that children are often far more competent in numerous ways than is commonly thought and also that growing up without responsibility is not necessarily the most effective way to promote children's wellbeing and best interests (Knutsson, 1997, p. 41). These findings imply also that excluding children from social, political or economic processes simply because they are young cannot be justified any more than can the exclusion of any other group in society. This is not to suggest that children should take on the full complement of adult rights or responsibilities. More to the point, they should have substantially more rights to participate in society. This is a matter of sheer pragmatism, since children often have sound ideas about their problems and needs and the possible solutions to these and are in any case better able to protect themselves when properly informed and given some say in decisions and processes affecting them. Such engagement may be especially important for children in middle childhood and adolescence.

Children's participation in social planning and action is being piloted by various non-governmental organisations and some governments in a range of situations throughout the world (Johnson, *et al.,* 1998; Guijt, *et al.,* 1994; Hart, 1997). In Colombia, the acceptance of children as participating citizens is a major educational objective and children play a significant role in the governance of the country's New Schools (Escuelas Nuevas) programme. In Senegal, members of the Working Children and Youth Union sit on the board of the National Programme to Eliminate the Exploitation of Children at Work.

Building childhood policy on a vision of inclusion, self-determination and self-protection carries many challenges. It entails changes in the way adults think and act. It requires respect for children's integrity and capacity for responsible thought and action. To do this, adults need to learn to trust children's choices. At the same time, great sensitivity must be shown towards children's existing responsibilities, in that initiatives to support and protect children should not add to the considerable family and community burdens many already bear. Also important, the responsibilities of childhood, including the responsibilities associated with participation, will inevitably change as children grow and mature. Education curricula certainly recognise children's growing maturity. But other areas of policy, such as child protection, public health, labour regulation, social welfare and juvenile justice, seldom accommodate growth and change in childhood in a systematic manner consistent with child development evidence. This suggests the need to examine and reform many of the laws, policies, procedures, regulations and programme strategies affecting adolescents and youth in particular.

It is now apparent that *supporting children's best interests requires the perspective not just that children need special protections, but that they have valid insights into their well-being, valid solutions to their problems and a valid role in implementing those solutions.* Such an approach acknowledges children not merely as beneficiaries of intervention by adults, or a future societal asset, but as competent social agents in their own right. The CRC provides for such an approach, although it is seldom translated effectively into policy or practice, which have tended toward a far more paternalistic outlook. *The task for policy makers and programme implementers is to find ways of respecting the spirit and intention of the CRC in relation to children's participation, whilst also paying due regard to the context and to the maturity and the vulnerabilities and attributes of children.*

References

GUIJT, I., FUGLESANG, A. and KISADA, Y. (eds) (1994) *It is the Young Trees that make a Forest Thick*, London, IIED and Norway, Redd Barna.

HART, R. (1997) *Children's Participation: the theory and practice of involving young citizens in community development and environmental care*, London, UNICEF Earthscan Publications Ltd.

JOHNSON, V., IVAN-SMITH, E., GORDON, G., PRIDMORE, P. and SCOTT, P. (1998) *Stepping Forward, Children and Young People's Participation in the Development Process*, London, Intermediate Technology Publication.

KNUTSSON, K. E. (1997) *Children: noble causes or worthy citizens?*, Aldershot and Brookfield VT, Ashgate Publishing, for UNICEF.

LEVISON, D., ANKER, R., ASHRAF, S., AND BARGE, S. (1998) 'Is child labour really necessary in India's carpet industry?' Chapter 5 in Anker, R., Barge, S., Rajagopal, S. and Joseph, M. P. (eds) *Economics of Child Labour in Hazardous Industries of India*, New Delhi, Hindustan Publisher.

SALAZAR, M. and GLASNIOVICH, W. A. (1991) *Child Work and Education: five case studies from Latin America*, Aldershot, Brookfield USA, Singapore, Sydney, UNICEF ICDC, Ashgate.

WORLD BANK (1998) *Assessing Aid: what works, what doesn't, and why*, Washington DC, The World Bank. Available at www.worldbank.org/research/aid [accessed December 2002]

Source

BOYDEN, J. and LEVISON, D. (2001) *Children as Economic and Social Actors in the Development Process: Working paper 2000:1*, Expert Group on Development Issues, Ministry for Foreign Affairs, Stockholm, Sweden, pp. 46–52.

Chapter 6

Children's participation in society

Perpetua Kirby and Martin Woodhead

CONTENTS

When you have studied this chapter, you should be able to:

1 Define the concept of participation, and show how participatory principles can be applied to a variety of settings, age groups and cultural contexts.

2 Describe Hart's ladder model of participation and discuss its usefulness and limitations.

3 Explain the case for 'listening to children' in decision making, as well as some of the practical issues involved.

4 Evaluate the potential role for young people in researching their schools and contributing to school improvement.

5 Describe the Child-to-Child approach to health issues and consider how it has been applied in practice.

6 Examine different strategies for involving children in democratic processes, including children's clubs, parliaments, and elections.

1 INTRODUCTION

Allow about 10 minutes

ACTIVITY 1   **Images of the child in proverbs**

Proverbs offer a useful starting point for thinking about the theme of this chapter. Here is a selection from various cultural contexts. Make a note of the range of ideas about childhood being expressed. Can you think of other proverbs on these themes?

Children should be seen and not heard (UK)

What children prepare will not be enough for dinner (Ethiopia)

Children are the wealth of the nation (Tanzania)

Children are innocent like angels; they can't do any harm (Pakistan)

A tree should be bent while it is still young (South Africa)

When a child knows how to wash his hands he eats with his elders (Ghana)

Children are an investment in the future (South Africa)

The egg should not be smarter than the duck (Vietnam)

It is the young trees that make the forest thick (Uganda)

You don't have to be old to be wise (Nigeria)

(adapted from Carnegie, 1998, pp. 148–9; UNICEF, 2002a, p. 23)

COMMENT

These proverbs express many recurring cultural discourses of childhood that have been discussed in earlier chapters, such as:

1   the child as innocent and vulnerable – in need of protection;

2   the child as potential – an investment for the future;

3   the child as immature and inexperienced – who requires guidance and training;

4   the child as a challenge – who needs to respect his/her elders and betters.

But the last two proverbs hint at another image of children, one of children as valued participants who enrich society by their presence, now, as children and young people, and not just as the adults of the future. This idea – of children's participation in society – is the starting point for this chapter.

This chapter continues the study of children's rights begun in Chapter 5, Section 4, but it also connects with many of the issues in earlier chapters of the book. The evidence of childhood adversities – especially poverty, ill health and violence – challenges comfortable images of childhood as a protected space, regulated by adults for the benefit of children. Beliefs that children are or should be innocent are too often inconsistent with the reality of children's lives. Adult society fails to provide millions of children with adequate protection, and at worst abuses and exploits them. Recognition of children's rights, their capacities for understanding and the evidence for their resilience suggests a positive alternative, within which children and young people are redefined as 'worthy citizens' and not just as 'noble causes' (Knuttson, 1997). Or, as Boyden and Levison (Chapter 5, Reading C, pp. 230–1) put it:

> … supporting children's best interests requires the perspective not just that children need special protections, but that they have valid insights into their well being, valid solutions to their problems and a valid role in implementing those solutions. Such an approach acknowledges children not merely as beneficiaries of intervention by adults, or a future societal asset, but as competent social agents in their own right.

One child's view: 'Adults make the decisions of children and children make the decisions of babies. And then babies make the decisions of a mouse, and then a mouse makes it for ants, and then ants make it for a small crumb' (quoted in Kirby, 2002, p. 63).

This perspective on childhood has far-reaching implications for adults' relationships with children and young people at home and in the community, as well as for professional practices in health, social care and education. It is especially significant for settings such as schools which are traditionally built around the authority of adults over children, who occupy a subordinate structural position (see Chapter 5, Section 4.2). It is a view of children which makes very specific demands in relation to groups whose voices have often been overlooked, notably very young children, and groups who have been marginalized or excluded, such as disabled children, minority groups and, in some societies, girls (UNICEF, 2002a).

At the same time, emphasizing children's rights to participate has been challenged as being at best idealistic and at worst dangerous rhetoric. It can be seen as threatening to undermine parents' and teachers' crucial role in educating children, and, when necessary, disciplining them. From this standpoint, children need greater protection, not less, for example from the harmful influence of uncontrolled access to modern media, or from the dangers of urban street life. Others are more concerned about the risks of allowing young people too much freedom, unless they have demonstrated their capacity to act responsibly. Images of wayward youth are just as powerful as images of dependent innocents. Risks from children 'out of control' are very real to those who have been victims of juvenile crime, as well as to those who have suffered at the hands of children who have been recruited as terrorists or soldiers (see Chapter 4). Finally, talk about children's rights to participation can seem irrelevant in contexts where many of their parents are denied rights. Even within liberal democratic societies, many adults are rarely consulted about the issues that affect them, notably in their workplace (see Burr and Montgomery, 2003).

Debates about children's participatory rights all too easily become polarized between those who are seen as upholding traditional values, emphasizing adult responsibility and control, versus so-called child liberationists. In this chapter we try to avoid either of these extremes. Section 2 explores the meaning of children's participation in society and some aspects of the debate surrounding this view of children. Sections 3, 4 and 5 use a series of practical examples to discuss the application of participatory principles. Finally, we will ask you to consider trends towards children's participation within a broader context.

2 THE CONCEPT OF PARTICIPATION

Participation is a multifaceted concept. It is about children's activity and agency being recognized; about children being treated with dignity and respect; about them being entitled to express their feelings, beliefs and ideas; about being listened to and about their voices being heard. It is about children being consulted on matters that affect them, and being given adequate information to be able to form an opinion. It is also about children making choices and influencing decisions, contributing to the understanding and solution of social issues.

Participation can be applied to any number of areas of children's lives, as the photographs below illustrate. It can be about respecting children's play and the ways in which they communicate and learn. It can include children's influence over what food they eat, what clothes they wear, which TV channels they watch and the time they go to bed. It can be about deciding which school a child attends and which subjects they take; who the child lives with following parental separation; or whether a sick child should undergo a particularly painful course of treatment. These examples centre on questions of individual children's agency and well-being. Other examples are about children's role in the institutions that shape their lives, for example, school management and governing bodies, or anti-bullying projects. Finally, principles of child participation can be applied to the

Participation is about children's activity and agency being recognized.

Participation is about being treated with dignity and respect.

Participation is about being consulted on matters that affect them.

Participation is about being entitled to express feelings, beliefs and ideas.

government policies and laws that affect children's lives, promoting or constraining their opportunities, including their entitlement, or lack of entitlement, to vote in elections. Figure 1 provides a framework for thinking about the implications of children's participatory rights for a wide range of settings and institutions.

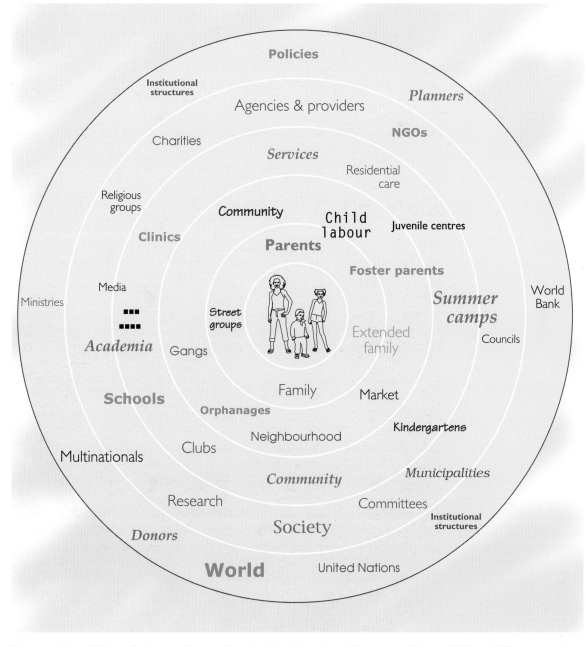

Figure 1 How children fit into settings and institutions (based on Johnson and Scott, 1998, p. 177).

Allow about 20 minutes

A C T I V I T Y 2   **Views on children's participation**

Before reading further, take time to consider your own views on children's participatory rights, using the examples of dilemmas below to help guide your thinking.

You have already come across one such example in Chapter 5, Section 4.1: the dilemma of the Norwegian children's ombudsman as to whether girls of sixteen should be allowed to make decisions about cosmetic surgery. How did you react to the ombudsman's decision to restrict the freedom of sixteen to eighteen year olds to make decisions about their bodies?

Now consider the following dilemmas. How do you react in each case?

1   Four-year-old Silvio has settled well into a nursery during the past term. He is very creative and loves to do paintings and craft projects, which he takes home with great pride. But he is very reluctant to do anything else. Silvio is very resistant to his teachers' efforts to introduce him to activities that will prepare him for school work. How far should Silvio be allowed to decide his priorities for learning?

2   Fourteen-year-old Jodie lives alone with her mother who has a mental health problem which makes her fearful of going outdoors. While the neighbours have always been very helpful, Jodie now takes charge of most of the shopping, going to the laundrette, etc., and she is often the one who calls the doctor or social worker when they need help. Now a meeting has been set up to discuss Jodie's future with a view to planning some alternative care arrangements. Jodie is very upset and feels she can do a better job than anyone else of caring for her mum. How far should Jodie be encouraged to continue taking on this responsibility?

3   City planners have set aside an area of land at the edge of a new estate for children and young people. There is a play area for the youngest children, an area for football, and an open shelter where teenagers can congregate. While the play area is frequently used by parents with young children, the teenagers prefer to 'hang out' near the railway station where they are constantly getting into trouble with shopkeepers and rail staff. They say the planners should have consulted young people before they decided what to provide. Should young people have a say in the planning of play and leisure facilities?

4   A local children's charity in a country with many extremely poor families offers support to a group of children who work in backstreet workshops to supplement their families' incomes. The children have been learning about the United Nations Convention on the Rights of the Child (UNCRC), and they decide to form a campaign group to fight for improvements in the way they are treated by their employers. They organize a march through the neighbourhood, with placards and chanting. But the police break up the march and some children get quite severely beaten. The organizers of the children's charity worry that they shouldn't have encouraged the children to express their views. Do you agree?

COMMENT

You might agree it is good to encourage Silvio's creativity, but still be concerned about the consequences of his resistance to activities that will prepare him for school. Four year olds cannot be expected to understand what school is going to be like, and the importance of academic achievement. But Jodie is much older and you may have felt her views should be respected. Even so, you may have felt she needed support, because she risks becoming isolated from her peers, or her schooling might suffer.

The city planning example is about how far the agencies responsible for children (which include central and local government, schools, health clinics, libraries, etc.) should take account of children's views, either directly through consultation and elected representation, or indirectly, for example, through a children's rights commissioner (see Chapter 5).

The final example raises a dilemma that can confront those working in situations where fundamental rights are not respected. Reactions to children asserting their rights are not usually as extreme as this, but it is very common for adults to feel threatened by the idea of young people taking action.

These examples raise a general issue that will recur throughout the chapter. Judgements about children's competence are crucial in deciding how far their wishes should be respected and how far they should influence decisions about what is in their best interests. These judgements may vary according to children's ages and abilities as well as their circumstances. This is true for individual cases, and also where groups of young people are concerned.

READING

Now read the Reading at the end of this chapter, 'The participation of children' by Gerison Lansdown. This is a long reading which introduces many of the issues raised by this chapter. Lansdown discusses the concept of children's participation and the implications of various articles in the United Nations Convention on the Rights of the Child. She then offers her own views on the debate.

Make a list of the arguments Lansdown offers for promoting children's participation, as well as her responses to objections that might be raised.

COMMENT

Gerison Lansdown starts from the principle that participation is a fundamental human right, and that children actively want to participate. She also claims that participation is beneficial to children themselves as well as to society. Finally, she challenges the conventional distinction between protectionist and participatory approaches to promoting children's well-being, citing several situations where adults have been better able to plan for the protection of children by ensuring those children's views are listened to.

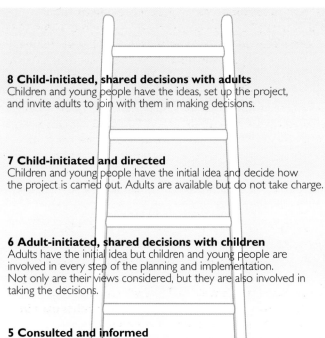

8 Child-initiated, shared decisions with adults
Children and young people have the ideas, set up the project, and invite adults to join with them in making decisions.

7 Child-initiated and directed
Children and young people have the initial idea and decide how the project is carried out. Adults are available but do not take charge.

6 Adult-initiated, shared decisions with children
Adults have the initial idea but children and young people are involved in every step of the planning and implementation. Not only are their views considered, but they are also involved in taking the decisions.

5 Consulted and informed
The project is designed and run by adults but children and young people are consulted. They have a full understanding of the process and their opinions are taken seriously.

4 Assigned but informed
Adults decided on the project and children and young people volunteer for it. Adults respect their views and the children feel fully informed.

3 Tokenism
Children and young people are asked to give their views, but they have little choice about the subject, or about the way they express themselves, or no time to formulate their opinions.

2 Decoration
Children and young people promote a cause, e.g. by singing, dancing or wearing t-shirts with slogans, but they do not really understand the issue, or play any part in organizing events.

1 Manipulation
Adults consciously use children's voices to carry their own messages.

In the second part of the extract, Lansdown examines the arguments against participation – notably, that it burdens children too early, when they lack sufficient competence; that adults' authority is too easily undermined; and that participation should be linked to children's capacities to take responsibility. More broadly, there is the argument that participation deprives children of their childhood, challenging traditional beliefs and values about children's innocence.

2.1 A ladder of participation?

As Lansdown suggests, many different types of initiative can be embraced under the broad heading of 'children's participation'. Initiatives vary in their scale and their goals, in the role of adults, and in the extent to which they promote children's power and influence. Roger Hart proposed using the metaphor of a ladder as a conceptual framework for thinking about all these different kinds of participation (see Figure 2).

Figure 2
The ladder of participation
(based on Hart, 1997, pp. 40–5).

Hart's initial interest was in children's participation in environmental projects, but the ladder metaphor has been applied much more widely. You may find it useful for thinking about the various examples in this chapter, although it is important to recognize the limitations of the metaphor. As we stated at the outset, participation is a multi-dimensional concept. It is not readily put on a linear scale. As Hart himself points out, the temptation is to judge children and projects according to how high they are up the ladder, as if the higher rungs are necessarily more desirable than the lower ones. But in some contexts it may be more appropriate for adults to take the lead. Also, according to their age and circumstances, children vary in how much initiative they feel able or wish to take. Hart would argue, however, that the lower, more tokenistic rungs of 'non-participation' are to be avoided in most circumstances.

Others have proposed, more radically, that the concept of children's participation is as much about adults' as about children's agendas: that it reflects a tension between encouraging children's self-realization and maintaining control over their lives (Prout, 2000). According to this view, 'the ladder' fails to represent those situations in which children take independent social action, which may be in opposition to (rather than in collaboration with) adult authority and agendas, through strikes, demonstrations and action groups. For example, consider the role played by young people in the struggle against apartheid in South Africa, discussed in Chapter 4, Section 4.3. As one student from Soweto wrote (in 1976), 'We cannot take it any longer. It is our parents who have let things go on far too long without doing anything. They have failed. We have been forced to fight to the bitter end' (Hoyles, 1979, p. 236).

Anti-apartheid demonstrators, Soweto, South Africa, 1976.

A very different but equally compelling example comes from a thirteen year old's account of a school strike in the small village of Burston in Norfolk, England, in April 1914, led by one of the children in the school, Violet Potter:

Burston School strikers, Norfolk, England, 1914.

We came on strike because our Governess and Master were dismissed from the Council School unjustly ... Violet Potter brought a paper to school with all our names on it, and all who were going on strike had to put a cross against their name. Out of seventy-two children sixty-six came out on strike.

(Hoyles, 1979, p. 230)

To summarize, the concept of children's participation conveys a positive image of inclusion, engagement and consensus. While these are fine ideals, their implementation in practice is inevitably constrained by children's status as a relatively powerless group within society, whose lives are in large measure regulated by adults 'in their best interests'. Of course, many adults also feel relatively powerless, especially if they live in extreme poverty or are socially excluded. In some situations children and adults may share a common cause in fighting against oppression and injustices.

We now go on to discuss children's participation in a range of settings, concentrating mainly on organized projects such as health programmes, school projects and children's clubs. Bear in mind, though, that we have had to be very selective in our choice of examples. Remember, too, that the principles of participation we are discussing also apply to more everyday relationships with children – at home, in shops and community facilities, on the street, on public transport.

SUMMARY OF SECTION 2

- Participation is about children taking part in and influencing processes, decisions and activities that affect them.

- Participation is a fundamental principle within the United Nations Convention on the Rights of the Child, which applies to a wide range of settings, including home, classroom and community, as well as to more formal involvement in school management and local and national government.

- Roger Hart's 'ladder of participation' has been an influential framework for evaluating different levels of children's participation.

3   LISTENING TO CHILDREN

UNCRC 1989 Article 12(1)
'States Parties shall assure to the child who is capable of forming his or her own views the right to express those views freely in all matters affecting the child, the views of the child being given due weight in accordance with the age and maturity of the child.'
(UNICEF, 2000b)

Listening to children is one of the first principles of child participation, as expressed in Article 12 of the UNCRC. Listening to children can be on a one-to-one basis, or it can be more formalized through consultations, representation in the management of services, or through children's parliaments.

In the Reading, Gerison Lansdown emphasized that listening to children does not necessarily mean accepting what they say, nor allowing them to take control over the decisions that affect them. But it does mean respecting children's attempts to make sense of their world, and their status as the key stakeholders in any decisions about what is in their best interests. It also means respecting the ways they communicate their understanding, feelings and wishes. In short, it means recognizing children 'as experts in their own lives' (Lansted, 1994, p. 42).

Listening effectively requires adults to create opportunities for children to express their feelings in ways appropriate to their abilities and interests, and to provide support for children who may find it difficult to communicate their feelings. In other words, it is about guiding and supporting their participation in a positive way, not just about judging whether they are competent to participate. (See Maybin and Woodhead, 2003, for further discussion of 'guided participation'.)

Listening isn't just about the words children say. This is especially the case with very young children, who communicate through their smiles or their cries, by whether they cling on to their care-giver or nuzzle up to them, long before they are able to put these feelings into words (Stern, 1985).

Listening to babies isn't about the words they say

Listening to young people who have communication impairments may require adults to make special efforts to ensure they don't feel socially excluded, as the example in Box 1 illustrates. It concerns two adults (Sharon and John) who have different views on how much Bobby understands about football. Initially, Sharon underestimates Bobby's understanding. John then intervenes to help Bobby demonstrate he knows exactly who won the match! For further discussion on participation with children with special needs, see Morris (1998).

The principle of listening to children has implications for children's treatment at home, at school, in hospitals and clinics, on public transport, in social work, and in the courts. Many of the required changes are about the quality of relationships with children, the styles of communication adopted, and the space created for children's voices to be heard.

The same principle can also be applied to larger-scale consultations with groups of children on, for example, improvements to child policies, provision or practices. For example, think back to the dilemma concerning children's use of play spaces in Activity 2 (Example 3). The children argued that consultation by town planners might have led to more appropriate provision for young people. Consultations of this kind now happen with increasing frequency. Many of these are about a specific issue in a locality, but consultations with young people may also inform national and international policies related to young people (Johnson and Scott, 1998).

For example, in the Reading Gerison Lansdown referred to a US-led campaign to end the employment of children under fifteen in the Bangladesh garment industry. The campaign failed to consult those affected, which had consequences far worse than if these children had remained in the factories. At that time – the early 1990s – working children's views went largely unnoticed in the international campaign to end child labour. More recently, organizations for working children have presented their views on the best ways to support young workers in countries of the South, at several major international meetings. One of the most effective organizations is Bhima Sangha, a union of working children based in Bangalore, India (Swift, 1999).

Box I   Did Bobby watch the game?

Bobby attends a special school in Scotland. He communicates through signs and through saying 'aye' or 'no' (and the adults use Scottish dialect in the conversation below). A visiting researcher called John has got to know Bobby well. One morning John is talking with a teaching assistant called Sharon about the football match on TV the night before, between rival teams Celtic and Rangers. Sharon (a Rangers supporter) turns to Bobby and asks:

Sharon: Bobby did you watch the game last night?

Bobby: Aye.

Sharon: Who won then?

Bobby: [*Puts his hands in the air*] uh, uh, uh,

Sharon: See he doesn't know. A don't think he really knows what's going on. A really don't think he understands.

John: Na na I don't agree Sharon, a think he knows.

Bobby: Aye, aye.

Sharon: So what was the score?

John: Look a know that he doesn't usually watch the football but am sure he seen this game. Ay Bobby, now you tell me with signs, how many did Rangers score?

Bobby: [*Puts one finger up*]

John: [*Without confirming he's right*] and how many did we [*Celtic*] get?

Bobby: [*Puts up one finger*]

John: So the score was one one?

Bobby: Aye [*said with triumph*]

John: And which team were lucky?

Bobby: Isss [*us*].

Sharon: That's really good Bobby a nivir realized that.

(adapted from Davis *et al.*, 2000, pp. 214–15)

Children are also being consulted through systematic research. For example, Save the Children Sweden carried out a consultation with 300 working children in a range of occupations in Bangladesh, Ethiopia, the Philippines, El Salvador, Guatemala and Nicaragua.

Participants in this study were mostly about ten to fourteen years old. Many were unable to read and write and could easily have felt intimidated by formal interviews or questionnaires, but within the context of their peer group they were both able and eager to share their views and experiences. Local adult facilitators worked with groups of children on a wide range of picture and story-based activities, with children mapping their daily lives, ranking the things they liked and disliked, as well as carrying out role-plays about difficult experiences they encounter with parents, teachers, employers and customers. In this way the study was able to inform international debate with children's own views on the ways in which they were harmed by their

Consulting working children: a group of farm boys in the Philippines use drawings to talk about their work.

work, as well as the reasons why they felt they had to work. Seventy per cent of participants in the study felt that combining work with going to school was the best solution in their circumstances. In Bangladesh, many children (especially girls) rated garment-factory work as preferable to alternatives available to them such as flower selling or domestic work (Woodhead, 1999; see also Mackinnon, 2003).

In this section we have begun to consider how the principle of listening to children can be adapted to children's competencies, circumstances and ways of communicating. We now look at two examples that draw attention to the way participatory principles can be applied with children at very different ages and stages of development.

3.1 Young children's perspectives on their nursery

Planning for very young children is usually seen as the responsibility of adults, on the assumption that parents, teachers and care workers know best; but what can be learned from asking about very young children's perspectives? Here, we focus on a study of three and four year olds within a nursery setting in London. Alison Clark and Peter Moss (2001) devised a range of methods, in what they called a 'Mosaic approach', to find out children's views and experiences. These included:

- short, informal interviews carried out with children (called child conferencing);
- children using disposable cameras to take photographs of 'important things';
- inviting children to take them on tours of the site, which children recorded, using a tape recorder;

- using children's drawings and photographs to create visual maps, from children's points of view;
- observations carried out to gain additional perspectives on children's experiences;
- interviews with parents and staff.

Through these methods, Clark and Moss built up a picture of the ways in which the children constructed meaning in the nursery. They learned about children's favourite places, the places in which they could feel a degree of privacy, the places where they liked to play with their friends.

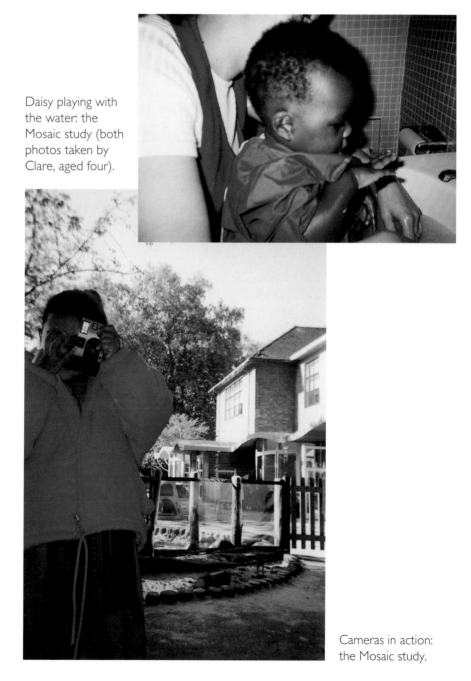

Daisy playing with the water: the Mosaic study (both photos taken by Clare, aged four).

Cameras in action: the Mosaic study.

Gaby was one of the three year olds at the nursery who took part in the Mosaic study. When she was given a disposable camera and asked to photograph 'important things', almost every photograph she took was of another child or children. When she took Clark on a tour of the nursery she explained that the conservatory was where she had lunch (as one of the younger ones), but added 'I can't wait to be big', explaining that older children eat in the Orange Room. She also talked about the activities she most liked, and about the role of adults. According to Clark and Moss, listening to young children in this systematic way enabled the adults involved with the nursery to understand more about what being at nursery feels like for children, while their parents gained insight into their child's experiences during the time they are apart. Sometimes parents and nursery workers were surprised by what they learned and by the children's capacities to understand nursery life. One parent went out and bought a camera for her three year old!

While the main goal of this study was to promote very young children's participation in the planning of their nursery, Clark and Moss also respected the children's rights to choose how they participated. For example, when they went on the tour of the nursery, the children were in charge of the recording. They carried the tape recorder in a little bag, they wore the clip mike, they controlled when the tape was recording and if a child felt uncomfortable carrying the bag, they could pass it on to someone else. Clark explained to the authors of this chapter why they wanted to enable young children to have some control over the process:

> I believe in research being a democratic process, and we thought the children were capable and that it was necessary to respect their willingness to take part or not, and so give them as much control as possible.

The Mosaic study was about finding ways to consult with even very young children about issues that affect their well-being (see also Cousins, 1999; Alderson, 2000a). The next example applies the same basic principles, but with very much older children. In this case, children were not just consulted in a research investigation. They contributed to designing, carrying out and interpreting the research itself.

3.2 Participation in school reform: students as researchers

As part of a strategy for school improvement, a comprehensive school in Bedfordshire, UK, began an initiative to involve school students as researchers in 1996. The school was attended by approximately 1,500 pupils aged thirteen to eighteen. Table 1 shows the different ways in which students were involved in research. (Note the parallel with Hart's ladder of participation in Figure 2.)

One of the teachers at the school, Louise Raymond, described how in some cases students took an active lead in research, either as co-researchers or researchers (Raymond, 2001). Small research teams of about six or seven students and a member of staff worked on a research issue chosen by the

Table 1 Four approaches to involving students in school research.

Data	Discussion	Dialogue	Significant voice
Students as data source	Students as active respondents	Students as co-researchers	Students as researchers
Asking students what they think via a questionnaire	Involving students in designing questionnaires and analysing results	Working with students to co-research specific areas of interest	Students identify and own the agenda for research issues that are important to them

Source: adapted from Raymond, 2001, p. 58

whole student body. Together, students and adults were trained in research and evaluation. Experienced student researchers sometimes helped deliver the training. The students used a range of methods in their research, including questionnaires, interviews, classroom observation and group discussions. Topics researched by the students included: evaluating and improving ways of teaching in science; school meals; and the use of praise slips as a form of motivation.

One of the most challenging proposals for research was about the support given to trainee teachers:

> ... students felt that, as a school, we were not being as honest about the trainees and how we used them in school as perhaps we could be. Quite simply, students recognised the fact that the expertise of some of these trainees, in terms of their subject knowledge, was fantastic, but that their skill in teaching was an area that, for some, was quite difficult. The students, effectively, were saying that they cared about their lessons and they wanted to be part of the process. They felt concerned about their progress and, after all, as many of them had said, 'These are *my* A levels'.

> (Raymond, 2001, p. 60)

Initially, the idea of students researching the quality of teaching met with resistance. It took two years for action to follow:

> The students' enquiry resulted in them making recommendations that students who had trainee teachers should be able to work in partnership with their normal teacher and the trainee to give feedback on lessons. At the time, I remember being extremely excited at putting these very simple recommendations into practice, but the culture and climate of the school at the time was just not right.

> What has become increasingly clear to me over the years is being able to accept that very simple fact. It is important to remember that all staff within a community need to feel comfortable with these types of initiatives.

> (Raymond, 2001, p. 60)

Box 2 contains two short extracts from articles by student researchers at the school.

Box 2   Students as Researchers: a viewpoint from two students

Beth

Schools cannot learn how to become better places for learning without asking the students … neither staff nor outside researchers are necessarily ideally placed to ask questions that allow people to get to the root of key issues, or subsequently get honest answers from students about things that matter to them.

[…]

Students as Researchers … changed how some staff at the school considered their students, encouraging them to think of students more as equals, and a source of help in making the most of their teaching. It also changed how students thought of themselves. They came to feel like a more valued and respected resource, and to recognise the fact that they were actually an education knowledge base.

(Crane, 2001, pp. 54–5)

Chris

When I entered the first year of upper school [at thirteen years old] I carried on as usual just having education done to me and not responding to anything other than what was inside the classroom …

I was trained in research methods and the ethics of research and formed with a group that was to be looking at profiling and assessment within the school. We spent approximately 6 months gathering data and preparing findings ready to feed into the senior management team …

This was my motivation to keep going … From some work that I had done [as a student researcher] I had influenced the school's feelings about profiling and assessment – so much so that they changed it, that gave me a great sense of achievement.

(Harding, 2001, p. 56)

Students and teachers discuss their research.

Allow about 15 minutes   A C T I V I T Y 3   **Involving students as researchers**

From this brief description of children as researchers, make a note of the likely benefits of children's participation for the teachers, the student researchers and the wider school community. What difficulties might arise from involving young people so centrally in the evaluation of aspects of their schooling?

COMMENT

When teachers work *with* students as researchers, it alters traditional, hierarchical teacher–student relationships. This is a potentially risky venture for teachers. They may worry about how students will behave if given more control. They may also open themselves up to unwelcome comments about their teaching practices. But according to those involved in the *Students as Researchers* project, this is balanced by the following benefits:

1   Students identify issues that are important to them, from their perspective, some of which teachers may otherwise overlook, as in the case of the role of trainee teachers.

2   Working *with* students can encourage teachers to perceive young people as equals and to see the value of what students have to offer adults. This helps to change their relationships with students.

3   Students enjoy being involved in research. It is easier for teachers to work with motivated students than those who would rather be elsewhere. At the same time, however, involving students as researchers no doubt creates extra work for teachers.

4   Students learn research and presentation skills. They gain a sense of achievement and a belief in their ability to make changes. They learn to respect other views and gain sensitivity in dealing with controversial issues.

5   When staff listen to students' views and changes are made, then the students benefit from improved teaching and a better school environment.

The *Students as Researchers* project illustrates one effective strategy for increasing young people's participation that has been extended more widely in Bedfordshire schools. It is important, however, to exercise a degree of caution about children's role as researchers. For example, Beth (in Box 2) believed that students give more honest responses to student researchers than they would to teachers. The assumption that young people are more honest with their peers than with adults may not always be true; it will depend on the issue and the context in which it is being considered.

Another project involving young people as researchers also raised questions about this assumption. In 1997, Save the Children UK supported seven young refugees to research a subject of their choice. The refugees were from the Horn of Africa, aged sixteen to twenty-one, and were living in London. They chose to research the educational support needs of other young refugees. In the following passage the workers who trained and supported the young researchers describe how the group accessed other young people to interview:

> The young researchers' interview skills varied within the group; some clearly had the ability to encourage interviewees to open up. However, they all collected useable data, although further practice and experience would have yielded more in-depth information.
>
> [...]

> Contrary to expectations, there was a very high refusal rate; almost three out of four people refused to be interviewed ... The young researchers ... felt that some of the interviewees were not freely open about the information they provided, particularly about sensitive issues such as personal experiences of bullying. Some of the young people were also clearly bored by the length of the interview, which lasted between half an hour and two hours.
>
> (Kirby *et al.*, 2001, p. 16)

In certain cases, young people may be *less* likely to open up about sensitive issues to people of their own age, people whom they know or will see again. In some instances they may prefer to talk to someone whose job and role are perceived as being independent and impartial.

It is also important to bear in mind that hierarchies of power affect relationships among peer groups, just as they affect relationships between young people and adults. The young refugee researchers found that just by becoming 'researchers' their status changed. Some of their interviewees worried that the young researchers were now working for the Home Office. It would also be a mistake to treat young people as a homogeneous group and assume that the benefits of their participation in research will apply in all situations. Gender, ethnicity, class, and even popularity may be as important as age in determining how much a young person will be open with others (in the same way as these factors are often important with adult researchers).

This still leaves the issue of whether children and young people can realistically acquire the necessary skills to carry out a well-planned investigation. Reviewing a number of research case studies undertaken in the UK involving young people as researchers, Alan Dyson and Nick Meagher conclude:

> Research is ... a highly technical process which many professionals spend an entire lifetime perfecting. Perhaps unsurprisingly, the experience of our case studies is that some young people lack the skills, expertise and attitudes to become involved in anything other than a peripheral role.
>
> In particular, the research process, by demanding resources which disadvantaged young people do not possess, provides further instance of their marginalisation and disempowerment. Attempts to involve young people which do not recognise this reality and are unprepared for its impact run the risk of doubly disenfranchising marginalised groups. If involving young people simply means involving those who are already most like professional researchers, then marginalized young people will effectively be excluded even from processes which are ostensibly designed to empower them.
>
> (Dyson and Meagher, 2001, pp. 65–6)

Dyson and Meagher draw attention to the risks of idealizing the potential for young people to carry out effective research, and the possibility that it might exacerbate their feelings of social exclusion. Their warning suggests that it may be a mistake to attempt simply to mimic traditional research techniques in studies involving child researchers. General principles of participatory work with children also apply to research – especially the importance of taking account of young people's interests, competencies and preferred ways of communicating their concerns.

SUMMARY OF SECTION 3

- 'Listening to children' requires adult sensitivity in adapting communication to children's abilities and interests.

- Larger-scale consultations with children are becoming more common as part of planning for children's services, as well as in the development of policies on their best interests.

- The Mosaic study illustrates how very young children can be consulted about their perspectives on their nursery.

- The *Students as Researchers* project illustrates how young people can contribute to processes of school improvement.

- In some situations, effective participation may be difficult to achieve, and research may sometimes require more technical knowledge than can be expected of young people.

4 PARTICIPATION IN CHILD HEALTH ISSUES: THE CHILD-TO-CHILD APPROACH

One of the earliest examples of participatory principles being applied on a large scale predates Article 12 of the UNCRC. Child-to-Child (CtC) is a radical approach to health education, where children's own potential in tackling health issues is recognized. It was initiated during the late 1970s by health and education professionals at the University of London, in preparation for the International Year of the Child (1979).

CtC offered an alternative strategy for tackling primary health care issues in the world's poorest countries – where infant mortality rates are very high and children are at risk from malnutrition and diarrhoeal infections, as well as from diseases preventable through vaccination (see Chapter 3). The approach is based on the belief that children can contribute to the health and well-being of themselves and others.

During the 1970s, approaches to health were inherently protectionist. They relied largely on interventions by 'experts': for example, setting up clinics and vaccination programmes, and teaching parents basic principles of child health. It was, however, becoming increasingly apparent that children's own role in the process was being neglected, and that they themselves could be seen as effective agents of change.

Increasing provision of primary schools in poorer communities meant that children were often more literate than their parents, and they tended to share new ideas with other children and adults more readily than their parents did. In traditional rural communities it was often children, especially girls, who were responsible for much of the care of their younger siblings – the very children most at risk (Weisner and Gallimore, 1977).

Though it predates the UNCRC, CtC was built in part on the principles of child participation. The other main principle embodied in the approach concerns education for social change. Inspired by Paolo Freire's literacy work with Brazilian peasants during the 1970s, CtC involves raising people's awareness of how their personal situation is linked with wider social issues, in this case by enabling children to learn about a community health issue and, in turn, inform others about the issue (Gibbs *et al.*, 2002).

CtC has now been applied in more than 70 countries, including affluent countries of the North as well as the poorest countries of the South where the scheme began. As the CtC movement has grown, lessons have been learned about the most effective ways of involving children. The original programmes were mainly about health promotion and about children passing on basic health messages to their peers and siblings – hence the name 'Child-to-Child'. These early programmes soon recognized the potential for children to influence adults too.

Some CtC programmes have extended beyond children's participation in health promotion to emphasize children's decision making and action. The Child-to-Child Trust, based at the University of London, states: 'The most effective programmes are those that involve children in decision making rather than merely using them as communicators of adult messages' (The Child-to-Child Trust, 2003). For example, children on a CtC project in south-east London have been supported to identify and take action on their own priority health issues. Their chosen topics have included elderly people, racism, murder, drugs, safe places to play, child abuse, children being hit and school uniform (Kirby, 2002).

Box 3 summarizes six steps within the CtC approach to child participation.

In Section 4.1 we examine a CtC project in rural Zambia. This project involves primary school children in tackling basic child health issues which are similar to those that inspired the originators of CtC during the 1970s. As you study this example, consider the ways in which the *context* of the participatory project – including the geographical location, parents' attitudes to children and the organizational culture of schools – can affect *how* children are involved. Think also about the level of children's participation, for example, how far they (or adults) are involved in planning the project, making key decisions and putting them into action.

Box 3 Six steps in the Child-to-Child approach to participation

1 *Identifying a local health issue and understanding it well*
Sometimes adults decide the health issue, but in other projects children choose the health issue they most want to focus on.

2 *Finding out more about the health issue*
Children use a range of methods, including looking in books and on the internet, writing letters or interviewing others with experience in the relevant field.

3 *Discussing what has been found out and planning action*
Children use their findings to decide what action they should take in relation to their specific health issue. Adults can help children evaluate the information they have collected and plan action.

4 *Taking action*
Children take action on the chosen health issue. The range and type of activities depend on the issue and on local circumstances in their community.

5 *Evaluation: discussing results*
The children and adults evaluate the project, looking at what worked well, what worked least well and how effective they were.

6 *Discussing how to be more effective next time and sustain action*
In some projects children are invited to improve on their activities and, if appropriate, to repeat or continue their action.

(adapted from the Child-to-Child Trust, 2003)

4.1 Child-to-Child in Zambia

Paul Mumba, a primary school teacher in rural Zambia, initiated a CtC project on the theme of child growth with the children in his school (Mumba, 2002). His starting point was two sets of issues. The first was about improving children's health; the second was about improving the quality and relevance of schooling, especially for girls.

1 The children in his class come from a poor rural community, where infant mortality rates are high and children's growth is often affected by malnutrition. Parents place value on having large families, with little spacing between children, which means babies are often weaned early and to an inadequate diet. National immunization programmes are available, but are not always taken up by parents. Most of the mothers lack the knowledge necessary to monitor the growth of their children, so early signs of illness are not detected.

2 The curriculum in primary schools is often seen by pupils as boring and irrelevant. Teaching is often very formal and oriented towards the passing of examinations, which for many rural children is unrealistic. This results in high drop-out rates, especially amongst girls, who are often under pressure to marry and become pregnant while still young.

Mumba wanted to adopt a more engaging way of teaching the health curriculum, to make it more relevant to the lives of his pupils, and, in turn, to help them contribute to achieving health for children in the community. He decided to focus the CtC project on the study of child growth. All households with young children were issued with growth monitoring charts known as 'under-five cards', and these were used as the main teaching aid in the CtC project.

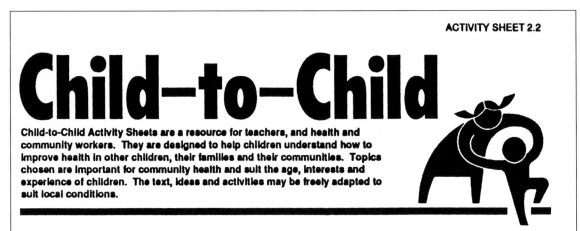

ACTIVITY SHEET 2.2

Child-to-Child

Child-to-Child Activity Sheets are a resource for teachers, and health and community workers. They are designed to help children understand how to improve health in other children, their families and their communities. Topics chosen are important for community health and suit the age, interests and experience of children. The text, ideas and activities may be freely adapted to suit local conditions.

FEEDING YOUNG CHILDREN 2: How do we know if they are eating enough?

THE IDEA

Children must have enough of the right kind of food for healthy growth and to fight infection.

Many children are not getting enough good foods. These children can develop normally if they are helped soon enough. There are three simple ways of finding out if an infant or young child is not getting enough food:
- by knowing how to recognise the signs of having too little food.
- by weighing young children regularly at the clinic and recording their weight on a chart.
- by measuring the upper arm of children under five years of age.

Children can learn to understand why children are undernourished, and how little children can be helped.

Extract from a CtC resource sheet. Teachers, health and community workers adapt activities to suit local conditions.

Mumba first taught children the importance of nutrition, using a weighing machine to relate the concept of food to weight. He then asked the children to bring in their own 'under-five card' from home and encouraged them to compare their charts in terms of differences in growth and health. The children began to ask their parents questions, such as:

> *Why is there a difference in weight and yet ages of the children are the same?*
>
> *Why don't parents feed us well?*

(Mumba, 2002, p. 2)

Parents offered some explanations, including reasons why their charts were incomplete – for example, they had stopped growth monitoring once the child had been vaccinated, or their priority was on nursing a newborn baby – or they told the children it was none of their business. But it became clear that some children's understanding was already better than that of their parents.

The children continued with a closer study of growth charts and discussed the causes of weight variation in the class. Over time their questions focused on the timing of births, nutrition, immunization, diseases and growth monitoring. They researched the answers to their questions by, for example, further discussions with parents and meeting with health professionals. The children visited the under-five clinic to witness immunization programmes, and their questions included:

> What are vaccines?
>
> Why are some vaccines given in the mouth? [polio]

(Mumba, 2002, p. 2)

The children then went home and checked the under-five cards for their siblings. They found that many of their brothers and sisters had not completed the immunizations. So they chose to monitor these siblings and regularly weighed them. They also encouraged their mothers to breast feed.

This project raised questions for the children about their own lives:

> What causes a woman to have a premature baby?
>
> Why are there so many children in some families?
>
> Why do some girls become pregnant at an early age?

(Mumba, 2002, p. 4)

Mumba explains why it was the girls who became especially engaged with these issues:

> Girls wanted to find out more on effects of abortions, miscarriages and children with low birth weight. They did not want to experience that when they become adults. A sense of responsibility was revealed as they discussed deeper issues affecting their lives. Questions arose on the correct age a girl should be married or pregnant. Most girls did not want to experience situations that would endanger their lives.

(Mumba, 2002, p. 3)

As their teacher, Mumba wanted to steer these young people towards finding people and places in the community that would help them find solutions to their concerns. He encouraged them to talk to medical professionals about the most sensitive issues (such as abortions, early marriages and premature babies). He also asked the children to survey their parents' response to involving children in child monitoring. These varied; some were not in favour, but the majority were positive about their children's learning. Some parents felt teachers should do all the teaching in class rather than sending children out into the community to find answers to questions, particularly parents who felt they lacked the competence to answer questions on school-related topics.

Participatory projects are frequently challenging to all involved. They disrupt conventional expectations about power, authority and the role of children. Paul Mumba acknowledges the risks he was taking in encouraging children to ask questions, seek information, and, in some cases, challenge their parents' child-care practices.

> According to our African culture, some of the topics explored ... were a taboo ... In fact a teacher would come into conflict with some members of the community if they discovered what went on in the classroom.

> (Mumba, 2002, p. 4)

The children, however, were very positive about the project. They felt they were promoting health knowledge and care to friends and family, and learning about how to be responsible parents in the future.

> *I am helping feeding my younger brother and sister.*
> *I am encouraging my mother to take the baby to the under-five clinics.*

> (Mumba, 2002, p. 5)

Allow about 30 minutes

ACTIVITY 4 **Features of a CtC project**

Make a list of the main features of this example of CtC in Zambia. Pay particular attention to these questions:

1   What role did the children's teacher play in initiating and facilitating their participation and guiding and controlling them, as well as enabling them to take action?

2   What role did children play? How much influence did they have in deciding the goals of the project and how these were to be achieved?

3   How much were children able to make a genuine contribution to the health issue?

COMMENT

While this project was very successful on several counts, it also highlights some of the inevitable constraints that surround putting children's participation into practice. First, the adult facilitator, the teacher, initiated the project and structured the sessions, as well as ensuring children's learning and general well-being. The children were not making decisions autonomously, but were always guided by their teacher, as well as by the structure of the CtC six-step approach.

Second, the project was implemented in a school, which placed organizational expectations and curriculum demands on children that restricted their freedom to decide priorities for the project. Third, parents' knowledge and attitudes influenced how much they supported the children's action.

Of course, you may feel the role of adults was not a 'constraint' at all, any more than it was in the *Students as Researchers* example (Section 3.2). You may think, on the contrary, that adults offering children support and direction and teaching them about the process of participation itself was essential to the success of the project.

In other respects, the Zambian context provided children with a rare opportunity to make a genuine contribution to their community. In a situation where adult health knowledge was poor, and adult literacy levels relatively low, the children were well placed to share their learning within the family. The children appear to have made a very significant impact on the basic health issues faced by children in their communities (although this was not formally evaluated), by promoting health messages to parents and taking a lead in monitoring younger siblings' growth. Interestingly, CtC projects carried out in south-east London found it more difficult to make a genuine impact, partly because of the complex infrastructure of existing health services within the urban community which diminishes children's potential role as health educators (Kirby, 2002).

Finally, it is important to bear in mind that the claimed benefits of child participation also include children's own well-being and development. The children's own comments illustrate that they have learned a lot about child nutrition (although again this was not formally evaluated).

Adult roles and children's participation

The examples above draw attention to the need for adults committed to encouraging children's participation to find new ways of interacting with children. Guiding participation is a dynamic process. Within this process, the balance between facilitating and instructing may shift between situations, between groups of children, and between activities. As we have seen, the role of adults is very different according to whether children are three, nine or fifteen years old. It will also vary according to children's experiences of participation, their interests and their preferred ways of communicating. Adult roles may vary from minute to minute, even with the same group of children. For example, an adult who is being very non-directive over children's plans may switch very rapidly to being highly directive if the fire alarm sounds.

Table 2 summarizes some of the adult roles observed in CtC projects in South London. In addition, of course, there are times when it is appropriate for adults to 'abstain' and allow children to undertake their own activities without any adult intervention.

Table 2 A range of adult roles in child participation.

Non-directive						Directive
Observer	Facilitator	Activator	Adviser	Informer	Instructor	Doer
Reflect and feed back on what is happening in the group.	Ask questions to find out what children want to do. Encourage inclusion. Provide resources to take action.	Challenge ideas and encourage children to develop their ideas further. E.g. may play devil's advocate.	Suggest ways in which events can move forward.	Tell children what is happening. Provide other information. May include adults' own views.	Tell children what to do and how to do it. E.g. ensure structure, discipline and safety.	Take action on behalf of children.

Source: Kirby, 2002, p. 80, based on Klein, 2001, p. 27

SUMMARY OF SECTION 4

- CtC began as an alternative strategy for tackling child health issues in the world's poorest countries. The six-steps model has since been applied more widely.

- A CtC project in rural Zambia aimed to teach health education in ways more relevant to the lives of pupils, especially girls. The project has helped children to contribute to achieving health in their community.

- Adults frequently play a key role in guiding children's participation. That role will depend on the children's age, abilities and circumstances, as well as the issue being addressed.

5 CHILDREN AND CITIZENSHIP

Earlier sections have discussed a range of projects designed to increase children's participation. These examples have drawn attention to the importance of organizational structures, adult guidance and child-centred communication styles through which children can develop a sense of agency in their lives, irrespective of their age, ability or circumstances. Increasing participation is, at root, about extending the goals of democracy to ensure that all citizens – including the youngest – are prepared and able to contribute to shaping their own lives, their community and wider society. This is one of Lansdown's arguments for participation in the Reading (see also Cutler, 2001; UNICEF, 2002a). In this final section we look briefly at young people's involvement in democratic initiatives, ranging from clubs and societies through to formal representation within local and national government. Many of these initiatives originate in well-established democracies in the affluent countries of the North, but not all. For our first example we turn to an experiment in children's democracy in a very different economic, political and cultural context – Nepal.

Young people campaign against labour and exploitation, New Delhi, India, 1999.

5.1 Children's clubs in Nepal

Nepal is one of the poorest countries in the world, where levels of schooling are relatively low and many children work. During the 1990s, an estimated 1,000 clubs were established as a focus for play, learning and community action. These clubs were not the first children's organizations in Nepal. For example, there were long-established boy scout and girl guide groups, but these were, for the most part, adult-directed organizations. By contrast, children's own role in managing their activities is emphasized in the children's clubs.

Members of the Chandra Surya Bal Samhua Children's Club, Nepal.

Many of the clubs originated in Child-to-Child schemes set up to improve health education and awareness in isolated communities (see Section 4). But the organization and functioning of the clubs has grown since then, fostered by two major non-governmental organizations working in Nepal – Save the Children Norway (SCN) and Save the Children US (SCUS). Most of the clubs involve children of eight to sixteen years, although sometimes seventeen and eighteen year olds are also members. Their organizational structure is similar to adult groups, with clearly defined roles. Box 4 contains brief descriptions of two of the clubs.

Box 4   Two children's clubs in Nepal

The Shrii Bagela Bal Club is in the Palpa district. The club has 26 members, 11 girls and 15 boys, with an elected structure of roles and responsibilities. The executive board has 11 older members, including a male chairperson. The club meets twice a month for two hours in a community centre also used by adult groups. At meetings the children pay an attendance fee. They plan activities such as building a flower garden, a volleyball programme, street dramas, competitions and clean-up campaigns. They also run informal activities such as singing and dancing. This club links up with twelve others in the district and children from each club attend regional meetings, where annual plans are shared.

The Chandra Surya Bal Samhua Club is in the village of Namuna Gaun, in the Chitawan district. Membership of the club reflects the ethnic mix of the village, including Brahmin, Chhetri, Tamang, Lama, Newar and Chaudhary. The village was devastated by floods in 1993, and since then it has been largely rebuilt by the community. The 25 boys and 15 girls in the club have been very actively involved in community development, and their role has been accepted and respected by adults. Building on Child-to-Child principles, they have taken on the task of monitoring the cleanliness of homes and toilets in the village, giving out rewards and charging fines accordingly. They also sponsor a few children to attend local schools. The club is open daily for one hour and all day Saturdays, and the children participate in a number of fun activities, including competitions, drama and drawing.

(adapted from Rajbhandari et al., 1999, p. 6)

A study of these clubs identified a wide range of activities engaged in by the children: artistic and cultural expression; play and sports; competitions; club management, administration and networking; national rallies (e.g. about children's issues); learning and skill development; development work and community awareness promotion. When the children were asked what they most valued, 'peer relations' was top of the list, that is, the chance to socialize and discuss and work together with other young people. This social dimension was the overriding factor shaping how they thought about the various club activities, such as games and art work, learning to read and write, tree planting schemes and other community activities (Rajbhandari et al., 1999).

A children's club treasurer goes over the accounts with club members, Nuwakot district, Nepal.

The children's clubs of Nepal also offer some striking examples of community action regarding the rights of disabled children. In one village in Bhaktapur disabled children from the children's club instigated a house-to-house survey to identify where there were other disabled children. If the child was not in school, the children counselled the parents to persuade them of the importance of sending the child to school. And where the family was too poor, the children tried to raise the money to ensure that the child could enrol at school. Disabled children have engaged in advocacy at a national level too.

At a child consultation day organized by the Disabled Human Rights Centre in Nepal, 25 disabled children worked together to identify priorities for action to overcome the profound discrimination and social exclusion they experience in their day-to-day lives. These included access to education, appropriate health care, equality of opportunity, changes in public awareness and the need for improved data about disability – both qualitative and quantitative. At a follow-up meeting, they also elaborated strategies for taking this agenda forward by raising their concerns through the media, with government, at school and with their local communities. The participating children were aged between fourteen and eighteen and included deaf, blind, and physically and intellectually disabled children (Lansdown, forthcoming).

The children's clubs in Nepal represent a very interesting experiment in child participation. But questions can be raised about how far they are truly child-run democracies. First, the clubs often originate in adult-led initiatives. Their government structure was introduced to the children in the training they received from SCN and SCUS and in advice received from the adult facilitators who support the groups. To begin with, children were not always encouraged to question or change the rules, for example, about meeting times or age limits. Although the goal is for children to make more decisions and manage their own activities, some clubs are still heavily influenced by dominant adults. Second, more boys attend the clubs than girls, and more boys hold official positions. This is mainly due to the girls' additional work responsibilities, and also reflects traditional gender divisions. Sometimes the poorest and lower-caste children are excluded because they cannot afford the fee or because they are not allowed to spend time at the clubs when they could be working to support their families. As the study of children's clubs concludes:

> The philosophy of the children's clubs is that they should offer an opportunity for children themselves to democratically organize and direct their own activities … even though a club may have no formal control by any adults, they can easily control the clubs in subtle ways just by virtue of their seniority. There is a need to minimize this kind of control. This does not mean at all that the clubs should be divorced from the adult community. There is a very important place for adults as advisers and supporters as the children need them. But the club's identity as an institution should be clear and respected and it should be as self-managing as possible.
>
> (Rajbhandari et al., 1999, p. 37)

5.2 Towards practical citizenship

Initiatives designed to increase children's democratic participation have become increasingly widespread since the UNCRC in 1989. This has been one of the functions of children's rights commissioners, who have been instrumental in setting up school councils, youth forums, children's parliaments and other forms of consultation, including via the internet (see Chapter 5, Section 4.1). Box 5 summarizes three further examples of children's participation, ranging from a local consultation about a children's hospital to an elected children's parliament.

These and other initiatives to promote children's civic engagement need to be set against a wider set of concerns expressed in many countries about how far young people are both ignorant of and feel excluded from representative democracy. For example, in 2002 the British government introduced citizenship as a national curriculum subject. An international survey of fourteen year olds' attitudes towards citizenship is relevant here. The authors of the study in England reported that fourteen year olds had a basic understanding of democratic values and institutions, but were sceptical about traditional party politics. However, they did recognize the importance of elections, and they were also open to other forms of active engagement, such as charity fund-raising and non-violent protests. Most important, the study found that schools that are organized to provide a model of democratic values – by encouraging students to discuss issues and take an active role in the life of the school – were most effective in promoting civic knowledge and engagement (Kerr et al., 2002). Note that Lansdown makes a similar point in the Reading, and cites other studies to support her argument.

Box 5 Children's civic participation

Derby children's hospital, UK, 1992

When a new children's hospital was to be built, 130 children were invited to participate in group discussions and workshops to find out what they wanted from the hospital. The children were drawn from local primary and secondary schools. The architects found the process instructive and creative. Some of the ideas from the children included better play areas and lowered reception desks where children could check in by themselves.

Youth councils, France

Youth councils have been in operation in France since the 1970s. Their role is to articulate the concerns of children and young people about their local communities. In 1991, the National Association for Children and Youth Town Councils was founded. Its first annual meeting was attended by 700 young people and 400 adults and subsequent meetings have been attended by government ministers.

Children's Parliament in Slovenia

In Slovenia, when parliamentary democracy was introduced in 1990, a Children's Parliament was also established. Each year, children in schools are introduced to a chosen topic and provided with the opportunity to learn about it in depth. More than 100 young people aged between thirteen and fifteen years are elected through their schools to meet at the Slovenian Parliament to discuss this issue. In the first year, the issue was 'A Safe and Healthy Environment'. But by the time of the second Parliament, the picture had dramatically changed. War had broken out in Slovenia, in Croatia and finally in Bosnia. The young people used the Parliament to express their concerns over the future and their complaints at the failure of the politicians to develop effective government.

(adapted from Lansdown, 2001, pp. 18–20)

A survey of children's views on daily life in schools in Great Britain and Northern Ireland provides further evidence that introducing concepts of citizenship needs to be practical, not just theoretical. This study asked children about the role of school councils, and their feelings about a wide range of other aspects of school life. Children who reported that their school had an effective school council generally had positive attitudes towards social and academic aspects of school life, whereas those who felt their school council was ineffective had more negative views. While these children's feelings about school organization were probably only one factor contributing to their disaffection, the study draws attention to the importance of how school councils are seen by children – as a real exercise in practical democracy or as tokenistic:

> It is illogical to expect students to understand lessons about rights and democracy and at the same time not to realise when their rights are

disrespected at school, or not to be sceptical about discrepancies between what teachers practise and preach …

The survey suggests that a council that is seen by students as token has as much or more negative impact than having no council. Simply starting a council, without ensuring that other aspects of the school improve, does not necessarily improve a school. It could increase disaffection about the tensions between rhetoric about democracy and reality in school life and about the school generally. Setting up a democratic council with the students involves related changes throughout the school in routines and relationships.

(Alderson, 2000b, pp. 132–3)

SUMMARY OF SECTION 5

- Increasing children's participation has been a major goal of children's rights commissioners, schools councils, youth forums and children's parliaments.
- Research suggests young people are most interested in practical democracy which directly impacts on their lives.
- The Nepal children's clubs illustrate how children can be encouraged to take responsibility for managing a project.

6 A FINAL THOUGHT

During the early decades of the twentieth century women in the UK and many other countries actively campaigned for recognition of their rights. They made progress towards their goal with the Representation of the People Act 1918, which gave married women over the age of 30 the right to vote. Equal suffrage with men was not finally achieved until 1928. But people under the age of twenty-one were excluded from voting rights, even though many were working full time, married and responsible for a family. The voting age was lowered from twenty-one to eighteen on 21 January 1970. But young people under the age of eighteen are still excluded from most aspects of political participation. One final issue to consider is this fixing on eighteen as the voting age in the UK and many other countries, and the case for extending voting rights to children.

Allow about 20 minutes

ACTIVITY 5   **Voting rights for children**

What are your views on the idea of extending voting rights to children? Make a list of arguments for and against children younger than eighteen being entitled to vote in national and local elections. You may find it helpful to look again at the discussion of this issue in the Reading, under the heading 'It strengthens a commitment to and understanding of human rights and democracy'.

COMMENT

From one point of view, children's participation in society will not have been fully achieved until such time as they are entitled to vote as full citizens. Since children as young as ten are considered old enough to take responsibility if they commit a serious crime in England and Wales, it seems inconsistent to argue they have to be eighteen before they can take responsibility for casting their vote in an election. Of course, an alternative view is that children can participate from an early age in lots of ways that are meaningful and appropriate to their age, but that voting rights assume they have reached a certain level of maturity and responsibility. According to this view, children younger than eighteen are still too innocent, too easily influenced by the opinions of others and incapable of fully understanding political issues, and their parents are much more capable of knowing what is in their best interests.

Bear in mind that similar claims were made about women only a few generations ago, when many husbands assumed they knew what was in their wives' best interests. Of course, the issue is different where children are concerned. Exclusion from voting rights was fixed by a woman's gender, whereas children's exclusion is temporary – until they grow up. Once again, considerations about children's maturity and competence are crucial, although there is not a close correspondence between a person's age and their capacities, of course. Note that older people as a group are not disenfranchised once they reach a certain age on the grounds that their mental faculties are likely to be failing, so why exclude young people as a group on the grounds that they are not yet mature enough?

Eighteen has the advantage of consistency with the international definition of childhood in the UNCRC. Even so, as noted by Lansdown in the Reading, voting rights have been extended to sixteen year olds in some countries. At the time of writing (2002), the Children's Rights Alliance for England (CRAE) and other children's rights groups were campaigning for voting

A sixteen-year-old voter in the Iranian parliamentary elections, February 2000. The polling station is at a synagogue in Tehran.

rights for sixteen year olds (CRAE, 2000). Their case seems reasonable enough, since children can legally leave school at sixteen, have sexual relationships and become parents, work and pay taxes and join the armed forces.

But sixteen also seems an arbitrary boundary in some ways. Why not extend voting rights to fourteen year olds, or ten year olds, or even younger? After all, in practice many 'mature and responsible' adults rely heavily on family, on friends and especially on the media to help them make up their minds on election day. Young people might in the same way be guided by discussion with parents and teachers as well as their peers. And encouraging children to participate in the electoral process might increase their interest, competence and sense of responsibility from an early age. Which view you, as an adult, take on this issue depends very much on your understanding of what childhood is, and what it should be. Of course, children's views just might be different.

REFERENCES

ALDERSON, P. (2000a) *Young Children's Rights: exploring beliefs, principles and practices*, London, Jessica Kingsley Publishers.

ALDERSON, P. (2000b) 'School students' views on school councils and daily life at school', *Children and Society*, **14**, pp. 121–34.

BURR, R. and MONTGOMERY, H. K. (2003) 'Children and rights' in WOODHEAD, M. and MONTGOMERY, H. K. (eds) *Understanding Childhood: an interdisciplinary approach*, Chichester, John Wiley and Sons Ltd/The Open University (Book 1 in The Open University course U212 *Childhood*).

CARNEGIE, R. (1998) 'Workshop on culture and children's participation' in JOHNSON, V., IVAN-SMITH, E., GORDON, G., PRIDMORE, P. and SCOTT, P. (eds) *Stepping Forward: young children's participation in the development process*, London, Intermediate Technology Publications.

THE CHILD-TO-CHILD TRUST (2003) 'Approach' [online] http://www.child-to-child.org/about/approach.html (accessed 6 February 2003).

CHILDREN'S RIGHTS ALLIANCE FOR ENGLAND (CRAE) (2000) *The Real Democratic Deficit: why 16 and 17 year olds should be allowed to vote*, London, CRAE.

CLARK, A. and MOSS, P. (2001) *Listening to Young Children, the Mosaic Approach*, London, National Children's Bureau/Joseph Rowntree Foundation.

COUSINS, J. (1999) *Listening to Four Year Olds*, London, National Early Years Network.

CRANE, B. (2001) 'Revolutionising school-based research', *Forum*, **43**(2), pp. 54–5.

CUTLER, D. (2001) *Taking the Initiative: promoting young people's involvement in public decision making in the UK*, London, Children and Young People's Initiative.

DAVIS, J., WATSON, N. and CUNNINGHAM-BURLEY, S. (2000) 'Learning the lives of disabled children' in CHRISTENSEN, P. and JAMES, A. (eds) *Research with Children: perspectives and practices*, London, Falmer.

DYSON, A. and MEAGHER, N. (2001) 'Reflections on the case studies: towards a rationale for participation?' in CLARK, J., DYSON, A., MEAGHER, N., ROBSON, E. and WOOTTEN, M. (eds) *Young People as Researchers: possibilities, problems and politics*, Leicester, Youth Work Press.

GIBBS, S., MANN, G. and MATHERS, N. (2002) *Child-to-Child: a practical guide*, Southwark, London, Groundwork/Health Action Zone/NHS.

HARDING, C. (2001) 'Students as researchers is as important as the National Curriculum', *Forum,* **43**(2), pp. 56–7.

HART, R. (1992) *Children's Participation: from tokenism to citizenship,* Florence, UNICEF, International Child Development Centre.

HART, R. (1997) *Children's Participation: the theory and practice of involving young citizens in community development and environmental care*, London, Earthscan/UNICEF.

HOYLES, M. (ed.) (1979) *Changing Childhood*, London, Writers and Readers Publishing Cooperative.

JOHNSON, V. and SCOTT, P. (1998) 'Institutions and power: introduction' in JOHNSON, V., IVAN-SMITH, E., GORDON, G., PRIDMORE, P. and SCOTT, P. (eds) *Stepping Forward: young children's participation in the development process*, London, Intermediate Technology Publications.

KERR, D., LINES, A., BLENKINSOP, S. and SCHAGEN, I. (2002) *England's Results from the IEA International Citizenship Education Study: what citizenship and education mean to 14 year olds*, NFER Research Report 375 [online] http://www.nfer.ac.uk/research (accessed 20 December 2002).

KIRBY, P. (2002) *Child-to-Child in South London: evaluation report*, London, Lambeth, Southwark and Lewisham Health Action Zone.

KIRBY, P., WUBNER, K., LEWIS, K. and HAYS YOUNG RESEARCHERS (2001) 'The HAYS Project: young people in control?' in CLARK, J., DYSON, A., MEAGHER, N., ROBSON, E. and WOOTTEN, M. (eds) *Young People as Researchers: possibilities, problems and politics*, Leicester, Youth Work Press.

KLEIN, R. (2001) *Citizens by Right: citizenship education in primary schools*, London, Save the Children/Trentham Books.

KNUTTSON, K. E. (1997) *Children: noble causes or worthy citizens?*, Florence, UNICEF.

LANSDOWN, G. (2001) *Promoting Children's Participation in Democratic Decision-Making*, Florence, UNICEF/Innocenti Research Centre.

LANSDOWN, G. (forthcoming) *Disabled Children in Nepal: progress in implementing the Convention on the Rights of the Child*, London, Rights for Disabled Children.

LANSTED, O. (1994) 'Looking at quality from the child's perspective' in MOSS, P. and PENCE, A. (eds) *Valuing Quality in Early Childhood Services*, London, Paul Chapman.

MACKINNON, D. (2003) 'Children and work' in MAYBIN, J. and WOODHEAD, M. (eds) *Childhoods in Context*, Chichester, John Wiley and Sons Ltd/The Open University (Book 2 in The Open University course U212 *Childhood*).

MAYBIN, J. and WOODHEAD, M. (2003) 'Socializing children' in MAYBIN, J. and WOODHEAD, M. (eds) *Childhoods in Context*, Chichester, John Wiley and Sons Ltd/The Open University (Book 2 in The Open University course U212 *Childhood*).

MORRIS, J. (1998) *Don't Leave Us Out: involving disabled children and young people with communication impairments*, York, York Publishing Services.

MUMBA, P. (2002) 'The growth monitoring chart: implementing quality education in a rural primary classroom in Zambia', unpublished paper presented at Child-to-Child Consultation, London, March 2002.

PROUT, A. (2000) 'Children's participation: control and self-realisation in British late modernity', *Children and Society*, **14**, pp. 304–15.

RAYMOND, L. (2001) 'Student involvement in school improvement: from data source to significant voice', *Forum,* **43**(2), pp. 58–61.

RAJBHANDARI, J., HART, R. and KHATIWADA, C. (1999) *The Children's Clubs of Nepal: a democratic experiment*, Kathmandu, Save the Children US/Save the Children Norway.

STERN, D. (1985) *The Interpersonal World of the Infant*, New York, Basic Books.

SWIFT, A. (1999) *Working Children Get Organised*, London, International Save the Children Alliance.

UNICEF (2002a) *State of the World's Children 2003*, New York, UNICEF.

UNICEF (2002b) 'Full Text of the Convention' [online] http://www.unicef.org/crc/crc.htm (accessed 12 October 2002).

WEISNER, T. S. and GALLIMORE, R. (1977) 'My brother's keeper: child and sibling caretaking', *Current Anthropology*, **18**, pp. 169–90.

WOODHEAD, M. (1999) 'Combatting child labour: listen to what the children say', *Childhood*, **6**(1), pp. 27–50.

READING

The participation of children

Gerison Lansdown

The concept of children's participation

The emerging recognition of children's right to be heard

At the World Summit for Children in 1990, children's role was to usher delegates to their seats, whilst dressed in national costume. In May 2002, at the UN General Assembly Special Session for Children held in New York, not only did several hundred children hold their own three-day Children's Forum, but they also participated throughout the full event as members of government delegations, chairpersons, speakers and contributors from the floor. A remarkable change had taken place over the intervening decade in terms of both the legitimacy and capacity of children in playing an active role in events that affect their lives. In every region of the world, there are now initiatives, projects and programmes in which children are participating in decision-making. They are beginning to shape the world around them, influencing politicians, policy-makers, child-focused professionals and the media with their own unique perspective on how the world looks from the viewpoint of a child.

Central to this process of change was the adoption, and subsequent near universal ratification of the Convention on the Rights of the Child. The Convention introduces a new philosophy towards children in which they are acknowledged as individuals, entitled to respect for their human dignity. It introduces the principle that children are entitled to express their views on all matters that affect them and have those views taken seriously.

[…]

This requirement to recognise the right of children to be heard, to have their views given serious consideration and to play an active role in promoting their own best interests, introduces a profound challenge to traditional attitudes towards children in most societies throughout the world.

[…]

Participation can be defined as children taking part in and influencing processes, decisions, and activities that affect them, in order to achieve greater respect for their rights. Recognising that children are entitled to do so does not imply that children have the same status as adults. Indeed, the Convention explicitly affords children special protection by virtue of their youth. Nor does it mean that adults no longer have responsibilities towards children. On the contrary, children cannot and should not be left alone to undertake the advocacy necessary to realise their rights. Structural problems such as poverty, discrimination and injustice cannot be dealt with simply through participation. Rather, what is implied by the Convention, and its philosophy of respect for the dignity of children, is that adults need to learn to work more closely in collaboration with children to help them articulate their lives and develop strategies to enhance their well-being.

The implications of the Convention on the Rights of the Child

Recognition of children's right to be heard is addressed most directly in Article 12, which states that:

1 *States Parties shall assure to the child who is capable of forming his or her own views the right to express those views freely in all matters affecting the child, the views of the child being given due weight in accordance with the age and maturity of the child.*

2 *For this purpose the child shall in particular be provided the opportunity to be heard in any judicial and administrative proceedings affecting the child, either directly, or through a representative or appropriate body, in a manner consistent with the procedural rules of national law.*

The Committee on the Rights of the Child has stressed that Article 12 is a general principle in the Convention, relevant to the implementation and interpretation of all other rights (Hodgkin and Newell, 1998). However, the concept of the child as subject of rights, entitled to respect as an individual is embedded in the entire philosophy of the Convention and expressed, explicitly or implicitly, in many of its articles:

Article 5 – parental provision of direction and guidance should be provided in accordance with respect for children's evolving capacity

Article 9 – children should not be separated from their families without the right to make their views known

Article 13 – the right to freedom of expression

Article 14 – the right to freedom of conscience, thought and religion

Article 15 – the right to freedom of association

Article 16 – the right to privacy and respect

Article 17 – the right to information

Article 29 – the right to an education that promotes the fullest possible development, and respect for human rights, peace and tolerance.

It is important to understand clearly what the Convention does and does not say …

Article 12 does not give children the right to control over all decisions affecting them, irrespective of levels of competence and understanding, nor to ride roughshod over the rights of their parents. However, it does introduce a radical and profound challenge to traditional attitudes, which assume that children should be seen and not heard. It is useful to elaborate the implications in order to clarify its scope and boundaries.

All children are capable of expressing a view – there is no lower age limit imposed on the exercise of the right to participate. It extends therefore to any child who has a view on a matter of concern to them. The emphasis on all children also needs to be understood together with the principle of non-discrimination in the Convention: children from marginalized groups – girls, disabled children, indigenous children, those from ethnic minorities, poor children and children from rural communities are equally entitled to be offered opportunities to express their views.

The right to express their views freely – if children are to be able to express their views, it is necessary for adults to create the opportunities for children to do so. In other words, Article 12 imposes an obligation on adults in their capacity as parents, professionals, policy-makers, and politicians to ensure that children are enabled and encouraged to contribute their views on all relevant matters. This may involve developing child-friendly processes to allow participation and the creation of 'spaces' which are sensitive to the needs of children of different ages and from different communities – accessible environments and language, recognition of the need for giving children time and exploring new ways of working together. The right to express views, does not, of course imply that children should be required to give their views if they are not willing or interested in doing so.

Have a right to be heard in all matters affecting them – the right to be heard extends to all actions and decisions which affect children's lives – in the family, in school, in local communities, at national political level. It is relevant to the implementation of all other rights – for example, children must be heard in respect of their education, health care, legal proceedings, or a change of name. It has relevance both to matters affecting an individual child, such as medical treatment or decisions relating to a child following the divorce of his or her parents, and also to children as a constituency, such as legislation, policy, resource allocation and programming (Pais, 1997). It is important to recognise that many areas of public policy and legislation impact on children's lives – issues relating to transport, housing, macro-economics and the environment all have implications for children.

To have their views taken seriously – it is not sufficient simply to listen to children. It is also important to take what they have to say seriously. Article 12 insists that children's views are given weight and should inform decisions that are made about them. Obviously, this does not mean that whatever children say must be complied with. However, it does mean that proper consideration must be given to children's views when decisions are being made.

In accordance with their age and maturity – the weight which must be given to children's views needs to reflect their level of understanding of the issues involved. This does not mean that young children's views will automatically be given less weight. There are many issues on which very small children are capable of understanding and contributing thoughtful opinions. Competence does not develop uniformly according to rigid developmental stages. The social context, the cultural environment, the nature of the decision, the particular life experience of the child and the level of adult support will all affect the capacity of a child to understand the issues affecting them.

Article 12 is a **substantive** right which demands that children are entitled to be actors in their own lives and to participate in the decisions which affect them. But, as with adults, democratic participation is not just an end in itself. It is the means through which to achieve justice, influence outcomes and expose abuses of power. In other words, it also a **procedural** right enabling children to challenge abuses or neglect of their rights and take action to promote and protect those rights. It facilitates children's contribution towards the promotion of their own best interests.

[...]

The case for promoting participation

The frequent and widespread failure of the adult world to act in ways which are effective in promoting the welfare of children, points to a need for a change of approach. A powerful case can be made for listening to children as part, though by no means all, of a strategy for promoting greater compliance with the obligations to children undertaken by governments when they ratified the Convention on the Rights of the Child.

It is a fundamental human right

All people, including children, have a right to express their views when decisions which directly affect their lives are being made. Whether it is an individual decision about where a child will live following her parents' divorce, or issues of broader impact such as the rules imposed at school, legislation on the minimum age for full time work, or representation of children in the media, children are entitled to articulate their concerns, participate in the development of policy and be taken seriously. Participation represents a means for children to advocate for their own cause and transform their situations.

[…]

It leads to better decisions

Children have a body of experience and knowledge which is unique to their situation. They have views and ideas which derive from that experience. Yet in too many countries, there is still a failure or even a refusal to recognise the legitimacy of children's contribution to decision-making. Much of government policy impacts directly or indirectly on children's lives, yet it is developed and delivered largely in ignorance of how it will affect the day-to-day lives of children, their present and future well-being. In practice, too often, adults either assume that they know best about what children need or children's interests are simply given no consideration.

[…]

Most countries in the world are concerned to improve educational opportunities and standards for children. Yet very few take any measures to find out from children themselves about what teaching methods work, whether the curriculum is relevant, what factors contribute to school drop-out rates and truancy, how to improve attendance rates, what is needed to promote better inclusion of girls, how to enhance good behaviour and promote effective discipline. The Committee on the Rights of the Child consistently asks governments to explain how Article 12 is implemented in the school system but progress remains slow (Hammarberg, 1998). There is a significant body of evidence which indicates that schools which do involve children and introduce more democratic structures are likely to be more harmonious, have better staff/pupil relationships and a more effective learning environment (Davies and Kirkpatrick, 2000). If the devastating drop-out rate of pupils in so many countries in the world is to be stemmed, schools will need to become places where children want to be, where they experience respect and engagement with their concerns. If they are to have a sense of ownership of the school with a commitment and responsibility towards it, then they need opportunities to be involved in the decisions, policies and structures that affect them on a daily basis.

National and international campaigns to end child labour have too often failed to address the reality of working children's lives. By failing to consult with children themselves as well as their families, the impact of such campaigns has sometimes been to worsen children's situation. In Bangladesh, for example, when children were laid off from garment industry jobs, after an American campaign to end the employment of children under 15 in this industry, many of them entered forms of employment which were less appropriate and more hazardous than the jobs from which they were sacked (UNICEF, 1997). Similarly, many programmes which have sought to remove children from the streets by providing them with institutionalised accommodation and education failed because they did not seek the views of the children themselves. Those programmes which have been effective are those which seek to empower children by working with them to enable their own experience to inform the development of appropriate interventions and services.

If the best decisions in respect of children are to be made, then it is important to obtain the best information available. Consulting children and drawing on their perceptions, knowledge and ideas are essential both to the development of effective public policy and positive outcomes for individual children.

It promotes the well-being and development of children

It is through learning to question, to express views and having opinions taken seriously, that children develop skills, build competencies, acquire confidence, and form aspirations. It is a virtuous circle. The more opportunities for meaningful participation, the more experienced and competent the child becomes which in turn enables more effective participation which then promotes improved development (Rajani, 2000) …

[T]he 'virtuous circle' effect is well evidenced by the example of a UK junior school which had been characterised by high levels of violence, disaffection and truancy. The new head teacher decided to involve the whole school community in making the school a safe and effective educational environment. She introduced a school council in which the children were involved in:

1   development of all school policies;

2   recruitment of staff;

3   circle time – time each day when the children could discuss issues of concern in the school;

4   the appointment of 'guardian angels' – children who volunteered to befriend other children who felt isolated or vulnerable;

5   child mediators who would help children resolve conflicts in the playground.

In other words, children's own skills, enthusiasm and creativity were engaged as part of the strategy for creating an effective school. As a result of these changes, the children were happier, achieved better educational results, and acquired considerable skills of negotiation, democratic decision-making and social responsibility (Alderson, 1997).

It strengthens a commitment to and understanding of human rights and democracy

In both well established and newly formed democracies, there is a need for children to experience the implications of democratic decision-making and respect for human rights. In those countries facing internal conflict and tensions which threaten democracy, such experience takes on an even greater significance. Children need opportunities to learn what their rights and duties are, how their freedom is limited by the rights and freedoms of others and how their actions can affect the rights of others. They need opportunities to participate in democratic decision-making processes within school and within local communities, and learn to abide by subsequent decisions that are made.

... This was recognised at the International Conference on Education in 1994 where delegates committed to '*take suitable steps to establish in educational institutions an atmosphere contributing to the success of education for international understanding, so that they become ideal places for the exercise of tolerance, respect for human rights, the practice of democracy and learning about the diversity and wealth of cultural identities*' (International Conference on Education, 1994). However, for most children to date, these words reflect little more than pious aspirations. Unfortunately, when democracy is taught in schools, it is often undertaken through simulation activities – for example, copying formal elections, running UN exercises – with no reference to the day-to-day arbitrary exercise of power in the school. What is needed is the development of participatory processes in all institutional settings with children to promote their understanding that these are what democracy is actually about.

Too many children in too many countries in the world feel that their views do not matter, that they cannot influence outcomes and that democracy does not work for them. At a formal level, most children are precluded from the right to vote in elections until they are 18 years old. Bosnia Herzegovina, Brazil, Croatia, Cuba, Iran, Nicaragua, Philippines, Serbia, Montenegro and Slovenia are the only countries which have reduced the voting age below 18 years. However, democracy can be understood in much broader terms as participation in civil society. Many groups who have traditionally suffered disadvantage – for example, women and disabled people, have increasingly entered into dialogue with politicians at local and national levels to promote and press for greater recognition of their concerns, as the instruments of parliamentary democracy have not proved sufficient to reflect their interests. Without the right to vote, children have an even stronger claim for comparable political participation.

It protects children better

The conventional approach towards child protection is predicated on a view that it is necessarily adults who must provide that protection. It is also sometimes argued that giving children rights will serve to place them outside adult protection – that if their views are listened to and taken seriously, they will make decisions and act in ways which place them at risk. This is to misunderstand the nature of the rights embodied in the Convention on the Rights of the Child. As argued earlier, the Convention does not give children full adult rights. Rather, it gives children the right to be heard and to gradually take increasing responsibility for decisions as their competence evolves. And where children are encouraged to articulate their concerns, and are provided with opportunities to express their views, they will be far better protected. In other words, children need to become protagonists in the realisation of their rights.

For example, the silence that has accompanied sexual abuse of children within families has served to protect only the abuser. Where it is recognised that children are entitled to challenge what is happening to them and mechanisms through which to do so are established, such abuse and violations of rights are far more easily exposed. Children who are encouraged to talk are empowered to act to challenge abuses of their rights and are not simply reliant on adults to protect them. On the other hand, children who are denied the right to express their views, and taught to be submissive and acquiescent, are more pliable and vulnerable to adult abuse. Furthermore, adults can only act to protect children if they are informed about what is happening in children's lives – and often it is only children who can provide that information. Violence against children in prisons, abuse in foster homes, racism in schools, misrepresentation of children in the media can only be tackled effectively if children themselves are enabled to tell their stories to those people with the authority to take appropriate action.

Children want to participate

[...]

There is considerable evidence that young people are increasingly disaffected from the formal political process in many European countries where patterns of both registration and voting amongst young people are low (Wilkinson and Mulgan, 1995). However, cynicism and lack of active engagement in existing political structures is not necessarily an indication of lack of interest in political issues. A survey carried out in Austria in 1997 of 800 13–17 year olds, asked them whether they wanted political information and participation. 93% wanted to be informed when new projects were planned in their municipality and 65% wanted youth consulting hours with politicians (Riepl and Riegler, 1997). The findings reveal a significant concern for greater involvement. A wider survey conducted by Euronet, a children's rights network, found that children felt that their views were consistently disregarded by the adult world and that not only did they want to be given a chance to be heard and taken more seriously, but also they had an important contribution to make (Lansdown, 2000).

Children offer a wide range of reasons for their interest in greater participation (Lansdown, 2002):

1   It offers them new skills

2   It builds their self-esteem

3   It challenges the sense of impotence often associated with childhood

4   It empowers them to tackle abuses and neglect of their rights

5   They have a great deal they want to say

6   They think that adults often get it wrong

7   They feel their contribution could lead to better outcomes

8   They feel it is right to listen to them when it is their life at issue

9   They want to contribute to making the world a better place

10 It can be fun

11 It offers a chance to meet with children from different environments, of different ages and experience

Addressing the arguments raised against children's participation

Children lack the competence or experience to participate

It is commonly argued that children's lack of competence and experience in understanding the world around them invalidates their claim to participation. However, competence is, to a great extent, a social construct rather than a biological given, determined by the child's own context and culture. And children have different levels of competence in respect of different aspects of their lives. Evidence from around the world provides testimony to children's capacities to take responsibilities in family life, in the field of work, in political negotiations, in creating democratic schools (International Save the Children Alliance, 2001). It has also been argued that the capacity for political understanding is a basic human attribute, evidenced in children by their inherent ability at a very young age to recognise and comply with rules (Stevens, 1973). Of course, a child will lack the extensive knowledge of, for example, an experienced educationalist. But even very small children can tell you what they like or dislike about school and why, can produce ideas for making a lesson more interesting, can offer help to and counsel other children. Provided they are given appropriate support, adequate information and allowed to express themselves in ways that are meaningful to them – pictures, poems, drama, photographs, as well as more conventional discussions, interviews and group work – all children can participate in issues that are important to them. The creation of settings which maximise their opportunities to explore and initiate activities themselves, is a means of fulfilling the spirit of the CRC.

Children must take responsibility before they are granted rights

One of the more effective ways of encouraging children to accept responsibility is to provide environments in which their rights are respected. Listening to children and taking them seriously encourages children to understand others, too, have a right to be heard which must also be respected. Adults do not have to prove that they will act responsibly before they are given the right to vote. And in many countries, they will have had no experience during their childhood and adolescence to prepare them for the responsibilities of adult citizenship. Providing opportunities for children to experience democratic decision-making can only strengthen commitment to and understanding of the importance of exercising responsibility within a democratic environment.

Children's participation is not part of our traditional culture

It is probably true to say that the practice of listening to children and taking their views seriously is not part of any traditional culture. But the fact that people have been treated in a particular way in the past does not justify continuing to do so, as new standards of respect for human rights evolve. Women have traditionally been denied access to power, to economic equality, to protection from violence, but it is now widely recognised that attitudes towards women must change and be backed up by legal protections to promote their equality with men. So it is with children; the Convention challenges all cultures to review their attitudes and behaviour towards children. The way in which these changes are introduced need to be sensitive to cultural traditions and religious beliefs, but these should not be used to deny children respect for the right to be heard. There has been criticism that some international NGOs import approaches and assumptions of participation from the North which are inappropriate in the environment in which they are working. Supporting initiatives in which children identify the issues of primary concern to them and are encouraged to evolve their own strategies for tackling them, will help overcome these difficulties, as the children themselves will be sensitive to how issues can be raised within their communities.

Giving children rights takes away their childhood

Article 12 does not impose an *obligation* on children to participate. Rather, it provides a *right* for children to do so. Children should not be forced into participatory initiatives for which they do not feel prepared. However, it is a romanticised view of childhood to imagine that most children are not making decisions and taking responsibilities from a very early age. Even small children in very protected environments might be involved in making decisions about friendships, coping with parental divorce and negotiating between parents in conflict, deciding what games to play and negotiating rules. And in many countries, young children are carrying significant burdens of child care within the family, participating in the labour market or caring for sick or disabled parents. Offering these children opportunities to articulate their concerns, is not imposing any further responsibilities on them. Rather, it is providing an opportunity to improve the quality of their lives and promote greater respect for their rights.

It will lead to lack of respect for parents

Listening to children is about respecting them and helping them learn to value the importance of respecting others. It is not about teaching them to ignore their parents. Indeed, Article 29 of the Convention clearly states that one of the aims of education is to teach children respect for their parents. Listening is a way of resolving conflict, finding solutions and promoting understanding – these can only be beneficial for family life. It can be difficult for some parents to respect children's rights to participate when they feel that they, themselves have never been respected as subjects of rights. This does not imply the need to retreat from encouraging children to participate but, rather, the need to be sensitive in doing so. Children should not be led to believe that they alone have a right to have a voice; wherever possible, their families should be involved in the process.

Children are not representative

When children are speaking on an issue, whether at a conference or to their national or local government, they are often accused of not being representative. Children can rarely be formally representative but this does not invalidate their contribution, provided they make no claim to speak for all children. Their own views may be based on experience of rights abuses within their community, on research undertaken with a wider group of young people, or on work undertaken within a project they are involved in. These experiences all provide legitimacy from which to speak, certainly no less so than many of the adults who make representations to governments. However, it is important that in seeking to raise awareness of children's concerns and to empower children to get involved in actions to promote and protect their rights, the voices of children from different experiences and perspectives are given a chance to be heard. It is also important, wherever possible, that child representatives are chosen by children themselves and not by adults on their behalf.

Some children become 'professionalised' child speakers

There is a danger that some children become almost 'professionalised' as speakers and representatives for their organisation with the result that they spend their lives in public arenas and away from the roots which provide the source and legitimacy for their contribution. The particular value of creating opportunities for children to be heard is that they are speaking from direct and continuing experience. It is important not to lose that. Some organisations have developed a non-hierarchical structure to avoid this happening or encouraged children to create many roles within their organisation. For example, Article 12, a UK child-led organisation, has a large steering committee all of whom can represent the organisation, as indeed, can any of the members. It has a rotating chair and it consistently seeks to create opportunities for younger as well as older children to participate in public events.

It is difficult to sustain participation

Projects and organisations involving children, by their very nature, will experience continual 'haemorrhaging' as the children grow up. It is important therefore to build in the capacity to involve new children and facilitate the transfer of skills from older to younger children. Some organisations develop the concept of young people advisers who can continue on in a supportive role once they have reached the maximum age range for the project.

Children can be manipulated by adult agendas

There is a danger that adults can use children to promote their own political agendas. It is important therefore that events and projects establish clear principles and ground-rules setting out how decisions are made and by whom and the respective relationships between adult and children. Whilst it may be the case that children are being used by adults in some initiatives, the likelihood is that as the children gain in confidence and skills through their involvement, they will increasingly wish to determine their own agenda and challenge attempts by adults to deflect them from their defined priorities.

References

ALDERSON, P. (1997) *Changing Our Behaviour: promoting positive behaviour by the staff and pupils of Highfield Junior School*, Highfield Junior School/Institute of Education, London.

DAVIES, L. and KIRKPATRICK, G. (2000) *The Euridem Project: a review of pupil democracy in Europe*, Children's Rights Alliance for England, London.

HAMMARBERG, T. (1998) *A School for Children with Rights*, UNICEF Innocenti International Child Development Centre, Florence.

HODGKIN, R. and NEWELL, P. (1998) *Implementation Handbook for the Convention on the Rights of the Child*, New York, UNICEF.

INTERNATIONAL CONFERENCE ON EDUCATION (1994) *Declaration and Integrated Framework of Action on Education for Peace, Human Rights and Democracy,* Article 2, 44th Session of the International Conference on Education, Geneva.

INTERNATIONAL SAVE THE CHILDREN ALLIANCE (ISCA) (2001) *Children's Rights*, A Second Chance, London.

LANSDOWN, G. (2000) *Challenging Discrimination against Children in the EU: a policy proposal by Euronet*, Brussels, Euronet.

LANSDOWN, G. (2002) *Promoting Children's Participation in Democratic Decision-making*, Florence, UNICEF, Innocenti Research Centre.

PAIS, M. S. (1997) 'The Convention on the Rights of the Child', in *The Manual of Human Rights Reporting*, UN, Geneva.

RAJANI, R. (2000) *Discussion Paper for Partners on Promoting Strategic Adolescent Participation*, UNICEF, New York.

RIEPL and RIEGLER (1997) *Jugendlicje reden mit,* unpublished report, Graz, Kommunale Beratungsstelle für Kinder and Jugendinitiativen.

STEVENS, O. (1973) *Children Talking Politics*, Mark Robertson, Oxford.

UNICEF (1997) *In Children's Words*, Dhaka, Bangladesh, UNICEF.

UNITED NATIONS (2002) *A World Fit for Children*, UN General Assembly Special Session for Children, A/S-27/19/Rev.1, New York.

WILKINSON and MULGAN (1995) *General Election: first time voters*, MORI, 1997 and Freedom's Children, Demos, London.

Source

LANSDOWN, G. (2002) 'The Participation of Children', unpublished draft paper. A later version of this paper was submitted to the United Nations Expert Group Meeting on Youth in Helsinki, 6–10 October, with a view to inclusion in the United Nations World Youth Report 2003.

ACKNOWLEDGEMENTS

Grateful acknowledgement is made to the following sources for permission to reproduce material in this book.

Chapter 1

Text

pp. 35–37: Field, N. (1995) 'The child as labourer and consumer: the disappearance of childhood in contemporary Japan', in Stephens, S. (ed.) *Children and the Politics of Culture*, Princeton (NJ), Princeton University Press; *pp. 37–40:* Werner, E. and Smith, R. (1982) *Vulnerable but Invincible*, New York, McGraw Hill; *pp. 41–44:* Hinton, R. (2000) 'Seen but not heard: refugee children and models for intervention' in Panter-Brick, C. and Smith, M. (eds.) *Abandoned Children*, Cambridge University Press.

Illustrations

p. 1: Penny Tweedie/Panos Pictures; *p. 4 (top):* Harmut Schwarzbach/Still Pictures; *p. 4 (middle):* Joanne O'Brian/Format Photographers; *p. 4 (bottom):* Martin Woodhead/The Open University; *p. 5 (top):* Paul Box/Report Digital; *p. 5 (bottom):* Bubbles; *p. 8:* Dorothea Lange/Library of Congress; *p. 10:* Bubbles; *p. 13:* Bubbles; *p. 14:* Claro Cortes IV/Reuters News Picture Service; *p. 15:* Sam Kittner/Panos Pictures; *p. 16 (top):* Jim Holmes/Panos Pictures; *p. 16 (bottom):* Nancy Durrell McKenna/Hutchinson Picture Library; *p. 22:* Mike Teruya/Free Spirit Photography; *p. 25:* courtesy of The Jewish Museum; *p. 26:* Bubbles; *p. 29:* Andrew Testa/Panos Pictures; *p. 31:* Deokumar/Rose Class/Photovoice.

Chapter 2

Text

pp. 80–85: UNICEF Innocenti Research Centre, Florence, Italy, *Innocenti Report Card* No. 1, June 2000. 'A league table of child poverty in rich nations'; *pp. 86–88:* Ashworth, A. (1998) *Once in a House on Fire*, Picador/Macmillan Publishers Ltd; *pp. 89–91:* Goldstein, D.M. (1998) 'Nothing bad intended: child discipline, punishment, and survival in a shantytown in Rio de Janeiro, Brazil', Scheper-Hughes, N. and Sargent, C. *Small Wars: the cultural politics of childhood*, University of California Press.

Figures

Figure 2: Poverty Reduction Begins With Children (2000) The United Nations Children's Fund (UNICEF), New York.

Illustrations

p. 45: Martin Woodhead/The Open University; *p. 47:* Jess Hurd/Report Digital; *p. 49:* Martin Woodhead; *p. 50:* Carlton Television; *p. 51:* The Hutchison Library; *p. 52:* Penny Tweedie/Panos Pictures; *p. 54:* Dariusz Klemens/Link Picture Library; *p. 57:* John Harris/Report Digital; *p. 59:*

Robert Aberman/The Hutchison Library; *p. 61:* Heather Montgomery; *p. 67:* Peter Bennett/Link Picture Library; *p. 70:* Jon Spaull/Panos Pictures; *p. 71:* Mira Bildarkiv, Stockholm; *p. 73:* Betty Press/Panos Pictures; *p. 75:* Alison Wright/Panos Pictures.

Tables

p. 53: Gordon, D. *et al.* (2000) *Poverty and Social Exclusion in Britain*, Joseph Rowntree Foundation.

Chapter 3

Text

pp. 130–133: Fadiman, A. (1997) *The Spirit Catches You and You Fall Down*, The Noonday Press, a division of Farrar, Straus and Giroux, Inc. Copyright © 1997 by Anne Fadiman. Reprinted by permission; *pp. 134–135:* Bellamy, C. (2002) 'Birth and broken promises', *The State of the World's Children*, pp. 9–13. Copyright © UNICEF; *pp. 136–139:* Dettwyler, K. (1998) 'The biocultural approach to nutritional anthropology: case studies of malnutrition in Mali', *Understanding and Applying Medical Anthropology*, Mayfield Publishing Company.

Figures

Figure 1: Administrative Committee on Co-ordination/Sub-committee on Nutrition (ACC/SCN) (2000) 'Low birthweight: report of a meeting in Dhaka, Bangladesh on 14–17 June 1999', eds J. Pojda and L. Kelly, *Nutrition Policy Paper* No. 19, Geneva, 2000. Copyright © United Nations System Standing Committee on Nutrition.

Illustrations

p. 93: Martin Woodhead/The Open University; *p. 95 (top):* WHO; *p. 95 (middle):* UNICEF; *p. 95 (bottom):* Martin Woodhead/The Open University; *p. 100:* Liba Taylor/Panos Pictures; *p. 101:* Isabella Tree/Hutchison Library; *p. 102:* Robert Harding Picture Library; *p. 103:* Jean-Leo Dugast/Panos Pictures; *p. 107:* Crispin Hughes/Panos Pictures; *p. 109:* Jorgen Schytte/Still Pictures; *p. 110:* Sean Sprague/Panos Pictures; *p. 111 (left and right):* Martin Woodhead/The Open University; *p. 114:* Catherine Panter-Brick; *p. 116:* Dermot Tatlow/Panos Pictures; *p. 119:* Professor K. A. Dettwyler, Texas; *p. 120:* Getty Images/Donna Day.

Chapter 4

Text

pp. 175–179: Olweus, D. (1999) 'Sweden', *The Nature of School Bullying*, Smith, P. K. *et al.* (eds), Routledge, Taylor and Francis Books Ltd; *pp. 179–183:* Cairns, E. (1987) *Caught in Crossfire: children and the Northern Ireland conflict*, Appletree Press Ltd; *pp. 183–185:* Ryle, J. (1999) 'Children at arms', *The Guardian*, 25 January 1999. Copyright © John Ryle; *pp. 185–186:* Macpherson, M. (1999) 'Letter to the editors of the New York

Review', *New York Review of Books*, 4 March 1999, reproduced by permission of Martin Macpherson.

Illustrations

p. 141: copyright © Corbis; *p. 144 (top):* Christa Stadtler/Photofusion; *p. 144 (middle):* Colin Edwards/Photofusion; *p. 144 (bottom):* S. Scott-Hunter/ Photofusion; *p. 145:* Giacomo Pirozzi/Panos Pictures; *p. 147:* Bryan & Cherry Alexander Photography; *p. 151:* Richard House/Hutchison Picture Library; *p. 152:* www.shoutpictures.com; *p. 156:* John Maier/Still Pictures; *p. 157:* Roy Peters/Report Digital; *p.158:* Howard Davies/Exile Images; *p. 160:* Associated Press, AP; *p. 161:* Scott Nelson/Getty Images; *p. 162:* Dr Alfred Brauner; *p. 164:* Giacomo Pirozzie/Panos Pictures; *p. 166:* Dr Alfred Brauner; *p. 167:* Jim Holmes/Panos Pictures.

Chapter 5

Text

pp. 220–223: Knutsson, K. E. (1997) *Children: noble causes or worthy citizens?*, Ashgate Publishing Limited. Copyright © United Nations Children's Fund 1997; *pp. 223–227:* Myers, R. (1992) *The Twelve Who Survive*, Routledge, Taylor and Francis Books Ltd.; *pp. 228–231:* Boyden, J. and Levison, D. (2001) *Children as Economic and Social Actors in the Development Process: Working Paper 2000:1*, EGDI. Copyright © Jo Boyden and Deborah Levison.

Illustrations

p. 187: Martin Woodhead; *p. 189:* Jeremy Horner/Hutchison Library; *p. 191:* Mary Evans Picture Library; *p. 192:* Mary Evans Picture Library; *p. 193:* Mary Evans Picture Library; *p. 194:* Barnardo's; *p. 196:* Save the Children Fund; *p. 197:* Save the Children Fund; *p. 200 (top):* Jorgen Schytte/Still Pictures; *p. 200 (bottom):* Martin Woodhead/The Open University; *p. 202:* Hulton Getty; *p. 204:* Jose Nicolas/Rex Features; *p. 210:* Martin Woodhead/The Open University.

Chapter 6

Text

p. 273–83: Landsown, G. (2002) 'The participation of children.' Unpublished draft paper. A later version of this paper was submitted to the United Nations Expert Group Meeting of Youth in Helsinki, 6–10 October 2002 with a view to inclusion in the *United Nations World Youth Report 2003*.

Illustrations

p. 233: Brenda Prince/Format; *p. 237 (top):* John Birdsall Photography; *p. 237 (bottom):* John Birdsall Photography; *p. 238 (top):* iD.8 Photography; *p. 238 (bottom):* Steve Eason/Photofusion; *p. 243:* Popperfoto; *p. 245:* Lucy Tizard/Bubbles; *p. 246:* Ulrike Preusse/ Photofusion; *p. 248:* Visayan Forum, Manila, The Philippines; *p. 249 (top and bottom):* with thanks to Clare for the use of her photographs which first appeared in Clark, A. and Moss, P. (2001) *Listening to Young Children: The Mosaic Approach*, National Children's Bureau/Joseph Rowntree Foundation; *p. 252:* Courtesy of Bedfordshire Schools Improvement Partnership; *p. 263 (top):* Sunil Malhotra/Reuters News Picture Service; *p. 263 (bottom):* Chandrika Khatiwada/Save the Children (Norway); *p. 265:* Jasmine Rajbhandary/Save the Children (US); *p. 269:* Enric Marti/Associated Press.

Extract

p. 258: Child-to-Child Trust, Institute of Education, University of London.

Figure

Figure 1: adapted from Johnson, V. and Scott, P. (1998) 'Institutions and power: introduction' in Johnson, V. *et al.* (eds) *Stepping Forward: young children's participation in the development process*, London, Intermediate Technology Publications; *Figure 2:* adapted from Hart, R. (1997) *Children's Participation: the theory and practice of involving young citizens in community development and environmental care*, London Earthscan/UNICEF.

Cover and title page photographs

top: Molly Cooper/Photofusion; *centre:* Martin Adler/Panos Pictures; *bottom:* Martin Woodhead.

Every effort has been made to locate all copyright holders, but if any have been overlooked the publishers will make the necessary arrangements at the first opportunity.

INDEX